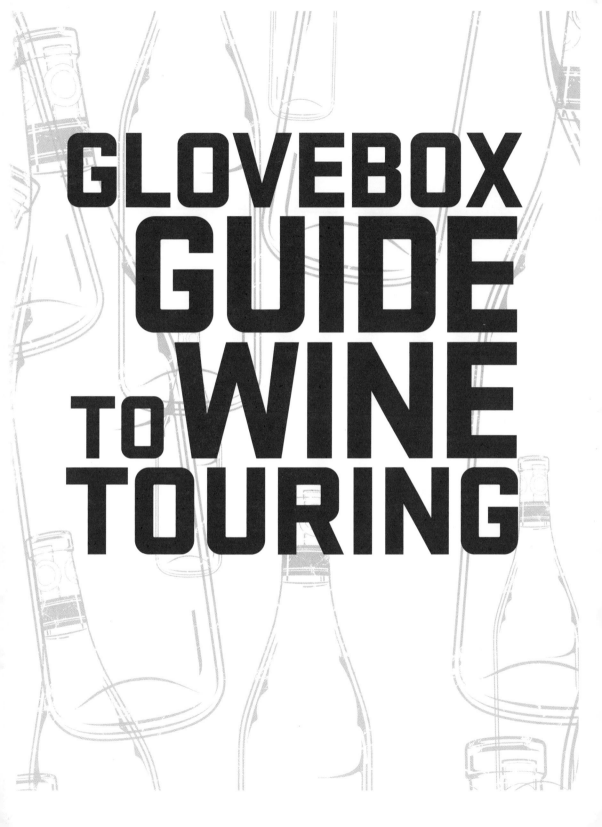

GLOVEBOX
GUIDE
TO WINE
TOURING

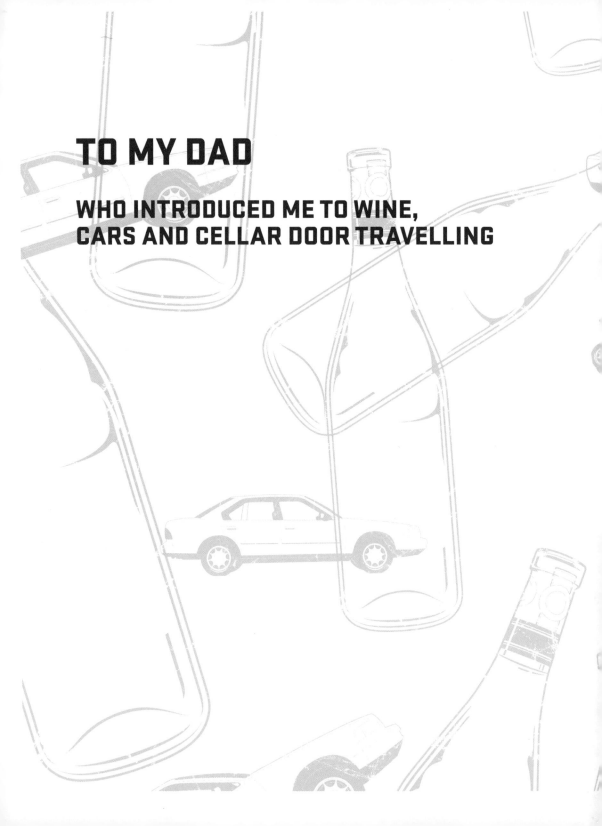

TO MY DAD

WHO INTRODUCED ME TO WINE, CARS AND CELLAR DOOR TRAVELLING

GLOVEBOX GUIDE TO WINE TOURING

GREG DUNCAN POWELL

MURDOCH BOOKS

CONTENTS

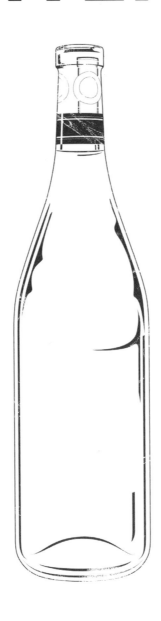

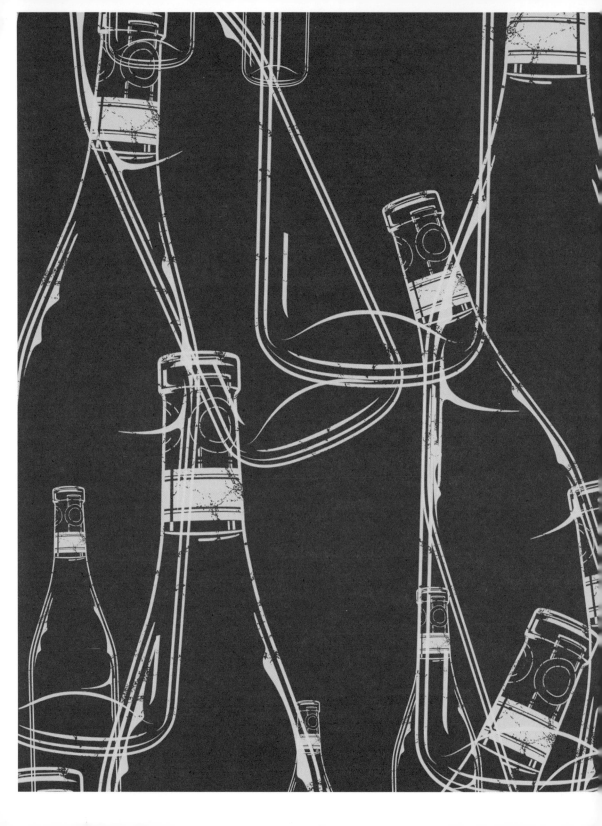

INTRODUCTION

Australians are an inventive lot. Nowhere is this more apparent than in the many inventions that make the ingestion of alcohol more efficient, fun and portable. We have the Esky, the wine cask and the stubby holder. But one of the things that we don't give ourselves credit for is the whole cellar door wine-tourism thing.

Yes, I know, cellar door trading has existed to some extent ever since there were vineyards and wineries. Farmers selling their produce onsite saved on transport and cut out the middlemen. But the way it has evolved in Australia is unique—anyone can travel to a wine region and make a day of going from cellar door to cellar door.

We take it for granted. Go to Bordeaux in France, rock up to a chateau and ask for a goût (taste) and see what sort of welcome you get. You will be shown the porte (door). There are less-famous spots in France where the chateaus are less ostentatious and the winemaker will give you a taste, but there is no tradition of cellar door tourism as we know it. It's the same in Chianti and in Piedmont. Champagne is set up for tourism but is so formal it takes the fun out of it.

Apart from the fact that our cellar doors are open to the public they're unique in the quantity of product available to taste. Typically, an Australian winery will have a fruit salad of grape varieties in its vineyards and offer everything from a sparkling wine through whites, rosés, reds and fortified wines.

When some wineries introduced the notion of charging for the taste (a fee usually refundable on purchase) most of us were horrified. Haven't we got a right to taste wine free of charge? No, we don't, but fortunately most wineries don't charge and you can taste some very fine products gratis.

There are 1647 Australian wineries out there with their doors open, and a wonderfully diverse world of climates, grape varieties, characters, dogs and wine awaits. With this book in your hand, you are equipped.

Bon voyage!

THE GENTLE ART OF CELLAR DOOR TASTING

Most people don't know it but when they go and taste wine at a cellar door they are learning far more than they think. While the taste of the wine may enter their sense through taste, smell and sight, other important information is seeping into their subconscious: the driveway, the dog, the signage, the attitude of the person pouring the wine—it all adds to the picture and whether or not you like the experience. It means that when you taste that wine away from its home, you have a vision of it that goes way beyond the look of the label or the liquid in the glass. The taste of the wine recalls the colour of the foliage in the vineyards, the softness of the light, the cleanliness of the toilets and the hairdo of the lady behind the counter. There is a fantastic French word for this—*terroir*—it sums up the unsummupable. It refers to all the things—sun, soil and site—that go into making wine from a specific spot taste the way it does. It's a wonderfully romantic notion that you can actually taste.

Experienced cellar door travellers are detectives. They can take a sniff as they step out of their car and determine the hygiene or otherwise of the winery. They become amateur viticulturists who can look at a vineyard and pick the rows of cabernet sauvignon from the shiraz, and analyse if the vineyard is biodynamic, healthy, sick, overcropped or underwatered.

Observant tasters pick up on a multitude of other cues that can tell them so much more than the spiel inside the cellar door. Check out the cars in the staff car park, the breed of dog lying in the sun, the roses in the garden, or the winemaker's boots; these are all things that will give an indication of why the wine tastes the way it does. It's all part of the challenge, part of the experience and it's what makes cellar door wine-tasting so much fun.

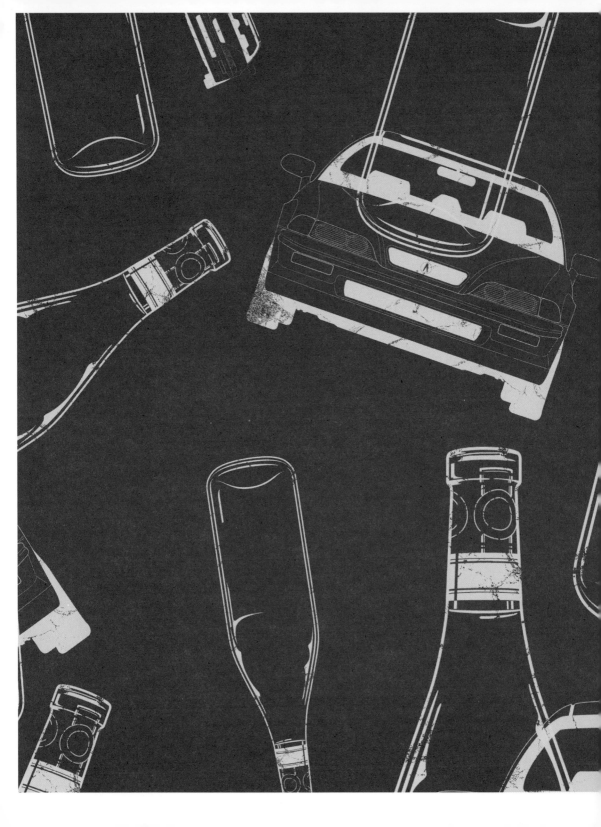

EATING

Food and wine seem to have a symbiotic, almost parasitical, relationship. Just as the plover picks the teeth of the crocodile and the remora hangs around the shark, wine and food tend to gravitate together. Put a few vineyards and wineries in a standard agricultural area full of fish and chips, pies and watery cappuccinos and within a year or so you'll find a cafe serving decent food, coffee worth drinking and maybe even a winery restaurant. Eventually, if the wine region keeps growing, someone might start making cheese, someone else starts farming a particular breed of pig and voilà! Suddenly the region is on the gastronomic map.

Take a look at Orange in New South Wales, Denmark in Western Australia and Stanthorpe in Queensland. They've all benefited in a food way from being surrounded by vineyards. And places such as the Mornington Peninsula and the Yarra Valley in Victoria and Margaret River in Western Australia feature food that is about as good as regional food gets. It's handy because tasting wine makes you hungry. Wine has a tendency to excite the gastric juices, and a day tasting wine without a decent luncheon is not recommended.

SEVEN TIPS FOR THE CELLAR DOOR TRAVELLER

Plan. Faced with a time limit, a host of cellar doors and a million wines to taste, a plan of attack is a must. Even if you don't stick to the plan and end up staying at one place too long, it's an essential way to start.

Spit. Even if you're not driving, spitting is the only way to go—if only to retain some sense of objectivity with what you taste. If you're embarrassed or worried about missing the bucket, have a bit of a practice in the bathtub before you leave home.

Focus. Australian cellar doors are renowned for having a huge range that can go from sparkling through umpteen varieties of white and red all the way to ports and muscats. If you taste the entire range it can take ages and it is a rare winery and wine region that can make fantastic examples of everything. It's best to narrow it down to the wine styles the region does best. For instance, in the Hunter Valley, stick to the semillon and shiraz rather than the pinot noir.

Resist. Don't feel you have to buy something. Even if there is pressure, don't succumb unless you want to buy the wine. Remember, there is no obligation.

Prepare. Beware of morningitis. I've observed that on a wine-tasting tour most people don't buy much wine in the morning but after lunch they find that all the wine tastes much better. This is because of morningitis. Most normal people who don't work in the wine industry aren't used to tasting wine at nine in the morning. A common scenario is that someone will rock up to their first winery, still with toothpaste on their breath and find that every wine tastes sour and bitter. The best advice is to taste a few wines to calibrate your palate and let it get used to the effects of acid and tannin before you apply judgment. I know it sounds a bit feral but don't clean your teeth before heading out for tasting. You'll be far more objective.

Get on the mailing lists of the wineries you like. There are often deals and special offers to mailing list customers, and if you're on the mailing list you're the first to know.

Drink. Drink what you buy! One of the saddest things about cellar door purchases is that they so often get hoarded away for that special occasion that never comes. The wine goes past its drinking peak and dies in the cellar untasted and unloved. That's wine crime.

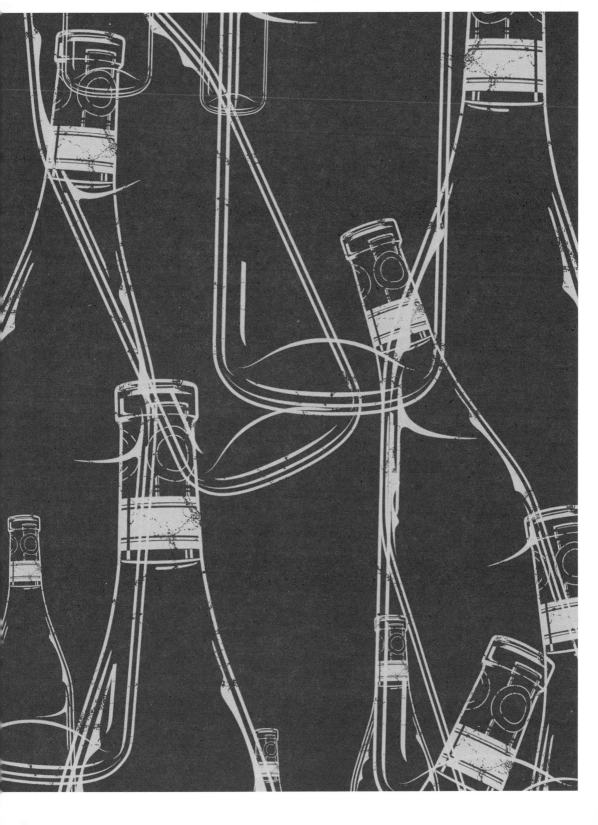

VICTORIA

Put your state-versus-state, mate-versus-mate prejudices to one side and understand that Victoria is number one when it comes to wine touring. It's a fact. Victoria has 522 cellar doors compared to its closest rivals South Australia and New South Wales, which are equal on about 350 each. So this is the biggest chapter, took the longest to research and the longest to write. But it's not just the number of cellar doors; in an age of rising fuel costs the good food/wine/coffee to kilometre ratio is higher in Victoria than anywhere else in the country. I know this is meant to be a book about wine but let's face it: a crappy cappuccino can ruin your day. In a short drive the state offers the gamut of the wine experience: fortifieds that rock your world, sublime bubbles, the best pinots, ballsy shiraz, stylish chardys, edgy Italians ... You name a wine style and it is being produced in a part of Victoria.

The diversity is all to do with varieties of climate and landscape. It goes all the way from stinking hot and flat up in Mildura to vines on the snowline in Whitfield and everything in between. If you can't find a wine or a wine region to like in Victoria you're very hard to please. Go forth and taste!

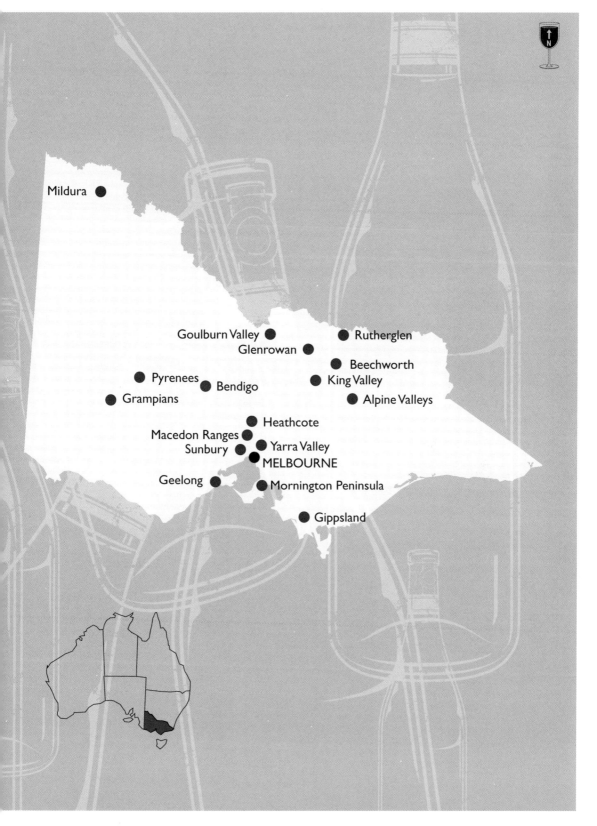

YARRA VALLEY

WINERIES

1. Yering Station
38 Melba Hwy, Yarra Glen
03 9730 0100

2. Sticks
179 Glenview Rd, Yarra Glen
03 9730 1022

3. De Bortoli
58 Pinnacle Ln, Dixons Creek
03 5965 2271

4. Tarrawarra Estate
Healesville Rd, Yarra Glen
03 5962 3311

5. Giant Steps/Innocent Bystander
336 Maroondah Hwy, Healesville
03 5962 6199

6. Badger's Brook
874 Maroondah Hwy, Coldstream
03 5962 4130

7. Dominique Portet
870 Maroondah Hwy, Coldstream
03 5962 5760

8. Oakridge
864 Maroondah Hwy
03 9738 9900

9. Domaine Chandon
727 Maroondah Hwy, Coldstream
03 9738 9200

WHERE TO EAT

A. Giant Steps/Innocent Bystander
336 Maroondah Hwy, Healesville
03 5962 6199

B. Bella Vedere Cucina
Badger's Brook Estate
874 Maroondah Hwy, Coldstream
03 5962 6161

C. Locale
De Bortoli, 58 Pinnacle Ln, Dixons Creek
03 5965 2271

handwritten: www.tarrawarra estate
handwritten: 28 ha cut bare.
handwritten: in middle tartan

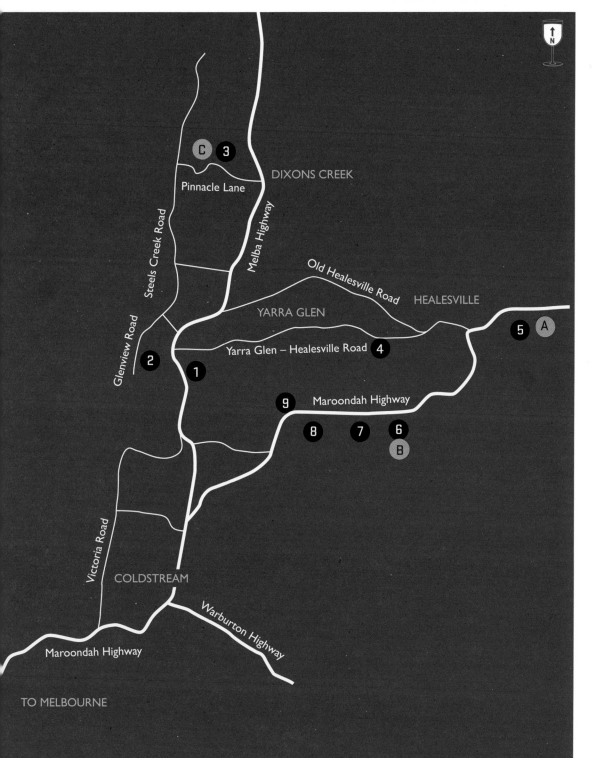

DIXONS CREEK

Pinnacle Lane

Steels Creek Road

Melba Highway

Old Healesville Road

HEALESVILLE

YARRA GLEN

Glenview Road

Yarra Glen – Healesville Road

Maroondah Highway

Victoria Road

COLDSTREAM

Warburton Highway

Maroondah Highway

TO MELBOURNE

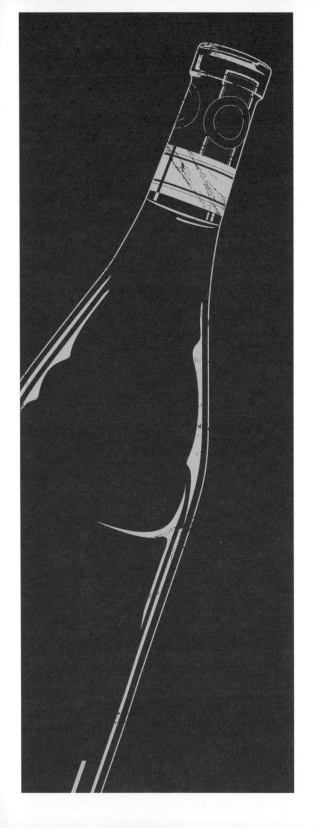

Snapshot

A drive through the Yarra Valley can make you feel like a pauper. As far as wine regions go it is the equivalent of a kid with rich parents who gets sent to all the right schools, gets all the right toys and is given a car when he or she turns 18. Just look at the driveways. Out of all the wine regions in this book, the Yarra Valley gets the driveway award. Tree-lined, beautifully gravelled winding masterpieces lead to architect-designed cellar doors. Melbourne money is everywhere. It would be easy to poke fun at the Yarra Valley for all its ponce and showiness were the wines not so damn good.

The background

Part of the reason it looks so 'designed' is that it is relatively new—the modern Yarra Valley, and the cellar doors and vineyards you see are recent. Paradoxically, the Yarra Valley is Victoria's oldest wine region. It was first planted in 1840 and has a real pedigree. One of the early vineyards was planted with 20,000 cabernet sauvignon cuttings from Château Lafite in Bordeaux.

During the late 1800s Yarra Valley wine had the name as the best in the country but fell into decline because of the vine louse, phylloxera; a population that was demanding fortified wine; and a government that was more interested in milk than wine. The Yarra vineyards were ripped out to provide grazing for bovines.

The rebirth didn't start until the 1960s and 1970s with the Mount Marys, the Seville Estates and the Yarra Yerings, plus a huge wave of investment in the 1980s. It is a big area with quite a range of climates, from the cool heights to the heat of the valley floor. Site selection for specific grape varieties means that the quality and diversity of Yarra wine has been getting better and better.

The wines

It used to be that the Yarra's cool climate dictated that pinot noir and chardonnay were the king and queen of the valley, but with some recent hot, dry vintages and much more knowledge about sites there is good shiraz and cabernet grown in the valley. There's sparkling wine, oh yes, and a little sauvignon blanc, too …

The prices

Yarra wine used to be some of the most expensive in the country but other regions have caught up and bigger wineries mean cheaper prices. Expect to pay about $18–$20 for the second labels and $30–$40 for the first labels. There is the odd bargain, too.

The layout

As Melbourne creeps ever closer, the borderline between suburbs and valley is getting more and more muddy, but it starts at about Diamond Creek driving from Melbourne and goes east to Warburton, south around Seville and north as far as Kinglake. In that area, there is a wide range of altitudes from 50 to 400 metres above sea level. Most of the cellar door action is on the Maroondah Highway, the Melba Highway and the Warburton Highway. Like any country region with intersecting roads, it can get confusing, but with a bit of north–south orientation and a good map you'll get the hang of it.

A suggested route

Entering from Melbourne along the Maroondah Highway you'll get to Yarra Glen and the place that sets the scene for the Yarra, **Yering Station** (38 Melba Hwy, Yarra Glen; open weekdays 10 am–5 pm, weekends 10 am–6 pm; 03 9730 0100; www.yering.com). The building is poncy, the views are magnificent and the wine lives up to the surroundings. One of the main style leaders in the valley, the entire range is actually pretty flash, particularly the pinot noir, chardonnay and shiraz viognier. The rosé should not be neglected, either.

From there, head up Glenview Road to what used to be the Yarra Ridge winery and is now **Sticks** (179 Glenview Rd, Yarra Glen; open daily 10 am–5 pm; 03 9730 1022; www.sticks.com.au), named after the nickname of (tall) winemaker and ex-Yarra Ridge man, Rob 'Sticks' Dolan. He came home when he bought the winery in 2005, pursuing the style and drinkability that made Yarra Ridge famous back in the 1990s. The pinot noir and shiraz are really good and there are some bargains to be had: $15 wines in the Yarra are quite rare!

Heading north on the Melba Highway will take you to **De Bortoli** (58 Pinnacle Ln, Dixons Creek; open daily 10 am–5 pm; 03 5965 2271; www.debortoli.com.au), a big winery but worth a visit simply to see where it's done and marvel at the quality of the wines. For such a huge operation, winemaker Steve Webber and his team make wines that taste artisan. From the chardonnay to the pinot rosé and the viognier and even the estate-grown sauvignon blanc, all are made with style and originality and are good to measure the rest of the valley against.

Backtrack until you get to the Healesville–Yarra Glen Road and you'll find **Tarrawarra Estate** (Healesville Rd, Yarra Glen; open daily 11 am–5 pm; 03 5962 3311; www.tarrawarra.com.au).

Winemaker Clare Halloran makes brilliant pinot noir and chardonnay, particularly the top-of-the-range $50 wines. Check out the art gallery, too.

Head into Healesville and it's pretty hard to miss the gigantic **Giant Steps/ Innocent Bystander** (336 Maroondah Hwy, Healesville; open weekdays 10 am–10 pm, weekends 8 am–1 am; 03 5962 6199; www.innocentbystander.com.au). Not only does it stay open later than any cellar door in the country, it features a restaurant, bakery and cheesemonger. It was brought from vision to reality by Phil Sexton, the man behind Redback, Matilda Bay and the beer revolution, and he is making the same splash with cellar doors. This one even roasts its own coffee. Giant Steps, named after Coltrane's classic track, is a groovy place and the wines don't let it down. The Innocent Bystander range is affordable at $20 and very good, particularly the pinot noir. The Giant Steps range starts at about $35 and the chardonnay from different vineyards in the valley is instructive to compare and contrast.

Take the Maroondah Highway back towards Melbourne and you'll discover **Badger's Brook** (874 Maroondah Hwy, Coldstream; open Wed–Sun 11 am–5 pm; 03 5962 4130; www.badgersbrook.com.au). The Storm Ridge range offers great value at sub $20 prices. The reds are generally better than the whites and the adjoining Bella Vedere Cucina bistro is a must for breakfast.

A little further up the road is the very French-looking cellar door of **Dominique Portet** (870 Maroondah Hwy, Coldstream; open daily 10 am–5 pm; 03 5962 5760; www.dominiqueportet.com). Dominique was the founder of Taltarni in the Pyrenees and has moved to the Yarra to pursue his muse. Winemaking duties are now shared with his son, Ben. The entire range is excellent and there's some top-class bubbly. Dominique also sells the most efficient and inexpensive Champagne stopper for those half-finished bottles.

Adjacent to Dominique is **Oakridge** (864 Maroondah Hwy; open daily 10 am–5 pm; 03 9738 9900; www.oakridgewines.com.au) with an understated cellar door but an increasing reputation. Winemaker David Bicknell has a real feel and skill with the fruit of the valley. The chardonnay, pinot noir and syrah are exemplary in the 864 range, the standard range and the $19 'Over the Shoulder' wines.

The Green Point Room at **Domaine Chandon** (727 Maroondah Hwy, Coldstream; open daily 10.30 am–4.30 pm; 03 9738 9200; www.domainechandon.com.au) should be visited at least once in a lifetime. Home to a host of stylish bubbles—my favourite is always the vintage blanc de blancs—and an increasing range of still wines; the chardonnay is particularly good.

Where to eat

Number one on your list should be **Giant Steps/Innocent Bystander** (336 Maroondah Hwy, Healesville; open weekdays 10 am–10 pm, and on weekends 8 am–1 am; 03 5962 6199; www.innocentbystander.com.au). It's a one-stop eating shop with a bistro, a cheesery and a bakery, and they even roast their own coffee beans.

At Badger's Brook is **Bella Vedere Cucina** (874 Maroondah Hwy, Coldstream; open Wed–Sun from 8.30 am for breakfast and lunch, Fri & Sat for dinner; 03 5962 6161; www.badgersbrook.com.au). The breakfast is sumptuous.

Locale (De Bortoli, 58 Pinnacle Ln, Dixons Creek; open Thu–Mon for lunch from noon, Sat for dinner from 6.30 pm; 03 5965 2271; www.debortoli.com.au) has a fantastic cheese room, which is a must-visit, and country-style Italian food that goes excellently with the wine.

MORNINGTON PENINSULA

WINERIES

1. Crittenden Wines
25 Harrisons Rd, Dromana
03 5981 8322

2. Foxeys Hangout
795 White Hill Rd, Red Hill
03 5989 2022

3. Ten Minutes by Tractor
1333 Mornington–Flinders Rd, Main Ridge
03 5989 6455

4. T'Gallant
1385 Mornington–Flinders Rd, Main Ridge
03 5989 6565

5. Morning Sun Vineyard
337 Main Creek Rd, Main Ridge
03 5989 6571

6. Paradigm Hill
26 Merricks Rd, Merricks
03 5989 9000

7. Merricks General Wine Store
3460 Frankston–Flinders Rd, Merricks
03 5989 8088

8. Moorooduc Estate
Derril Rd, Moorooduc
03 5971 8506

WHERE TO EAT

A. Merricks General Wine Store
3460 Frankston–Flinders Rd, Merricks
03 5989 8088

B. Foxeys Hangout
795 White Hill Rd, Red Hill
03 5989 2022

C. Montalto Vineyard and Olive Grove
33 Shoreham Rd, Red Hill South
03 5989 8412

D. Tractor Restaurant and Wine Bar
1333 Mornington–Flinders Rd, Main Ridge
03 5989 6080

E. Max's at Red Hill Estate
53 Shoreham Rd, Red Hill
03 5931 0177

F. Salix Restaurant & Bistro
166 Balnarring Rd, Merricks North
03 5989 7640

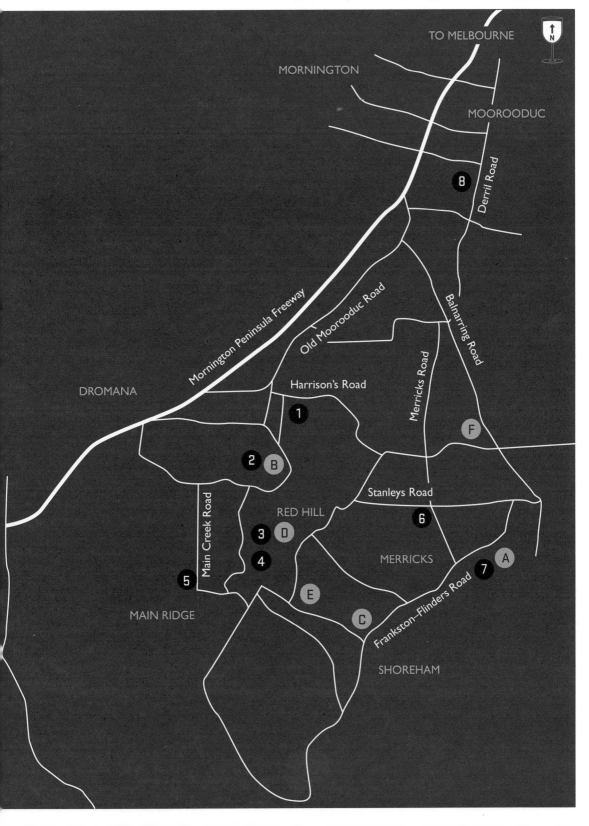

TO MELBOURNE

MORNINGTON

MOOROODUC

Derril Road

8

Mornington Peninsula Freeway

Old Moorooduc Road

Balnarring Road

Merricks Road

DROMANA

Harrison's Road

1

2 **B**

Main Creek Road

RED HILL

3 **D**

Stanleys Road

F

6

MERRICKS

4

5

E

7 **A**

Frankston–Flinders Road

MAIN RIDGE

C

SHOREHAM

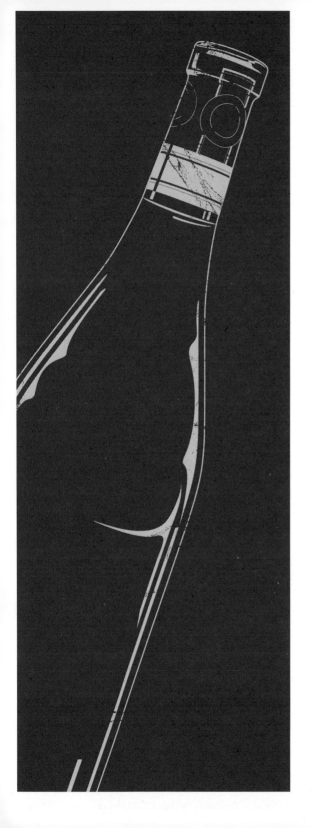

Snapshot

When it comes to cellar door travelling, scenery and gastronomy, it's hard to beat the Mornington Peninsula. A short drive from Melbourne, the sausage-shaped peninsula offers several different climates in a small amount of space, and a level of sophistication in wine and food unmatched by most wine regions. For classy pinot noir and chardonnay in scenic settings it doesn't get much better.

The background

Apart from a few plantings by part-timers, the modern vine history on the peninsula began in the 1970s when Baillieu Myer planted Elgee Park with cabernet sauvignon and riesling, both of which are now lesser varieties. Nat White from Main Ridge planted his immaculate Main Ridge Vineyard at Red Hill in 1975 to pinot noir and chardonnay. Waves of investment followed. Old apple orchards were grubbed out and replanted with vines. Lawyer and doctor money flooded in, along with investment schemes. Trellises and vineyards popped up everywhere.

Soon it became apparent that the cabernet was a no-go in all but the warmest of sites and the peninsula's strong suits were the Burgundians—pinot noir and chardonnay. In the 1990s, driven by the enthusiasm of Kevin McCarthy and Kathleen Queely for the variety, pinot gris/grigio came to the peninsula and Australia. These days, the peninsula grows a diverse range of varietals but if you don't like pinot noir or chardonnay you probably won't get the best of what the Mornington Peninsula has to offer.

The wines

Cool-climate specialists such as pinot noir, chardonnay and pinot gris/grigio are favourites. There's a little bit of viognier and some shiraz, the odd cabernet and some decent sparkling.

The prices

The price of land can often dictate the price of wine, and it does on the peninsula. Add that cost to the handmade nature of both the grape growing and the winemaking and prices are not cheap. Expect to pay $25–$50 for the good stuff.

The layout

There are vineyards spread all over the peninsula from Mornington almost down to Flinders. Most are in a band across the middle of the peninsula between Dromana and Shoreham. Assuming you're coming from Melbourne, it's best to arrive at Dromana from the freeway first then head up over Red Hill to the ocean side of the peninsula and pick some of those off before heading back in the direction of Melbourne. Alternatively, take the ferry across to Queenscliff and the Geelong wine region from Portsea.

A suggested route

First stop should be **Crittenden Wines** (25 Harrisons Rd, Dromana; open daily 11 am–4 pm; 03 5981 8322; www.crittendenwines.com.au). This is home to one of the peninsula's pioneers, Garry Crittenden. The wine is now made by his son, Rollo. An excellent chardonnay, pinot noir and very good tempranillo are just the beginning. There's stylish, comfortable accommodation here, too.

Head up White Hill Road towards Arthur's Seat and at the top you'll see the signs to **Foxeys Hangout** (795 White Hill Rd, Red Hill; open weekends & public holidays 11 am–5 pm; 03 5989 2022; www.foxeys-hangout.com.au). Foxeys has an interesting range of wines that are not typical of the peninsula. There's good sparkling red, an interesting shiraz, a fortified shiraz, a vermentino and the peninsula's ubiquitous velvety pinot noir. It's a lovely spot to hang out except if you're a dead fox.

From Foxeys, head up the Mornington–Flinders Road in Main Ridge and you'll soon come to **Ten Minutes by Tractor** (1333 Mornington–Flinders Rd, Main Ridge; open daily 11 am–5 pm; 03 5989 6455; www.tenminutesbytractor.com.au) named because that's the time it takes to drive between the two main vineyards by tractor—not wind-assisted. It's a shrine to peninsula pinot noir and chardonnay. There's a wide range of each and they are all excellent examples. There's also a very good winery restaurant.

T'Gallant (1385 Mornington–Flinders Rd, Main Ridge; open daily 10 am–5 pm; 03 5989 6565; www.tgallant.com.au) is now owned by Foster's but still retains the funky character imbued by Kathleen Queely and Kevin McCarthy. Kevin is still the winemaker and is still experimenting. The whole range shows off his skills but the pick is still the pinot gris/grigio.

Head south towards Main Creek Road and you'll come to a winery you've probably never heard of. **Morning Sun Vineyard** (337 Main Creek Rd, Main Ridge; open Thu–Sun 10 am–5 pm; 03 5989 6571; www.morningsunvineyard.com.au) is the retirement project of Italian Mario Toniolo, which has grown beyond retirement size. Winemaker Owen Goodwin is doing a great job and the pinot grigio is particularly tasty. Don't leave without a bottle of Signor Toniolo's fruity, fresh olive oil.

From Morning Sun Vineyard, head towards Merricks Road. **Paradigm Hill** (26 Merricks Rd, Merricks; open first weekend of every month & public holidays noon–5 pm; 03 5989 9000; www.paradigmhill.com.au) has some good wines and is a scenic place to taste it. It's a different cellar door experience. Viticulturist Ruth Mihaly hands out nibbles while winemaker Dr George Mihaly talks you through the range seated at a table rather than standing at a bar. The pinot noir is very good and the riesling is pretty stylish, too.

Head down Merricks Road towards the coast and you'll come to **Merricks General Wine Store** (3460 Frankston–Flinders Rd, Merricks; open weekdays 9 am–5 pm, weekends 8 am–5 pm; 03 5989 8088; www.mgwinestore.com.au). Not only is this a good place for brekkie or a coffee or even lunch, you can taste a range of wines here made by the indefatigable Kathleen Queely under labels Elgee Park, Baillieu Vineyard and her own, Queely. She's a dab hand with pinot noir and has a left-of-field blending philosophy that works.

On your way back to Melbourne, drop in on **Moorooduc Estate** (Derril Rd, Moorooduc, open Thu–Mon 11 am–4 pm & every day in January 11 am–4 pm; 03 5971 8506; www.moorooduc-estate.

com.au). The rammed-earth buildings suit the organic nature of the wines. The Moorooduc Chardonnay is the absolute showpiece and regularly one of the best on the peninsula—and that's saying a lot.

Where to eat

Where to start? **Merricks General Wine Store** (3460 Frankston-Flinders Rd, Merricks; open weekdays 9 am–5 pm, open weekends 8 am–5 pm; 03 5989 8088; www.mgwinestore.com.au) is a good place. For a coffee, breakfast and lunch, chef Janine Richmond matches the food to the menu very nicely.

Foxeys Hangout (795 White Hill Rd, Red Hill; open weekends & public holidays 11 am–5 pm; 03 5989 2022; www.foxeys-hangout.com.au) is a bit like a modern wine bar and is a good spot for a light lunch.

Montalto Vineyard and Olive Grove (33 Shoreham Rd, Red Hill South; open daily 11 am–5 pm; 03 5989 8412; www.montalto.com.au) is one of the more imposing-looking cellar doors and the restaurant is pretty good, too.

Tractor Restaurant and Wine Bar (1333 Mornington–Flinders Rd, Main Ridge; open Wed–Sun from noon, Thu–Sat for dinner from 6 pm; 03 5989 6080; www.tenminutesbytractor.com.au) is an unusual winery restaurant because it has a very good wine list that features wine that isn't made onsite.

At the top of Red Hill is **Max's at Red Hill Estate** (53 Shoreham Rd, Red Hill; open daily noon–5 pm, Fri & Sat from 7 pm; 03 5931 0177; www.maxsrestaurant.com.au) has a spectacular view and the food has an Italian accent.

Salix Restaurant & Bistro at Willow Creek Vineyard (166 Balnarring Rd, Merricks North; open daily for lunch from noon, Fri & Sat for dinner from 6 pm; 03 5989 7640; www.willow-creek.com.au) has views of the rolling vineyard-covered hill, the food has a French/Spanish touch and the wines are pretty flash, too.

GEELONG

WINERIES

1. Shadowfax
K Rd, Werribee
03 9731 4420

2. Clyde Park Vineyard
2490 Midland Hwy, Bannockburn
03 5281 7274

3. Lethbridge
74 Burrows Rd, Lethbridge
03 5281 7221

4. Leura Park Estate
1400 Portarlington Rd, Curlewis
03 5253 3180

5. Bellarine Estate
2270 Portarlington Rd, Bellarine
03 5259 3310

6. Scotchmans Hill
190 Scotchmans Rd, Drysdale
03 5251 3176

7. Pettavel
65 Pettavel Rd, Waurn Ponds
03 5266 1120

8. Brown Magpie Wines
125 Larcombes Rd, Modewarre
03 5261 3875

WHERE TO EAT

A. Clyde Park Vineyard
2490 Midland Hwy, Bannockburn
03 5281 7274

B. Shadowfax
K Rd, Werribee
03 9731 4420

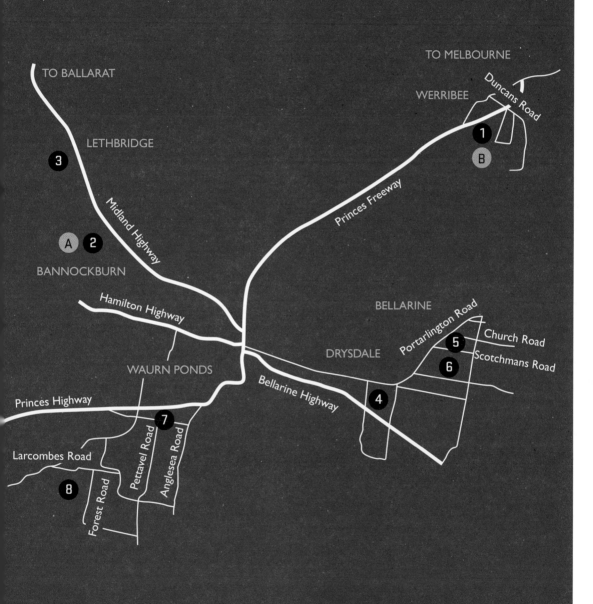

TO MELBOURNE

WERRIBEE

Duncans Road

1

B

TO BALLARAT

LETHBRIDGE

3

Princes Freeway

Midland Highway

A **2**

BANNOCKBURN

BELLARINE

Hamilton Highway

Portarlington Road

DRYSDALE

Church Road

5

WAURN PONDS

Scotchmans Road

6

Bellarine Highway

4

Princes Highway

7

Pettavel Road

Anglesea Road

Larcombes Road

8

Forest Road

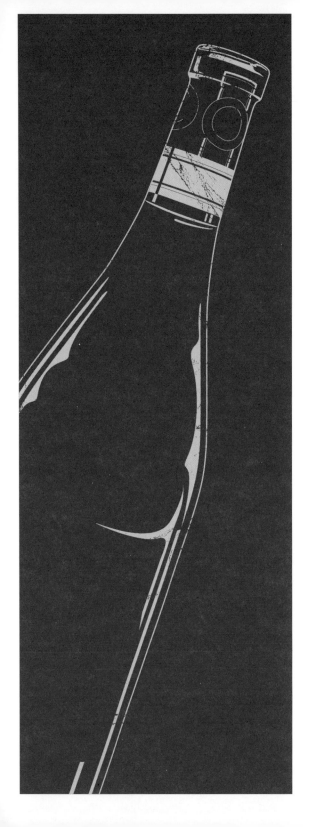

Snapshot

Geelong is a paradoxical place. It's the fifth-largest non-capital city in Australia and, with the car factories, has a dark blue-collar side, but then head out to Queenscliff music festival or Torquay, Victoria's surf city, and you get a whole different idea of the place. The wineries are no different. There's a sophistication and wine quality here that most regions envy. It produces some of the best pinot noir, chardonnay and shiraz in the country.

The background

Geelong's wine history is a bit like its footy team. Successes have been a long way apart. It's Australia's oldest wine region and by the 1860s there were more than 200 hectares of vineyards in Geelong, which is only slightly smaller than it is now. But Geelong is where the notorious, vineyard-wrecking, hope-destroying vine louse known as phylloxera entered Australia. The Victorian government in its wisdom offered a bounty for uprooted vineyards and so the vineyards came to an end.

The revival didn't occur until the 1960s and since then gurus such as Gary Farr (Bannockburn and now By Farr) have made the region famous. Where the gurus go others will follow and so they have. Weather is notoriously nasty, with low rainfall, aggressive summers, wind and hail. But as we all know, good wine is not made by coddling vineyards.

The wines
The region is red-dominant with 65 per cent of vineyards being red and mostly made up of pinot noir and shiraz. Chardonnay is the great white from the region but there's also some decent sauvignon blanc, pinot gris/grigio and riesling produced, too. Don't neglect the viognier, either.

The prices
Weather is an issue in Geelong. It can flatten crops, and prices reflect the difficulty and the inherent labour-intensiveness of the agriculture. It's not cheap.

The layout
The region starts at Werribee, goes south then north-west up the Midland Highway to Bannockburn, west on the Princes Highway and east on the Bellarine Peninsula. There is a huge variety in climate.

A suggested route
Coming from Melbourne, you shouldn't drive past **Shadowfax** (K Rd, Werribee; open daily 11 am–5 pm; 03 9731 4420; www.shadowfax.com.au), a large, money-is-no-object operation overseen by clever winemaker Matt Harrop. The wines are stylish and balanced across the range. The range of shiraz from different vineyards and regions is instructive to taste and the chardonnay is a beauty.

Head off the freeway up the Midlands Highway and you'll get to **Clyde Park Vineyard** (2490 Midland Hwy, Bannockburn; open weekends & public holidays 11 am–5 pm; 03 5281 7274; www.clydepark.com.au). Once owned by the legendary Gary Farr, Clyde Park still makes a very smart pinot noir and chardonnay, and there's a casual eatery.

Further along the road you come to **Lethbridge** (74 Burrows Rd, Lethbridge; open Thu–Sun 11 am–5 pm; 03 5281 7221; www.lethbridgewines.com.au), a recent arrival (established 1996) and one of the big movers. With a dedication to organic, sustainable wine practices, the winery is built from straw bales for its insulation properties. The wines are really good, particularly the riesling and the shiraz.

Head out towards the Bellarine Peninsula on Portarlington Road and you'll come to **Leura Park Estate** (1400 Portarlington Rd, Curlewis; open weekends 10.30 am–5 pm, daily in Jan; 03 5253 3180; www.leuraparkestate.com.au). Check out the 25D'Gris Pinot Gris and the shiraz in particular.

Bellarine Estate (2270 Portarlington Rd, Bellarine; open 11 am–4 pm; 03 5259 3310; www.bellarineestate.com.au) has nice views, a decent shiraz and an added bonus—the Bellarine Brewing Company—which has some pretty good brews, notably 'The Heads' Ale.

Scotchmans Hill (190 Scotchmans Rd, Drysdale; open daily 10.30 am–4.30 pm; 03 5251 3176; www.scotchmanshill.com.au) is one of the Geelong pioneers and has grown significantly without becoming overblown and losing its way. The chardonnay, pinot noir and Cornelius Pinot Gris are beauties and the Swan Bay has a good chardonnay and pinot below $20.

Heading out west along the Princes Highway you come to **Pettavel** (65 Pettavel Rd, Waurn Ponds; open daily 10 am–5.30 pm; 03 5266 1120; www.pettavel.com). With one of the prettiest labels in the business and an imposing cellar door, there's a good late-harvest riesling and the occasional supple pinot noir.

A bit off the beaten track is one of the newbies to the region, **Brown Magpie Wines** (125 Larcombes Rd, Modewarre; open daily noon–3 pm; 03 5261 3875; www.brownmagpiewines.com). It's named not after magpies that roll in mud but because of the colour of the unique warblers that inhabit the property. Check out the magpies, and the shiraz and pinot noir in particular.

Where to eat

Clyde Park Vineyard (2490 Midland Hwy, Bannockburn; open weekends 11 am–5 pm; 03 5281 7274; www.clydepark.com.au) is a good spot for a casual bite.

Shadowfax (K Rd, Werribee; open daily 11 am–5 pm; 03 9731 4420; www.shadowfax.com.au) has antipasto plates and good wood-fired pizzas.

MACEDON RANGES

WINERIES

1. Hanging Rock Winery
88 Jim Rd, Newham
03 5427 0542

2. Curly Flat
263 Collivers Rd, Lancefield
03 5429 1956

3. Cobaw Ridge
31 Perc Boyers Ln, East Pastoria
03 5423 5227

4. Granite Hills
1481 Burke and Wills Track, Baynton
03 5423 7264

5. Candlebark Hill
Fordes Ln, Kyneton
03 9836 2712

6. Big Shed Wines
1289 Malmsbury Rd, Glenlyon
03 5348 7825

Snapshot

One of the great things about wine touring in Victoria is the relatively short distances you have to travel to enter entirely new wine terrain. Just a short drive from Melbourne is the Macedon Ranges, a place that looks and feels as if it could be in another state. Rocky, quaint, rural quiet and hilly—it's a pretty place to drive around, with some unique country and some unique wines.

The background

Burke and Wills have given their names to the Burke and Wills Track as they headed north towards the never-never with their caravan of camels, comfy chairs and superfluous stuff. There were a few vineyards planted in the wake of Burke and Wills but Macedon didn't light up the radar of wine watchers until Virgin Hills, a legendary red established in the 1970s that set many others off down the cool-climate path. At about the same time, Knight's Granite Hills set a new standard for riesling and shiraz. Recently, the quality of pinot noir and chardonnay coming from Curly Flat has refocused the wine tosser's pitiless gaze once more on the region.

The wines

It's cool-climate territory and consequently there are some pretty good sparklings; chardonnay also does well and riesling has made a mark because of the Knight's Granite Hills. On the red side of the spectrum, pinot can be great and shiraz does well, too. Cobaw Ridge makes a great red from lagrein, an Italian variety from Trentino.

The prices

Expect standard $20-plus cool-climate pricing from all except Hanging Rock and Big Shed, which have a few bargains.

The layout

The Calder Highway runs through the region and most of the wineries are to the east of the highway around the town of Lancefield. The cellar doors are spread out but the driving is far from boring with ever-changing landscape.

A suggested route

If you're heading up the Calder Highway from Melbourne, turn off at Woodend and follow the signs to **Hanging Rock Winery** (88 Jim Rd, Newham; open daily 10 am–5 pm; 03 5427 0542; www.hangingrock.com.au). There's a huge range of wines and varietals both from locally grown Macedon fruit and from elsewhere. There are sub $20 wines that are pretty good; the sparklings are excellent.

From Hanging Rock head towards Lancefield. It's a bit hard to find but **Curly Flat** (263 Collivers Rd, Lancefield; open weekends 1 pm–5 pm, or by appointment; 03 5429 1956; www.curlyflat.com) is worth seeking out. It is home to some of the best chardonnay and pinot noir in Macedon, if not the country.

From Lancefield, direct your travels towards Baynton and follow the signage to **Cobaw Ridge** (31 Perc Boyers Ln, East Pastoria; open Thu–Mon noon–5 pm; 03 5423 5227; www.cobawridge.com.au). The landscape says it all—hungry soil and granite boulders sticking out of the ground everywhere. This is not a fun place to be a grapevine but that's what it's all about. Good vignerons are sadists. The entire range of wines is really good but the lagrein and shiraz viognier are favourites.

Granite Hills (1481 Burke and Wills Track, Baynton; open Mon–Sat 10 am–6 pm, Sun 1 pm–6 pm; 03 5423 7264; www.granitehills.com.au) is further from Kyneton than Cobaw Ridge, and was once known as Knight's Granite Hills. It's legendary in pioneering cool-climate winemaking, and the shiraz and riesling are well worth the drive.

Closer to Kyneton is **Candlebark Hill** (Fordes Lane, Kyneton; open Sundays by appointment; 03 9836 2712) a tiny, family run operation which does a particularly tasty cabernet blend.

Heading east towards Daylesford, you come to **Big Shed Wines** (1289 Malmsbury Rd, Glenlyon; open daily 10 am–6 pm; 03 5348 7825; www.big shedwines.com.au). There's a wide range of wines from local and Victorian fruit. The estate pinot is pretty good and there are bargains to be had.

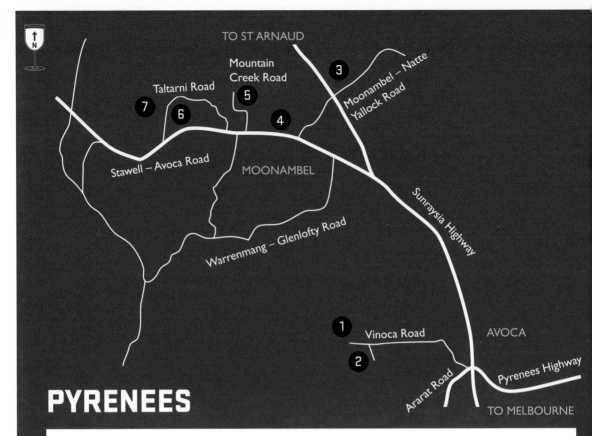

PYRENEES

WINERIES

1. Blue Pyrenees Estate
Vinoca Rd, Avoca
03 5465 1111

2. Mount Avoca
Moates Ln, Avoca
03 5465 3282

3. Redbank
1 Sally's Ln, Redbank
03 5467 7255

4. Summerfield
5967 Stawell–Avoca Rd, Moonambel
03 5467 2264

5. Warrenmang Vineyard & Resort
188 Mountain Creek Rd, Moonambel
03 5467 2233

6. Taltarni
Taltarni Rd, Moonambel
03 5459 7918

7. Dalwhinnie
448 Taltarni Rd, Moonambel
03 5467 2388

Snapshot

Pretty as a picture, the Pyrenees looks nothing like the pass at Roncesvalles—like most of the European names used for Australian spots there's a fair bit of poetic licence involved. It doesn't matter; it's a lovely name for a lovely region. Wooded hills encircle a valley that contains the towns of Moonambel and Avoca and some excellent wine. Some of the best features are the magnificent gum trees bordering pretty green vineyards shrouded in the blue haze that descends from the hills.

The background

In much the same way as Colonial Light named the Barossa after a battle that he had fought in Spain, the Pyrenees got its name from battle experience. Major Thomas Mitchell observed the hills in 1836 and somehow saw a similarity to the foothills of the French/Spanish Pyrenees he had fought in as a young soldier. Avoca got its name after the Vale of Avoca in Ireland.

By any measure the Pyrenees has a bizarre wine history. Like so many central Victorian wine regions, there was gold before vines. The place is still potholed with gold mines. The yellow metal was discovered in the mud of Four Mile Flat and by 1854 Avoca had a booming population of 16,000. It wasn't until 1887 that vines were planted and wine produced. The enterprise proved successful and was sold to a Methodist minister in 1929, who promptly smashed all the winemaking gear and ripped out the vines.

In 1963 Rémy Martin of Cognac fame made a decision almost as bizarre as buying a winery just to smash it up. They planted a vineyard dedicated to making brandy! When the brandy balloon promptly burst, Rémy went into sparkling-wine production. In the 1970s the Pyrenees led the central Victorian wine push with Redbank, Taltarni, Mount Avoca and Dalwhinnie, all of whom are still producing the goods today.

The wines

You could look at the climate with its rather hot summers and say that the Pyrenees might be somewhat limited in its wine styles, but you'd be wrong. This is a region that produces good sparkling wine from Blue Pyrenees and Taltarni, as well as magnificent reds. The weakness is probably the whites but there is the occasional white surprise, too.

The prices

Pricewise, the Pyrenees is about average. At the high end you can pay $30 and up but there are quite a few very good sub $20 wines.

The layout

Most of the vineyards sit between the Pyrenees range to the west and the St Arnaud National Park to the north along the Sunraysia Highway. The region is divided between the larger town of Avoca and the smaller town of Moonambel—about a 25-kilometre drive.

A suggested route

If you're entering from Melbourne, you come to Avoca first. Go through town and hang a left onto Duke Street, turn right into Vinoca Road and you're heading for **Blue Pyrenees Estate** (Vinoca Rd, Avoca; open weekdays 10 am–4.30 pm, weekends & public holidays 10 am–5 pm; 03 5465 1111; www.bluepyrenees.com.au). Here, you'll find some very good sparkling wines—particularly the Midnight Cuvée—but also a host of well-priced still wines. The sauvignon blanc and chardonnay are good and there's an excellent merlot and a killer cab sav.

Close by is **Mount Avoca** (Moates Ln, Avoca; open daily 10 am–5 pm; 03 5465 3282; www.mountavoca.com.au), one of the veterans of the Pyrenees offering excellent value for the cellar door traveller. The merlot and shiraz are particularly worth checking out.

Head from there towards Moonambel: there's a Y-intersection with one road heading to Moonambel and the other to St Arnaud. Take the road to St Arnaud and you'll come to the rustic cellar door of **Redbank** (1 Sally's Ln, Redbank; open Mon–Sat 9 am–5 pm, Sun 10 am–5 pm; 03 5467 7255; www.sallyspaddock.com.au). It can be confusing because Yalumba bought the Redbank brand but the winery and the town of Redbank have retained the name. Sally's Paddock is the legendary red blend and still worth a taste.

Back on the Stawell–Avoca road heading toward Moonambel you'll come to **Summerfield** (5967 Stawell–Avoca Rd, Moonambel; open daily 9 am–5 pm; 03 5467 2264; www.summerfieldwines.com). This is one of the best red-wine producers in the region. The standard wines taste like reserves and the reserves taste like uber reserves.

Drive up the road, hang a right-hand turn and you'll eventually come to **Warrenmang Vineyard & Resort** (188 Mountain Creek Rd, Moonambel; open daily 10 am–5 pm; 03 5467 2233; www.warrenmang.com.au), which is the indefatigable Luigi Bazzani's realised vision. The restaurant is one of the best in the region and the wines are great, particularly the reds—they are very expensive, though.

Back on the main road, turn right on Taltarni Road and not surprisingly you'll arrive at **Taltarni** (Taltarni Rd, Moonambel; open daily 10 am–5 pm; 03 5459 7918; www.taltarni.com.au). Here, you'll find a vast range of wines. The cabernet and cab blends are usually the pick of the bunch, as well as Taltarni's top-notch sparkling rosé.

Further up the road is the highlight—at least in wine and site terms—**Dalwhinnie** (448 Taltarni Rd, Moonambel; open daily 10 am–5 pm; 03 5467 2388; www. dalwhinnie.com.au). Immaculate vineyards and visionary winemaking combine to create memorable chardonnays and sumptuous shiraz. A glass of the latter with a cheese plate on the deck looking at the spectacular view is one of the Pyreneean highlights.

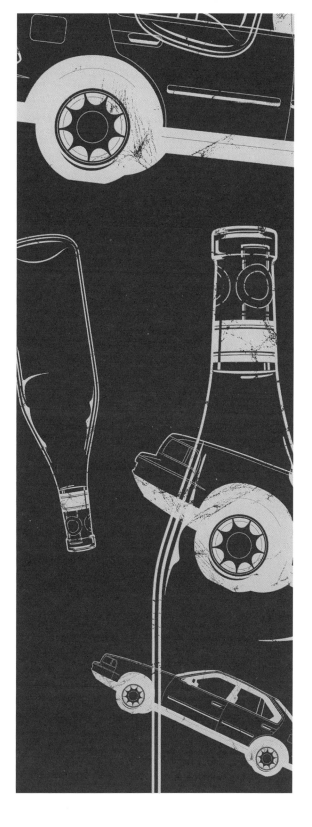

HEATHCOTE

WINERIES

1. Shelmerdine
cnr Northern Hwy and Lancefield Rd,
Tooborac
03 5433 5188

2. McIvor Estate
80 Tooborac–Baynton Rd, Tooborac
03 5433 5266

3. Heathcote Winery
183–185 High St, Heathcote
03 5433 2595

4. Munari Wines
1129 Northern Hwy, Heathcote
03 5433 3366

5. Barnadown Run
390 Cornella Rd, Toolleen
03 5433 6376

6. Mount Burrumboot Estate
3332 Heathcote–Rochester Rd,
Colbinabbin
03 5432 9238

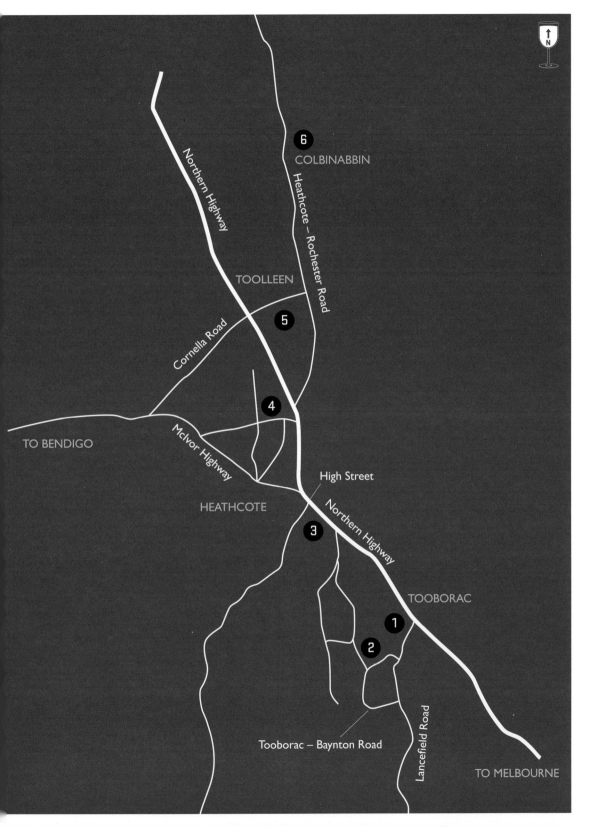

N

6 COLBINABBIN

Northern Highway

Heathcote – Rochester Road

TOOLLEEN

5

Cornella Road

4

TO BENDIGO

McIvor Highway

High Street

HEATHCOTE

Northern Highway

3

TOOBORAC

1

2

Tooborac – Baynton Road

Lancefield Road

TO MELBOURNE

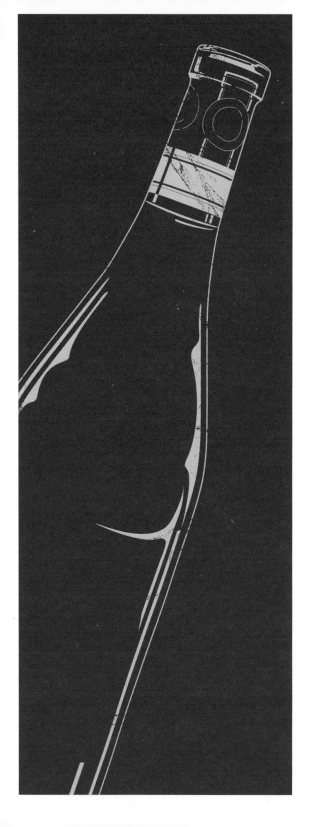

Snapshot

If any region has dirt as notorious as Coonawarra, it is Heathcote and the famous decomposed Cambrian greenstone. It's 500 million years old and is the weathered top of Mount Camel, which has washed down to the slopes where most of the vines are planted. That soil affects the structure of the reds, giving firm but supple tannins that have to be tasted to be believed.

The background

Being so close to Bendigo, Heathcote was swept up in the gold rush but not so much in the vine-planting craze. The modern wine history began with the Osicka Vineyard, which was established in the 1950s.

Jasper Hill was planted in 1975 and after Cambrian fever hit in the 1990s, a host of vineyards were planted—many for wineries outside the region looking for something special from the magic dirt.

The wines

Shiraz is the big one. Actually, only 10 per cent of the vineyard area is white. The cabernet is good and there is the odd decent sangiovese, too.

The prices

When you're the flavour of the month you'd normally expect flavour-of-the-month prices. Strangely that's not the case here and generally prices are in the $15–$30 range.

The layout

The region is in a 30-kilometre radius around the town of Heathcote and north along the Heathcote–Rochester Road.

A suggested route

Coming from Melbourne (60 kilometres away) is **Shelmerdine** (cnr Northern Hwy and Lancefield Rd, Tooborac; open daily 10 am–5 pm; 03 5433 5188; www.shelmerdine.com.au), one of the bigger concerns, which makes wine from several regions. The Heathcote Shiraz shines.

South-west of Shelmerdine is **McIvor Estate** (80 Tooborac–Baynton Rd, Tooborac; open weekends & public holidays 10 am–5 pm; 03 5433 5266; www.mcivorestate.com.au), a newer winery making a splash. Soothing surroundings and views from the little cellar door add to the appeal of the spicy shiraz, but don't neglect the sangiovese.

Next stop is in town at **Heathcote Winery** (183–185 High St, Heathcote; open daily 10 am–5 pm; 03 5433 2595; www.heathcotewinery.com.au). The shiraz is the pick and the prices are pretty good.

Head north on the Northern Highway and on your left you'll come across **Munari Wines** (1129 Northern Hwy, Heathcote; open Tue–Sun 11 am–5 pm; 03 5433 3366; www.munariwines.com) has excellent shiraz and a delicious cabernet sauvignon.

Up the Heathcote–Rochester Road is **Barnadown Run** (390 Cornella Rd, Toolleen; open daily 10 am–5 pm; 03 5433 6376; www.barnadownrun.com.au) with some decent reds that can be a little up and down.

Not far away is **Mount Burrumboot Estate** (3332 Heathcote–Rochester Rd, Colbinabbin; open weekends & public holidays 11 am–5 pm; 03 5432 9238; www.burrumboot.com), a friendly cellar door with a big range of varietals, a good petit verdot, tempranillo and a handy shiraz.

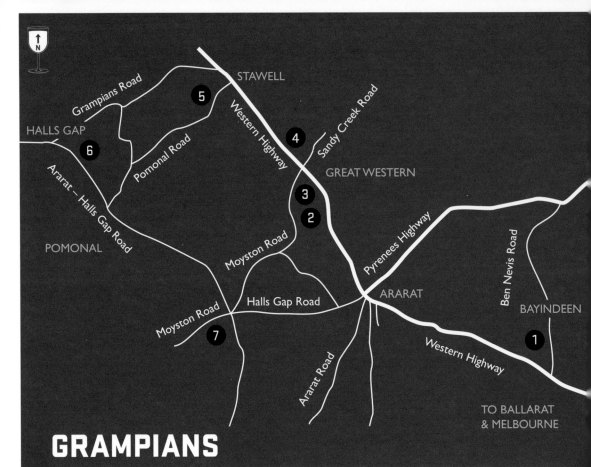

GRAMPIANS

WINERIES

1. Mount Langi Ghiran
80 Vine Rd, Bayindeen
03 5354 3207

2. Grampians Estate
1477 Western Hwy, Great Western
03 5356 2400

3. Seppelt Great Western
36 Cemetery Rd, Great Western
03 5361 2239

4. Best's Wines
111 Best's Road, Great Western
03 5356 2250

5. Donovan Wines
RMB 2017 Pomonal Road,
Stawell
03 5358 2727

6. The Gap Vineyard
Ararat–Halls Gap Road, Halls Gap
03 5356 4252

7. Clayfield Wines
25 Wilde Lane, Moyston
03 5354 2689

Snapshot

The name may not roll off the tongue with the same familiarity as the Yarra Valley or Rutherglen but this is holy ground as far as wine goes. It's the area around Great Western, and the towns of Ararat and Stawell (you know, the spot where they hold the running race known as the Gift). The most famous names are Bests and Mount Langi Ghiran, both of which have hung their shingle on shiraz. Here in this tough country, shiraz takes on a sublime beauty and why the Grampians isn't bigger, more famous and more travelled when patriotic Australians love shiraz so much is one of wine's great mysteries.

The background

Gold. Most central Victorian wine districts have a modern history that begins with the yellow metal and nowhere is it more visible than here. The 'drives' of Seppelt Great Western are tunnels lined with bottles—the remnants of mines. The Bests were butchers feeding the miners meat, which financed the planting of a vineyard in 1866. Across the road, Frenchies Jean Pierre Trouette and Anne Marie Blampied started Great Western Estate about the same time. The French influence continued when Charles Pierlot arrived and in the 1890s made the best sparkling wine yet produced in Australia. Since then, the sparkling reputation for Great Western has been surpassed by other cooler regions but the drives at Seppelt are still full of fizz and pretty amazing to look at.

The wines

Shiraz, shiraz, shiraz. Is there anything else than Grampians shiraz? Well, yes. But three-quarters of the grapes in the vineyards are red. There's a bit of riesling and this is also the birthplace of sparkling red.

The prices

Mount Langi's top-of-the-line shiraz is $85, which is pretty good value considering how good it is. Most of the wines in the region sit around the $20–$30 mark.

The layout

The region exists around Great Western, Ararat and Stawell along the Western Highway and within a 30-kilometre radius. A couple of wineries have situated their cellar doors wisely in the main strip at Great Western.

A suggested route

Coming from Melbourne, the first winery you get to is the legendary **Mount Langi Ghiran** (80 Vine Rd, Bayindeen; open weekdays 9 am–5 pm, weekends & public holidays 10 am–5 pm; 03 5354 3207; www. langi.com.au). Established in 1969 and guided by the celebrated winemaking skills of Trevor Mast, it has since been sucked into a large wine conglomerate but the wine quality has not retreated. From the delicious flagship—the Mount Langi Shiraz at $70—to the Billi Billi Shiraz at about $15, the quality is excellent. There's also another Langi cellar door at the north-west end of the region at the other vineyard.

Grampians Estate (Great Western Wine Centre, 1477 Western Hwy, Great Western; open daily noon–5 pm; 03 5356 2400; www.grampiansestate.com.au) is the old Garden Gully and shiraz is still the focal point. The sparkling shiraz is a beauty.

Next door is **Seppelt Great Western** (36 Cemetery Rd, Great Western; open daily 10 am–5 pm; 03 5361 2239; www.seppelt.com.au). The 'drives' are three kilometres of underground tunnels and are all very good and interesting but don't forget the wines, especially the shiraz. The St Peters is a beauty and the sparkling red is still one of the best.

Also in Great Western is **Best's Wines** (111 Best's Road, Great Western; open Mon–Sat 10 am–5 pm Sun 11 am–4 pm; 03 5356 2250; www.bestswines.com). With vines dating back to the 1860s it's living history. Shiraz is the trump card (it's

excellent), but there's also a good riesling chardonnay and the pinot noir can be surprisingly good.

Up the highway from Best's is the town of Stawell and **Donovan Wines** (RMB 2017 Pomonal Rd, Stawell; open Mon–Sat 10 am–5 pm and Sun 12 pm–5 pm; 03 5356 2482). It's an unsung label with a shed for a cellar door. Sometimes there are some real bargains and the shiraz is great.

Follow the Grampians road to Hall's Gap and hang a left into Pomonal road back towards Ararat and you'll come to **The Gap Vineyard** (Ararat–Halls Gap Road, Halls Gap; Wed–Sun 10 am–5 pm, daily during school holidays 10 am– 5 pm; 03 5356 4252; www.langi.com.au).

Then head further down the Ararat– Halls Gap road and you'll come to Moyston, the little spot that gave its name to the famous red of the 1970s Seppelt Moyston Claret. A couple of kilometres past the town is **Clayfield Wines** (25 Wilde Ln, Moyston; open Mon–Sat 10 am–5 pm, Sun 11 am–4 pm; 03 5354 2689). Shiraz is a speciality and the quality is excellent. The Massif Grampians Shiraz is a bargain at $25.

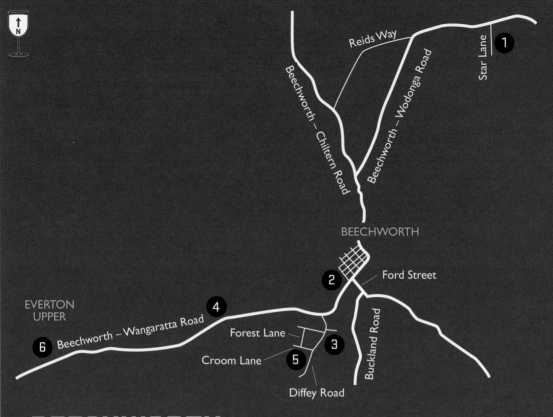

BEECHWORTH

WINERIES

1. Star Lane Vineyard
1 Star Ln, Wooragee, via Beechworth
03 5728 7268

2. Bridge Road Brewers
Old Coach House, Ford St, Beechworth
03 5728 2703

3. Pennyweight Winery
13 Pennyweight Ln, Beechworth
03 5728 1747

4. Amulet Vineyard
Wangaratta Road, Beechworth
03 5727 0420

5. Smiths Vineyard
27 Croom Ln, Beechworth
03 5728 2364

6. Indigo Vineyard
1221 Beechworth–Wangaratta Rd,
Everton Upper
03 5727 0233

Snapshot

Mention Beechworth to a wine snob and, like that reaction when a doctor belts a knee with one of those little hammers to test the reflexes, the word Giaconda will involuntarily pop out. It's one of the great cult labels with a mind-blowing chardonnay and a killer pinot and it's in Beechworth. It doesn't have a cellar door (open by appointment) but there are plenty of wineries you might never have heard of mining the Beechworth dirt for great fruit.

The background

Don't be in too much of a rush to get on the road and taste the wine as the town of Beechworth is worth a visit. The streets, the buildings and the houses make it easy to imagine life here during the heady days of the gold rush when the vineyards were first being planted. Like most places, the vine fell from fashion until late last century. The revival occurred in the 1980s courtesy of Giaconda and Sorrenberg. It's been a slow growth but Beechworth continues to march on.

The wines

Diverse. Giaconda is famous for its magnificent chardonnay, Sorrenberg makes the best gamay in the country, while Castagna and Star Lane make stunning shiraz. There are even some decent sherries.

The prices

Pricey. Not much here that you can buy with a $20 note.

The layout

The region is about 30 kilometres end-to-end either side of C315—the Beechworth–Wodonga Road.

A suggested route

From the north you hit **Star Lane Vineyard** (1 Star Ln, Wooragee, via Beechworth; open weekends 10 am–5 pm; 03 5728 7268; www.starlane.com.au), which is 15 kilometres from Beechworth and produces some really smart reds, particularly the shiraz.

In Beechworth itself is **Bridge Road Brewers** (Old Coach House, Ford St, Beechworth; open Mon–Wed 11 am–4 pm, Thu–Sun 11 am–6 pm; 03 5728 2703; www.bridgeroadbrewers.com.au). Brewer Ben Kraus is a winemaker who is also very well versed in the art of producing tasty beer. At Bridge Road there's a bar alongside a pizza and pie kitchen in a 150-year-old coach house and the Robust Porter is a beauty.

Not far out of Beechworth is **Pennyweight Winery** (13 Pennyweight Ln, Beechworth; open daily 10 am–5 pm; 03 5728 1747; www.pennyweight.com.au), an unirrigated, organic, biodynamic family concern, which has some good pinot noir and some intriguing sherries.

Close by Pennyweight Winery on the road to Wang is **Amulet Vineyard** (Wangaratta Road, Beechworth; open weekends and public and school holidays; 10 am–5 pm; 03 5727 0420; www.amulet wines.com.au) which specialises in scenery and Italian varieties. There's also the ubiquitous shiraz and a very good cider made from local apples.

Smiths Vineyard (27 Croom Ln, Beechworth; open weekends & public holidays 11 am–5 pm; 03 5728 2364; www. smithsvineyard.com.au) has the oldest vineyard in the region, dating back to 1978. The chardonnay and 310 Shiraz can rock.

Indigo Vineyard (1221 Beechworth–Wangaratta Rd, Everton Upper; open daily 11 am–3 pm; 03 5727 0233; www.indigovineyard.com.au) is part of the Brokenwood group, owners of the largest vineyard in the district, which provides fruit for Brokenwood as well as Indigo. The wines are made at Brokenwood and show the region's strengths. Check out the chardonnay in particular.

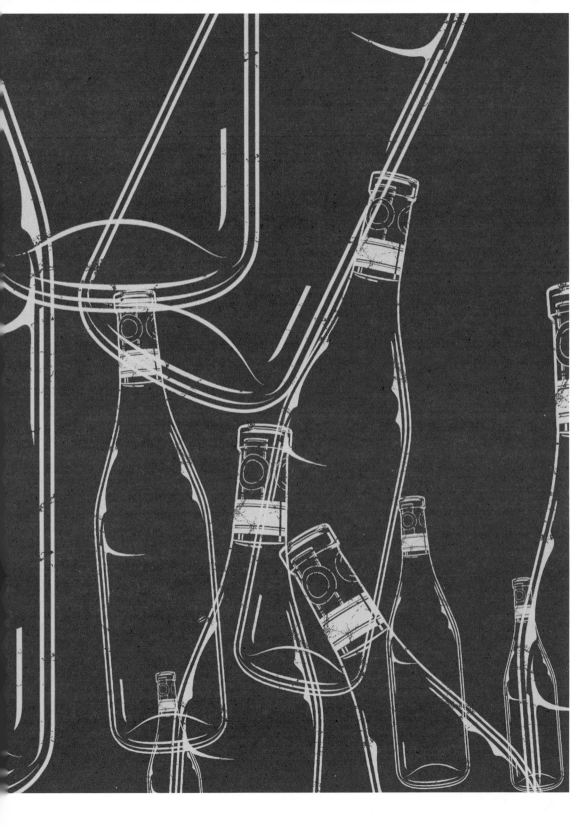

RUTHERGLEN

WINERIES

1. Morris Wines
Mia Mia Rd, Rutherglen
02 6026 7303

2. Jones
Jones Rd, Rutherglen
02 6032 8496

3. Rutherglen Estates
Tuilieries Complex, 13–35 Drummond St,
Rutherglen
02 6032 7999

4. Chambers Rosewood Vineyard
Barkly St, Rutherglen
02 6032 8641

5. Pfeiffer Wines
167 Distillery Rd, Wahgunyah
02 6033 2805

6. Cofield Wines
Distillery Rd, Wahgunyah
02 6033 3788

7. All Saints
All Saints Rd, Wahgunyah
02 6035 2222

8. St Leonards
St Leonards Rd, Wahgunyah
02 6033 1004

9. Campbells
Murray Valley Hwy, Rutherglen
02 6032 9458

10. Stanton & Killeen
Jacks Rd, Rutherglen
02 6032 9457

WHERE TO EAT

A. Parker Pies
86–88 Main St, Rutherglen
02 6032 9605

B. The Pickled Sisters Cafe
Distillery Rd, Wahgunyah
03 6033 2377

C. The Terrace at All Saints Estate
All Saints Rd, Wahgunyah
02 6035 2209

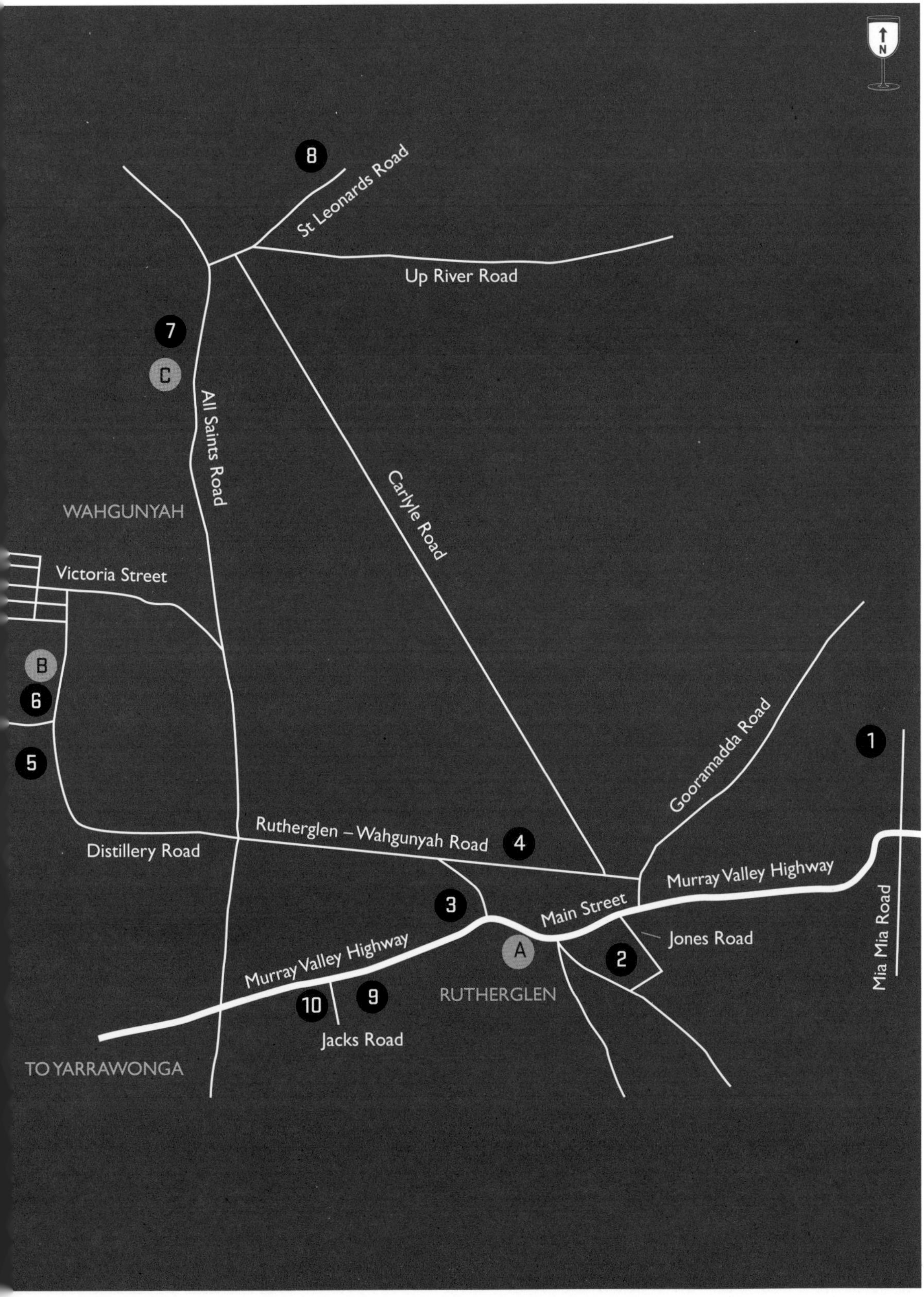

N

8

St Leonards Road

Up River Road

7

C

All Saints Road

WAHGUNYAH

Victoria Street

Carlyle Road

B

6

5

Distillery Road

Rutherglen – Wahgunyah Road

4

Gooramadda Road

1

3

Murray Valley Highway

Main Street

Murray Valley Highway

Jones Road

A

2

10

9

RUTHERGLEN

Mia Mia Road

Jacks Road

TO YARRAWONGA

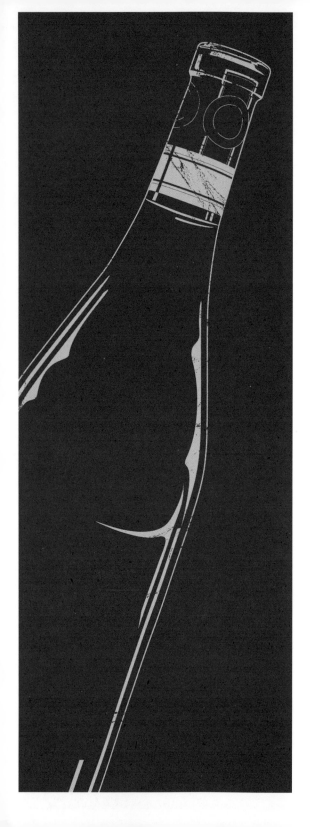

Snapshot

If you had a friend from overseas visiting and wanted to show them a truly Australian-looking wine region, it would be hard to go past Rutherglen. The countryside, the eucalypts and the harsh Murray River all have a classically Aussie look. Some of the buildings have a bit of the old hardwood-plank-shed look about them and there's even some authentic bulldust.

From a wine point of view it's not bog-standard chardonnay and shiraz country; the wines are very unique. Rutherglen produces a strange style of fortified wine known as liqueur muscat and liqueur tokay, an amazing liquid by any standards. Then there's the general use of unusual varieties such as durif—it's worth a look.

The background

Believe it or not, it wasn't until 1824 that Hume and Hovell crossed the Murray River, which Hume (of highway fame) named after himself (fortunately it didn't stick), and discovered the flat grazing land on the other side. Before long, squatters had infested the area and gold was found in 1860, giving birth to a town that was named by a gold-digger after his birthplace. Vines had already been experimented with successfully and when the gold boom really hit, those names so familiar with

Rutherglen and fortified wine such as Morris, Campbell, Gehrig and Sutherland Smith were in business.

Unfortunately, the boom didn't last. Fortified wine had its day in the sun during the latter part of the 1800s and early part of the 1900s but then fell into decline. Rutherglen went from being God's own wine country to one of the least-valued wine regions during the cool-climate madness. Now we are in the midst of a Rutherglen rebirth. A new generation of Browns, Gehrigs, Campbells and Cofields is re-energising Rutherglen. The wines are less old-fashioned and the famous fortifieds are as good as they ever were.

The wines

Rutherglen has justly achieved fame for its liqueur muscat and tokay and for a long time bore a deserved reputation for big, bruising reds. Younger winemakers, better gear and a basic understanding that not too many people hang onto wine for 20 years before drinking it means that the reds have got better—or at least more drinkable. They've lost a fair bit of grunt and tannin and gained a little bit more finesse.

Durif is the unusual variety. 'Invented' by one Dr Durif by crossing peloursin with shiraz, for a long time it was thought to be the same variety that is known in the US as petite syrah (a very inappropriate name for such a ball-busting grape variety). It's not. The taste of durif lies somewhere between shiraz and cabernet—imagine warm-climate cabernet with a rustic edge and that's durif. Whites have never been one of the region's strong points—it's too warm. That said, there is the odd surprise.

The prices

There are bargains to be had! You could argue that being able to buy fortified wine that dates back to the days of the horse and cart is a bargain no matter what the price. The fortifieds have a tiered price range, which means you can buy in at below $20 or go up to triple figures for a blend with components that are older than the Anzacs. Most of the table wines haven't had the inflationary marketing of trendier regions so good reds can be had for under $20.

The layout

Rutherglen is west of the Hume Highway. Heading south, exit just after Wodonga or heading north, turn left at the Murray Valley Highway before you hit the border (there are plenty of signs). There's the subregion of Wahgunyah close to the border and it's an easy place to find your way around. If you get lost in Rutherglen, sack your co-driver.

A suggested route

From the eastern side, the first winery you get to off the Murray Valley Highway is **Morris Wines** (Mia Mia Rd, Rutherglen; open Mon–Sat 9 am–5 pm, Sun 10 am–5 pm; 02 6026 7303; www.morriswines.com). A huge multinational wine company, Pernod Ricard, now owns it but you would never know. David Morris is still the winemaker and there are some treasures at the cellar door that are a bit hard to get in retail land. The blue imperial red made from cinsaut is worth a taste and the old fortifieds are still bargains.

In the town of Rutherglen itself you'll find **Jones** (Jones Rd, Rutherglen; open Mon, Tue & Fri 11 am–4 pm, weekends & public holidays 10 am–5 pm; 02 6032 8496; www.joneswinery.com). It's a heritage-listed building complete with a family-bought-back-the-farm story. As the name of the road indicates, the Joneses have a long history in the region—1860 to be exact. The winemaker Mandy Jones spent considerable time in Bordeaux and reds display an identifiable style. The shiraz and durif are especially good and the chardonnay is one of the best in the region.

Also in town is **Rutherglen Estates** (Tuilieries Complex, 13–35 Drummond St, Rutherglen; open daily 10 am–6 pm; 02 6032 7999; www.rutherglenestates.

com.au), a relative newcomer (established in 2000) but one company that is pushing Rutherglen into new territory. With interesting blends, experimental varietals and energetic marketing, you'll hear more from it.

If you follow Drummond Street in to Scott Street, and turn right into Barkly, you'll find **Chambers Rosewood Vineyard** (Barkly St, Rutherglen; open Mon–Sat 9 am–5 pm, Sun 10 am–5 pm; 02 6032 8641; www.chambersrosewood.com.au), which is one of the quaintest cellar doors in the country. No architect-designed stuff here. The fortified wines are brilliant; the table wines less so.

Head back along the Rutherglen–Wahgunyah Road and you'll come to the romantically named Distillery Road and the turn-off to **Pfeiffer Wines** (167 Distillery Rd, Wahgunyah; open Mon–Sat 9 am–5 pm, Sun 10 am–5 pm; 02 6033 2805; www.pfeifferwinesrutherglen.com.au). There's a vast range, a pretty good gamay and the vintage port is a beauty.

Up the road a bit further is **Cofield Wines** (Distillery Rd, Wahgunyah; open Mon–Sat 9 am–5 pm, Sun 10 am–5 pm; 02 6033 3788; www.cofieldwines.com.au), one of the wineries that has been given fresh life by passing the winemaking baton to the next generation. Winemaker

Damian Cofield has a modern touch. Highlights are the durif and the occasional sparkling red.

Close by is **All Saints** (All Saints Rd, Wahgunyah; open Mon–Sat 9 am–5.30 pm, Sun 10 am–5.30 pm; 02 6035 2222; www.prbwines.com.au). You can't miss it. The driveway is straight out of Brideshead Revisited and the building that houses All Saints looks like a castle and was modelled on one. A new generation of Browns is running the place and the wines are becoming more modern in style. The fortifieds are great and the imaginatively blended table wines are a long way from the way All Saints table wine used to taste.

St Leonards (St Leonards Rd, Wahgunyah; open Fri–Sun 10 am–5 pm, weekends only in winter; 02 6033 1004 www.prbwines.com.au) is a scenic old winery on the banks of the river and a good place for reds.

Take the Carlyle Road back to town, drive west and you'll come to **Campbells** (Murray Valley Hwy, Rutherglen; open Mon–Sat 9 am–5 pm, Sun 10 am–5 pm; 02 6032 9458; www.campbellswines.com. au) and a wide range of fortifieds and table wines. Apart from the excellent Merchant Prince Rare Rutherglen Muscat, there are a couple of classic reds: the Barkly Durif and the Bobbie Burns Shiraz.

Across the road is **Stanton & Killeen** (Jacks Rd, Rutherglen; open Mon–Sat 9 am–5 pm, Sun 10 am–5 pm; 02 6032 9457; www.stantonandkilleenwines.com.au). With a cellar door that looks a bit like an old-style garage and arguably some of the best liqueur muscat and tokay in the region, it's typically Rutherglen. Don't forget to try the durif ...

Where to eat

Parker Pies (86–88 Main St, Rutherglen; open Mon–Sat 8 am–5 pm, Sun 9 am–4.30 pm; 02 6032 9605; www.parkerpies. com.au) is the spot for a pie.

The Pickled Sisters Cafe (Distillery Rd, Wahgunyah; open Wed–Sun 10 am–4 pm, Sat from 6 pm; 03 6033 2377; www.pickledsisters.com.au) is based at Cofield Wines with an indoor/outdoor eating area and it serves local produce.

The Terrace at All Saints Estate (All Saints Rd, Wahgunyah; open Wed–Sun for lunch from noon, Saturday for dinner from 6 pm; 02 6035 2209; www.prbwines. com.au) is a little like dining in a castle.

BENDIGO

WINERIES

1. BlackJack Wines
3379 Calder Hwy, Harcourt
03 5474 2355

2. Leamon Estate
5528 Calder Hwy, Bendigo
03 5447 7995

3. Balgownie Estate
Hermitage Rd, Maiden Gully, Bendigo
03 5449 6222

4. Sandhurst Ridge
156 Forest Dr, Marong
03 5435 2534

5. Pondalowie Vineyard
6 Main St, Bridgewater on Loddon
03 5437 3332

6. Water Wheel Vineyards
Raywood Rd, Bridgewater on Loddon
03 5437 3060

7. Passing Clouds
Kurting Rd, Kingower
03 5438 8257

8. Blanche Barkly
Rheola Rd, Kingower
03 5438 8223

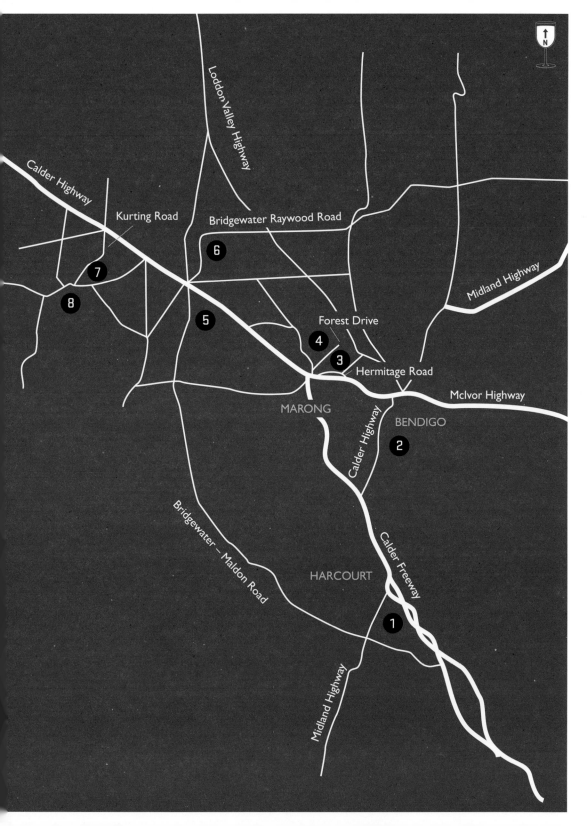

Snapshot

Some wines resemble the region and climate they're grown in and Bendigo's chunky, gutsy reds are a sort of vinous mirror to the harsh climate and the tough-looking bush they come from. If you don't like your reds shy, and you find the word elegant pejorative, Bendigo is for you.

The background

Bendigo epitomised the Victorian gold rush. More gold was found in Bendigo between 1850 and 1900 than anywhere else in the world. Liquor followed the miners. Vines were planted, wine was made but both dried up when the gold and the miners departed.

The renaissance occurred in 1969 when Stuart Anderson planted vines at Balgownie. Those big, spicy wines excited palates used to what the established regions produced. They smelt and tasted like the Australian bush, winemakers were intrigued and more followed. In the 1980s, Château Leamon and Passing Clouds were the names that the snobs and knobs were quoting. The region has lost some of its gloss since, but still produces fantastic reds.

The wines

Vineyards in the region are more than 90 per cent red. There's a bit of chardonnay and a bit of sauvignon blanc but if you don't like red you're not going to like Bendigo.

The prices

Great. Not being trendy and flavour of the month does pay dividends for the cellar door traveller—$25 is an expensive wine.

The layout

It's spread out in about a 25-kilometre radius of the town of Bendigo.

A suggested route

Coming from the south on the Calder Highway you come to **BlackJack Wines** (3379 Calder Hwy, Harcourt; open weekends 11 am–5 pm; 03 5474 2355; www.blackjackwines.net.au). Named after an American sailor who jumped ship for the gold rush back in the day, gutsy reds are the stock in trade. Chortle's Edge is a big, ballsy $18 shiraz and the Block 6 Shiraz is a beauty.

Leamon Estate (5528 Calder Hwy, Bendigo; open daily 10 am–5 pm; 03 5447 7995) is one of the pioneers of Bendigo (established in 1973 and formerly called Château Leamon). The shiraz is the trump here—both the reserve and the $20-ish standard wine—and there's also a decent riesling to break up the red monotony.

Further towards the north is **Balgownie Estate** (Hermitage Rd, Maiden Gully, Bendigo; open 11 am–5 pm; 03 5449 6222; www.balgownieestate.com.au). This is the original Balgownie that was devalued when it was purchased by one of the mega wine companies and is now having a revamp. The shiraz is the wine to taste but there's a pretty good chardonnay, too.

Sandhurst Ridge (156 Forest Dr, Marong; open daily 11 am–5 pm; 03 5435 2534; www.sandhurstridge.com.au) was established in 1990. It's a quiet achiever producing really good wines with great success but not much fanfare. There's a sauvignon blanc for those craving whites but as with most of Bendigo, it's the shiraz that rocks.

Pondalowie Vineyard (6 Main St, Bridgewater on Loddon; open weekends & public holidays noon–5 pm; 03 5437 3332; www.pondalowie.com.au) is a relative newbie (established 1997) but is showing a dab hand with some of the newer varieties, notably tempranillo.

Close by is **Water Wheel Vineyards** (Raywood Rd, Bridgewater on Loddon; open weekdays 9 am–5 pm, weekends noon–4 pm; 03 5437 3060; www.waterwheelwine.com). Winemaker Peter Cumming is down to earth and his prices and wines reflect it. They're honest, flavoursome and not shy.

The Memsie red blend is a ripper at $13 and the sauvignon blanc can be good, too.

West of there is **Passing Clouds** (Kurting Rd, Kingower; open weekends noon–5 pm, weekdays by appointment; 03 5438 8257; www.passingclouds.com.au), another legend of the district that got its name because the clouds would pass by without depositing any rain. The reds are the thing, particularly Graeme's Blend shiraz cabernet and the Angel Cabernet Sauvignon.

Close by is **Blanche Barkly** (Rheola Rd, Kingower; open weekends & public holidays 9 am–5 pm; 03 5438 8223), reclusive as far as marketing goes but occasionally producing a very good cabernet from an old, struggling vineyard.

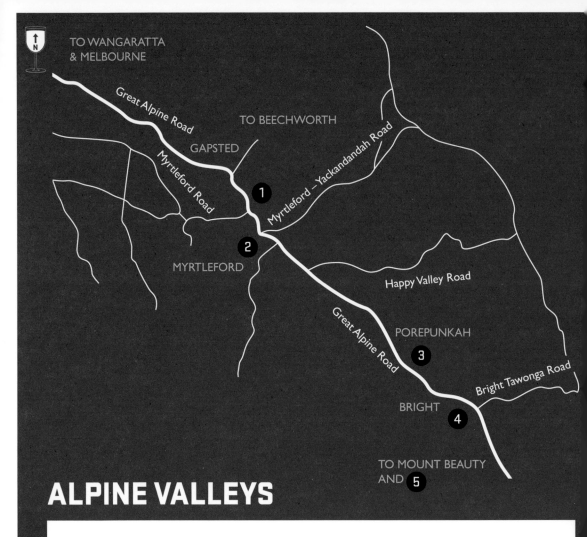

ALPINE VALLEYS

WINERIES

1. Gapsted
Great Alpine Rd, Gapsted
03 5751 1383

2. Michelini Wines
Great Alpine Rd, Myrtleford
03 5751 1990

3. Boynton's Feathertop Winery
Great Alpine Rd, Porepunkah
03 5756 2356

4. The Bright Brewery
121 Great Alpine Rd, Bright
03 5755 1655

5. Annapurna Wines
Simmons Creek Road, Mount Beauty
03 5754 4517

Snapshot

The phrase 'cool climate' gets thrown around in the wine business willy-nilly and you can go to some so-called frigid regions on a 35 degree day and think the term employs some poetic licence. Not so in the Alpine Valleys where snow and brisk mountain air give the word 'cool' punch. It's tricky viticulture and vineyards suffer bushfires in summer and frost and snow in winter. But when all the planets align, the results can be fantastic, with flavours in the grapes that almost seem concentrated. It's a large region and is not highly populated with cellar doors but it's home to some of the prettiest vine scenery in the state.

The background

This region was first populated during the gold rush. Then later, with the post-war immigration of Italians, tobacco became a major crop (there's even a charming little town named Smoko) and the corrugated-iron tobacco-drying sheds can still be seen from the roadside. Typical Italian mixed farming has blessed the region with a wide range of produce from apples to chestnuts to olives.

The wines

The region is relatively new and is yet to hang its hat on any particular variety. Sauvignon blanc does well, and chardonnay, too. Italian varieties show promise, merlot is pretty good and there's the occasional stunning cool-climate shiraz.

The prices

For such labour-intensive viticulture, prices aren't too bad. Gapsted has plenty of sub $20 wines and even some quaffers for less than $10! Michelini prices are competitive, too.

The layout

The Alpine Valleys consist of four valleys around four rivers—the Ovens, Buffalo, Buckland and Kiewa. Most of the cellar doors lie between the two pretty towns of Myrtleford and Bright.

A suggested route

Coming from Melbourne, the first winery you arrive at is **Gapsted** (Great Alpine Rd, Gapsted; open daily 10 am–5 pm; 03 5751 1383; www.victorianalpswinery.com.au), one of the bigger operators and home to the evocatively named 'ballerina canopy'—a trellising system that exposes the grapes to the sun. The range is good throughout, the chardonnay is a regular standout and there's the occasional killer merlot.

Michelini Wines (Great Alpine Rd, Myrtleford; open daily 10 am–5 pm;

03 5751 1990; www.micheliniwines.com.au) is home to tobacco farmers turned grape growers turned winemakers. There's a big range of Italian varieties as well as the standard French grapes, and the whites tend to be better than the reds. The chardonnay is the pick and prices are good.

Closer to the beautiful town of Bright is **Boynton's Feathertop Winery** (Great Alpine Rd, Porepunkah; open daily 10 am–5 pm; 03 5756 2356; www.boynton. com.au). Winemaker Kel Boynton is a human dynamo who makes smart wine—a very good sauvignon blanc—but like many of the wineries in the region, the merlot shouldn't be ignored, either.

In Bright itself is **The Bright Brewery** (121 Great Alpine Rd, Bright; open daily noon–evening; 03 5755 1655; www.bright brewery.com.au) a high-quality boutique brewery specialising in hearty ales.

Off on its own at Mount Beauty and well worth the detour is **Annapurna Wines** (Simmons Creek Road, Mount Beauty; open Fri–Sun and holidays 11 am–4 pm; 03 5754 4517; www.annapurnawines.com.au) named after one of the highest Himalayan peaks. Mount Beauty doesn't come close to that altitude but the views are spectacular, the vineyard is a picture and the bubbly and the chardonnay are particularly good. There's a café at the cellar door as well.

GIPPSLAND

WINERIES

SOUTH GIPPSLAND

1. Phillip Island Vineyard and Winery
44 Berrys Beach Rd, Phillip Island
03 5956 8465

2. Djinta Djinta Winery
10 Stevens Rd, Kardella South
03 5658 1163

WEST GIPPSLAND

3. Cannibal Creek
260 Tynong North Rd, Tynong North
03 5942 8380

4. Wild Dog Winery
Warragul–Korumburra Rd, Warragul
03 5623 1117

EAST GIPPSLAND

5. Narkoojee
170 Francis Rd, Glengarry
03 5192 4257

6. Nicholson River Winery
57 Liddells Rd, Nicholson
03 5156 8241

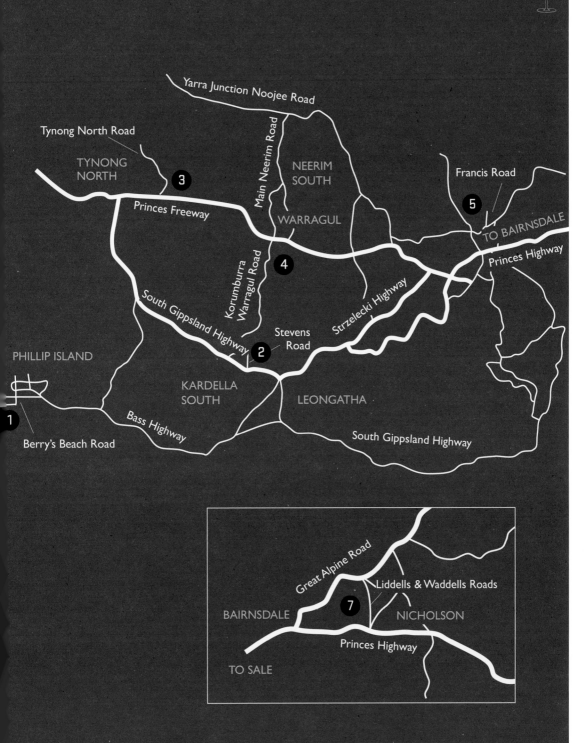

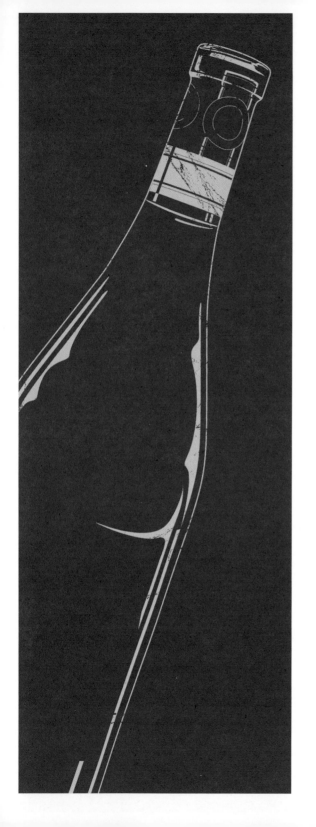

Snapshot

Gippsland is the most far-flung and sparsely populated wine region in the state. It goes all the way from the Phillip Island Winery down in Bass Strait up to the Nicholson River winery near Lakes Entrance (about 300 kilometres), and as you'd expect from such vastness there's a lot of diversity in the climate and wine style. It's not a region where you can buzz from one winery to another—it's best approached in bits.

The background

Like most of Victoria, Gippsland didn't miss out on vine planting in the mid 1800s, which occurred mostly around Bairnsdale. It didn't dip out on the vine renaissance of the 1970s, either. Not all have survived but Nicholson River does date back to 1978.

The wines

It's predominantly red and predominantly pinot noir although there is some shiraz and cabernet and chardonnay mixed in there to make it interesting. There is a smattering of other grape varieties but pinot noir is the variety that put it on the map.

The prices

Prices are typical of small wineries producing varieties such as pinot noir. There's not much below $25.

The layout

For practical and climatic reasons the region is split into three bits. South Gippsland is the area south of the Strzelecki Ranges down to the Bass Strait and includes Phillip Island and Wilsons Promontory. West Gippsland is the area around Warragul and the Latrobe Valley and surrounding hills. East Gippsland includes the cities of Sale, Bairnsdale and Lakes Entrance.

A suggested route

In South Gippsland, start with **Phillip Island Vineyard and Winery** (44 Berrys Beach Rd, Phillip Island; open daily noon–5 pm; 03 5956 8465; www. phillipislandwines.com.au). The same family famous for Diamond Valley in the Yarra Valley established it and given that link it's no surprise that the chardonnay and pinot noir are excellent.

Djinta Djinta Winery (10 Stevens Rd, Kardella South; open weekends & public holidays 10 am–6 pm; 03 5658 1163; www. djintadjinta.com.au) is just north-west of Leongatha and does a nice line in marsanne and roussanne, which they blend and call Classique.

If you're in West Gipplsand, **Cannibal Creek** (260 Tynong North Rd, Tynong North; open weekdays 11 am–5 pm; 03 5942 8380 www.cannibalcreek.com.au)

is a small, organically run vineyard with a friendly cellar door and some pretty good wines, especially the pinot noir, the sauvignon blanc and the chardonnay.

The ferociously named **Wild Dog Winery** (Warragul–Korumburra Rd, Warragul; open daily 10 am–5 pm; 03 5623 1117; www.wilddogwinery.com) is one of the stars of West Gippsland and not too far a detour from the Princes Highway. Quality is good with the shiraz and riesling being the picks.

In East Gippsland, **Narkoojee** (170 Francis Rd, Glengarry; open daily 10.30 am–4.30 pm; 03 5192 4257; www.narkoojee. com) is off the beaten track north of Traralgon but the wines are worth the detour. It produces one of the best chardonnays in the region and a great merlot in the good years. The cabernet is pretty good, too.

Nicholson River Winery (57 Liddells Rd, Nicholson; open daily 10 am–4 pm; 03 5156 8241; www.nicholsonriverwinery. com.au) has struggled against the elements since 1978 and now produces some excellent wines from a well-established vineyard. The chardonnay is the most famous but the reds can be worth taking home, too.

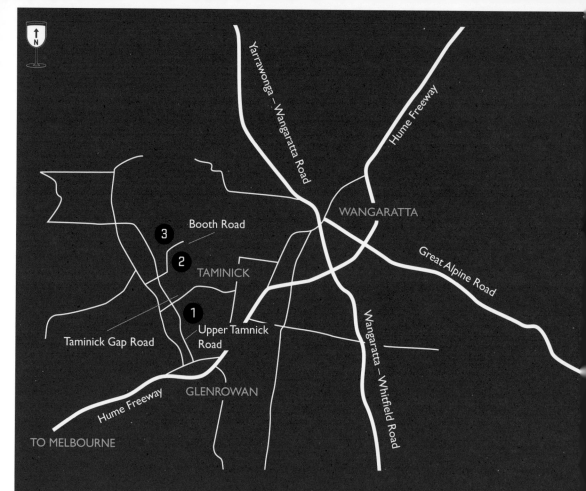

GLENROWAN

WINERIES

1. Baileys of Glenrowan
cnr Taminick Gap & Upper Taminick Rds,
Glenrowan
03 5766 2392

2. Auldstone
296 Booth Rd, Taminick, via Glenrowan
03 5766 2237

3. Taminick Cellars
339 Booth Rd, Taminick, via Glenrowan
03 5766 2282

Snapshot

Glenrowan will always be linked to Ned Kelly's glorious fight and capture but it has quite a wine history, too. The country looks tough, like the bushrangers who used to hide in it, and, like the bushrangers, the wines are none too elegant.

The background

Before Ned and his gang or shiraz there was gold and entrepreneurs taking money from lucky and unlucky miners. Once the gold ran out, shopkeepers turned to farming and viticulture.

The wines

Shiraz is king and rightly so. The shiraz is gutsy, grunty and sometimes brutal but very good. Like Rutherglen, there are some good fortifieds, too.

The prices

Cheap! Taminick Cellars is in the Stone Age as far as prices go but don't tell them!

The layout

It's not a large region and if you're in the neighbouring areas of Rutherglen or the King Valley, Glenrowan should definitely be on the touring list. All the cellar doors are north of Glenrowan, pretty much along the same drag.

A suggested route

The first one you're going to get to travelling from Glenrowan is **Baileys of Glenrowan** (cnr Taminick Gap & Upper Taminick Rds, Glenrowan; open daily 10 am–5 pm; 03 5766 2392; www.baileysofglenrowan. com.au). Once known as Baileys Bundara, it's been there since 1866 and has history dripping from it. The shiraz is the pick of the table wines and the Founder Muscat and Tokay are bargains at $24 or so.

Next is **Auldstone** (296 Booth Rd, Taminick via Glenrowan; Thu–Sat & school holidays 9 am–5 pm, Sun 10 am–5 pm; 03 5766 2237; www.auldstone.com.au), a renovation project with a winery and vineyard that was around in the 1800s. There's some decent shiraz and the sparkling shiraz is definitely worth a taste.

Taminick Cellars (339 Booth Rd, Taminick, via Glenrowan; open Mon–Sat 9 am–5 pm, Sun 10 am–5 pm; 03 5766 2282; www.taminickcellars.com.au) is like stepping back in time. Check out the grizzled old vines that line the driveway. The whole range features bargains but make sure you have a look at the old-vine shiraz and the bargain-priced trebbiano.

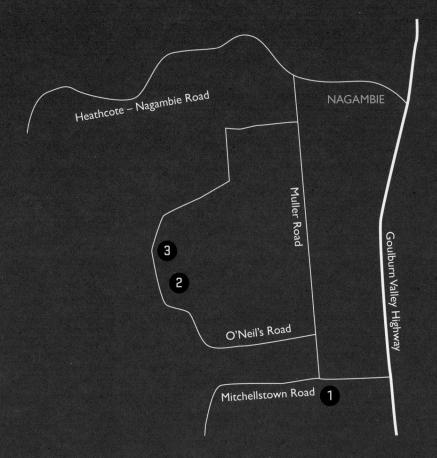

GOULBURN VALLEY

WINERIES

1. Mitchelton
Mitchellstown Road, Nagambie
03 5736 2221

2. Tahbilk
254 O'Neils Rd, Tabilk, via Nagambie
03 5794 2555

3. Dalfarras
254 O'Neils Rd, Tabilk, via Nagambie
03 5794 2555

Snapshot

Goulburn Valley used to be first on the list for cellar door travellers. These days other regions have eclipsed it, but the valley is home to two historic wineries, Tahbilk and Mitchelton, some smart wine and it isn't much of a detour from the Hume Highway.

The background

The history of the region begins and ends with Tahbilk, which was planted in 1860 with 700,000 vines and, unlike the majority in that era, they have actually survived. There's even a shiraz made from those old vines. Purchased by the Purbrick family in 1925 (the same family is still in charge), it is up there with Seppelt Great Western as one of the great wine relics in Victoria. In 1969 Mitchelton was established and set a new benchmark for what could be achieved in the region. Don Lewis made some of the best riesling and shiraz in the late 1980s.

The wines

Shiraz and chardonnay are dominant here. This region also pioneered marsanne and the marsanne/roussanne blend.

The prices

Sub $20 wines are the norm not than the exception. Tahbilk Marsanne at $15 is still one of the best-value whites going around.

The layout

The region sits astride the Goulburn Valley Highway north of Seymour and close to the Hume Highway—it's a pleasant detour.

A suggested route

Heading north, one to visit is **Mitchelton** (Mitchellstown Rd, Nagambie; open daily 10 am–5 pm; 03 5736 2221; www. mitchelton.com.au). The weird 55-metre tower is a landmark and the range of wines is huge. The riesling has a long pedigree and is a beauty. The Preece Shiraz is excellent value as is the Cabernet Sauvignon, and if you take home the Print Shiraz at about $50 you won't be disappointed.

Close by is **Tahbilk** (254 O'Neils Rd, Tabilk, via Nagambie; open Mon–Sat 9 am–5 pm, Sun 11 am–5 pm; 03 5794 2555; www.tahbilk.com.au). It used to be called Chateau Tahbilk: the chateau has gone. The marsanne is still one of the great $15 wines and the 1860 Vines Shiraz is historic although the standard shiraz is much better value. There are special deals for cellar door customers and the Dalfarras wines, which are owned and made by the Purbricks, can also be tasted at the Tahbilk Wetlands Cafe.

Dalfarras (see Tahbilk listing for address details) does some interesting blends—check out the shiraz viognier and cabernet sangiovese; at $16, they're bargains.

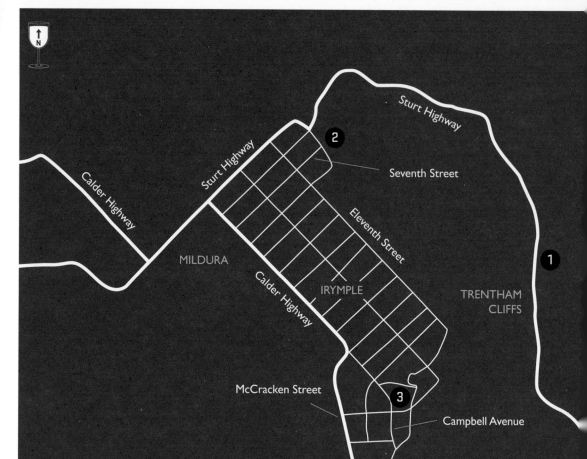

MILDURA

WINERIES

1. Trentham Estate
Sturt Hwy, Trentham Cliffs
03 5024 8888

2. Tall Poppy Wines
34A Seventh St, Mildura
03 5022 7255

3. Neqtar Wines
Campbell Ave, Irymple
03 5024 5704

Snapshot

Despite being responsible for 80 per cent of the state's production, this is the most unfashionable wine region in Victoria. It's broad-acre viticulture, big wine companies and relies on the water resources of the Murray River. It is under threat from the whole climate change issue but Mildura is a unique city and if you're in the area the region is worth a look and a taste.

The background

Mildura exists because of Alfred Deakin and the irrigation scheme he championed. He and the Chaffey brothers, William and Edward, helped build Mildura and turn the area into a fruit bowl. How were they to know about climate change?

The wines

Pretty much everything is available. From the stock-standard varieties, chardy and shiraz, to petit verdot and Italian varietals.

The prices

This is winemaking on a big scale and the prices reflect that—if you're paying more than $20 it's probably too much.

The layout

The region follows the Sturt Highway from Robinvale/Euston to Mildura. There are vineyards as far as the eye can see but not too many cellar doors.

A suggested route

Coming from the south-east, the first cellar door you arrive at is the best. **Trenthham Estate** (Sturt Hwy, Trentham Cliffs; open daily 9.30 am–5 pm; 03 5024 8888; www.trenthamestate.com.au), which, strictly speaking, is in New South Wales. The range is huge and prices go from the Murphy's Lore brand at about $8 all the way to $20. All the wines are pretty good, the chardonnay regularly outperforms its price and, against all expectation in the hot climate, Trentham actually does a decent pinot noir now and again.

In Mildura itself is **Tall Poppy Wines** (34A Seventh St, Mildura; open weekdays 8.30 am–5 pm; 03 5022 7255; www.tallpoppywines.com), which is the head office for the company and a spot where enthusiasts can buy wine by the case. Mainly an exporter, Tall Poppy's wine quality is pretty good, particularly the petit verdot.

Neqtar Wines (Campbell Ave, Irymple; open Mon–Sat 10 am–4.30 pm; 03 5024 5704) is on the border of where Mildura ends and the vineyards begin. The wines aren't show stoppers but they're pretty good value.

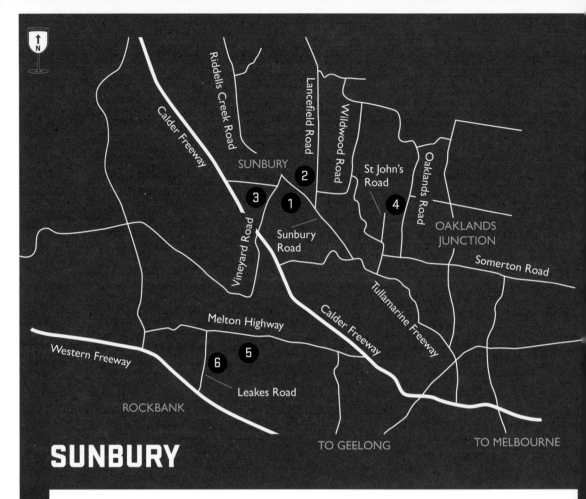

SUNBURY

WINERIES

1. Craiglee
Sunbury Rd, Sunbury
03 9744 4489

2. Goona Warra
790 Sunbury Rd, Sunbury
03 9740 7766

3. Andraos Bros Wines
150 Vineyard Rd, Sunbury
03 9744 4489

4. Wildwood
St John's Rd, Oaklands Junction
03 9307 1118

5. Galli Estate
1507 Melton Hwy, Rockbank
03 9747 1444

6. Witchmount Estate
557 Leakes Rd, Rockbank
03 9747 1188

Snapshot

A rock concert in the 1970s put Sunbury on the map and the name is probably more synonymous with Billy Thorpe & the Aztecs than wine but that's no reason to leave it off your itinerary. In the 1980s Sunbury became famous among wine snobs courtesy of a winemaker named Pat Carmody and his Craiglee Shiraz. Surprisingly, it hasn't grown much since then. The Craiglee Shiraz is still a beauty and being so close to Melbourne and the airport, it is one of the most accessible wine regions in Victoria.

The background

Sunbury has quite a historical pedigree. The bluestone winery of Goona Warrra (which got its name before Coonawarra) was built way back in the 1850s and Craiglee followed a few years later. Both labels and some of the buildings still survive.

The wines

Shiraz rules and quite rightly. Goona Warra has a clever cabernet franc merlot blend that is worth a try and there's a bit of chardonnay and pinot noir, too.

The prices

For cool-climate and handmade, it's not too bad. There are some sub $20 wines but expect to pay $25 for the good stuff.

The layout

Most of the wineries in the region are to the east of the Calder Highway within five kilometres of the Sunbury township. It's flat, fairly unimpressive scenery but the history and the wines make up for the lack of spectacular views.

A suggested route

As you head past the airport, the Tullamarine Freeway becomes Sunbury Road and the first winery on the left is **Craiglee** (Sunbury Rd, Sunbury; open Sun & public holidays 11 am–5 pm; 03 9744 4489; www.craiglee.com.au), home to the famous spicy shiraz, which is still relatively cheap for such an iconic wine at $45. There's also an excellent chardonnay and pinot noir, too. Pat Carmody is a lovely bloke.

Across the road is **Goona Warra** (790 Sunbury Rd, Sunbury; open Sun–Fri 10 am–5 pm, Sat noon–5 pm; 03 9740 7766; www.goonawarra.com.au). The bluestone building is a beauty, the trio of shiraz, pinot noir and chardonnay is pretty good, and the merlot cabernet franc blend is worth a taste.

Off the main drag and up the appropriately named Vineyard road is **Andraos Bros Wines** (150 Vineyard Rd, Sunbury; open weekends and public holidays 11 am–5 pm; 03 97444489; www.

andraosbros.com.au). This is another Sunbury resurrection story which dates back to the 1860s. The cabernet is a favourite.

The winery closest to the airport is **Wildwood** (St John's Rd, Oaklands Junction; open daily 10 am–6 pm; 03 9307 1118; www.wildwoodvineyards.com.au). The spot is surprisingly elevated and you can see the skyscrapers in the distance and a glimpse of the bay. It's a carefully maintained property and the wines likewise. The cabernet franc merlot blend is a favourite and the chardonnay is very good, too.

Head back across the Calder Highway to the Melton Highway to **Galli Estate** (1507 Melton Hwy, Rockbank; open daily 10 am–5 pm; 03 9747 1444; www.galliestate.com.au), which is easily the biggest producer in the region and the most likely Sunbury producer you're likely to see in a wine shop. The range is large and very good with fruit from Heathcote as well. Shiraz and chardonnay are the picks and there are some decent reds for less than $18.

Continue along the Melton Highway then turn left onto Leakes Road where you'll find **Witchmount Estate** (557 Leakes Rd, Rockbank; open Wed–Sun 11 am–5 pm; 03 9747 1188; www.witchmount.com.au). Witchmount has been around since 1991

and has garnered a reputation for its shiraz and for weddings at its function centre. The Lowen Park chardy is great value.

KING VALLEY

WINERIES

1. Sam Miranda of King Valley
cnr Snow & Whitfield Rds, Oxley
03 5727 3888

2. Brown Brothers
Milawa Bobinawarrah Rd, Milawa
03 5720 5500

3. Wood Park Wines
17 Milawa-Bobinawarrah Rd, Milawa
03 5727 3367

4. John Gehrig Wines
80 Gehrigs Lane, Oxley
03 5727 3395

5. Boggy Creek Vineyards
1657 Boggy Creek Rd, Myrrhee
03 5729 7587

6. Pizzini Wines
175 King Valley Rd, Whitfield
03 5729 8278

7. Politini Wines
65 Upper King River Rd, Cheshunt
03 5729 8277

8. Chrismont
251 Upper King River Rd, Cheshunt
03 5729 8220

9. Dal Zotto
Main Rd, Whitfield
03 5729 8321

WHERE TO EAT

A. Rinaldo's
Main Rd, Whitfield
03 5729 8000

B. Milawa Cheese Factory Bakery and Restaurant
17 Milawa Bobinawarrah Rd, Milawa
03 5727 3589

C. Sam Miranda of King Valley
cnr Snow & Whitfield Rds, Oxley
03 5727 3888

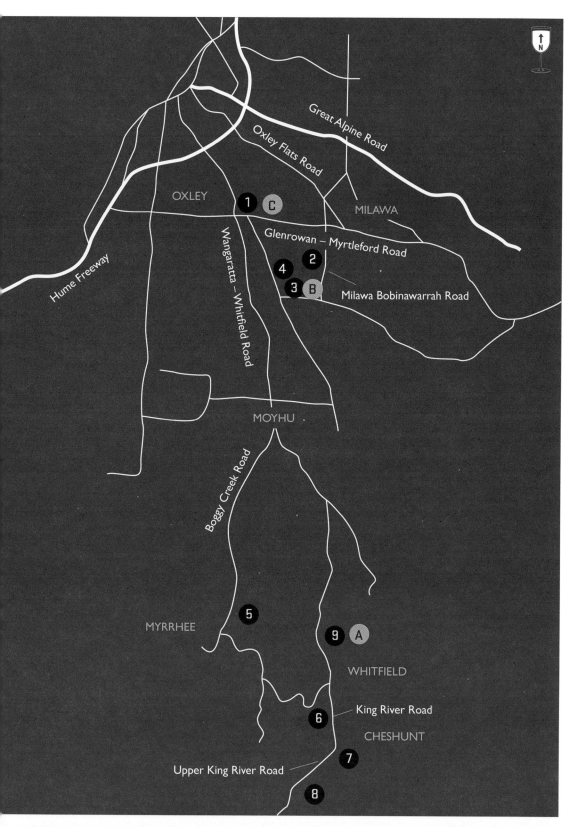

N

Great Alpine Road

Oxley Flats Road

OXLEY **1** **C**

MILAWA

Glenrowan – Myrtleford Road

4

2

3 **B**

Milawa Bobinawarrah Road

Wangaratta – Whitfield Road

Hume Freeway

MOYHU

Boggy Creek Road

MYRRHEE

5

9 **A**

WHITFIELD

King River Road

6

CHESHUNT

7

Upper King River Road

8

Snapshot

My first experience of this region was as a student back in the mid 1980s when we used to travel from Melbourne up the snow road to Mount Hotham. It was extreme skiing—we were so broke we had to sleep in a tent! A very necessary stop on the way was at Brown Brothers at Milawa to stock up on wine and other fortified fluids to help us survive. Back then Brown Brothers was it as far as cellar doors went.

The King Valley was full of tobacco growers but as that industry gave its last emphysemic gasp, the tobacco growers turned to grape growing and a wine region was born. It is home to some of the most dynamic wine goings-on in Australia. This is the number one spot for Italian varieties and that Italian influence is there to taste in the food at the local restaurants as well.

The background

The long history of the King Valley is the history of the Brown Brothers. George Harry Brown arrived in Bendigo in 1857 looking for gold. He found it when he married the local schoolteacher and when her dad died they moved to Milawa—the old man's house. Vines were planted and the company has followed a unique and undeviating course ever since. Credit for the diversity of grape varieties we now have in Australia can be sheeted back to the Browns. The Browns encouraged the tobacco farmers to try growing grapes, urging them to grow interesting, different varieties and guaranteeing to buy the fruit. It has given a particular flavour to the region. It's a place where the bog-standard chardy and shiraz are not the norm.

The wines

What sort of wine would you like, Sir or Madam? There's pretty much everything here, from very good sparklings through to fortifieds and loads of interesting Italians. There are also some weirder things going on. A glass of petit manseng, anyone? The key words are variety and quality.

The prices

At Brown Brothers there's the entire gamut of prices from low to high. In general, the average price for a bottle of wine in the region is about $25.

The layout

It's not a large region, and driving from Oxley to Milawa and down the pretty Wangaratta–Whitfield Road to Whitfield and Cheshunt is an easy day's driving and tasting.

A suggested route

Coming from the Hume Highway, head towards Oxley. At the junction of the Glenrowan–Myrtleford Road (Snow Road) and the Wangaratta–Whitfield Road is **Sam Miranda of King Valley** (cnr Snow & Whitfield Rds, Oxley; open daily 10 am–5 pm; 03 5727 3888; www.sammiranda.com.au), a relatively new (established 2004) spot in the valley. Sam is the same Miranda who used to be associated with Griffith and wine casks but that business was sold and this is a different thing entirely. There are some good reds and Sam now owns Symphonia Wines, which specialises in tannat, saperavi and petit manseng, wines that are definitely worth a taste.

Up the Snow Road a few kilometres is Milawa and **Brown Brothers** (Milawa Bobinawarrah Rd, Milawa; open daily 9 am–5 pm; 03 5720 5500; www.brownbrothers.com.au). The cellar door has more cellar door customers and more wine for tasting than any other. There are more than 50 wines being poured at the cellar door. Treats are the experimental wines that are only available at the cellar door in a slightly different livery. At the pricier end, the Patricia range is excellent.

Just up the road is **Wood Park Wines** (Milawa Cheese Factory, Milawa; open daily 10 am–5 pm; 03 5727 3367; www.woodparkwines.com.au), home to charismatic wines made by John Stokes. The chardonnay and cab shiraz can be good.

John Gehrig Wines (80 Gehrigs Lane, Oxley; open daily 9 am–5 pm; 03 5727 3395; www.johngehrigwines.com.au) is an old label energised by new-generation winemaker Ross Gehrig. There's a wide range of wines and some interesting sparkling from non-standard grape varieties, notably the cremant de chenin and the red, cremant de gamay.

From there, head down through Moyhu, turn right on to the Boggy Creek Road—it's dirt but not too bad—you'll come to **Boggy Creek Vineyards** (1657 Boggy Creek Rd, Myrrhee; open 10 am–5.30 pm; 03 5729 7587; www.boggycreekwines.com.au). It's a bit isolated but the wines are getting better and better and it makes for a scenic round trip. Check out the pinot gris, in particular.

Next stop is one of the highlights, **Pizzini Wines** (175 King Valley Rd, Whitfield; open daily 10 am–5 pm; 03 5729 8278; www.pizzini.com.au). The Pizzinis were grape growers before they got into winemaking and do both jobs very well. The Italian varietals in particular are particularly authentic, and the sangiovese and nebbiolo are fantastic. Don't forget to taste the white, verduzzo.

Further towards Cheshunt is **Politini Wines** (65 Upper King River Rd, Cheshunt; open daily 11 am–5 pm; 03 5729 8277; www.politiniwines.com.au). Like the Pizzinis, the Politinis were grape growers who decided to take the plunge into the winemaking vat. The merlot is a beauty for only $16.

Close by is **Chrismont** (251 Upper King River Rd, Cheshunt; open daily 11 am–5 pm; 03 5729 8220; www.chrismont.com.au). Run by Arnie and Jo Pizzini, the specialties here are the red marzemino and the pinot grigio.

Back in the town of Whitfield you'll come to the funky cellar/restaurant door that is **Dal Zotto** (Main Rd, Whitfield; open daily 10 am–5 pm; 03 5729 8321; www.dalzotto.com.au) with wines made by the poetically named Otto Dal Zotto and his son Michael. Otto comes from the town of Prosecco in Italy so it's not surprising that the prosecco is brilliantly authentic. The entire range of Italian varietals is worth taking home.

Where to eat

King Valley is blessed with good eateries. **Rinaldo's** at Dal Zotto (Main Rd, Whitfield; open Thu–Sun for lunch, Sat from 6 pm for dinner; 03 5729 8000; www.dalzotto.com.au) has good Italian food and local produce from chef Adam Pizzini's many relatives.

Milawa Cheese Factory Bakery and Restaurant (17 Milawa-Bobinawarrah Rd, Milawa; open daily 9 am–5 pm; 03 5727 3589; www.milawacheese.com.au) is famous for its cheese and is a good spot for lunch, too.

Sam Miranda of King Valley (cnr Snow & Whitfield Rds, Oxley; open daily 11 am–3 pm for lunch; 03 5727 3888; www.sammiranda.com.au) is one of the newer spots, with an Italian-styled menu.

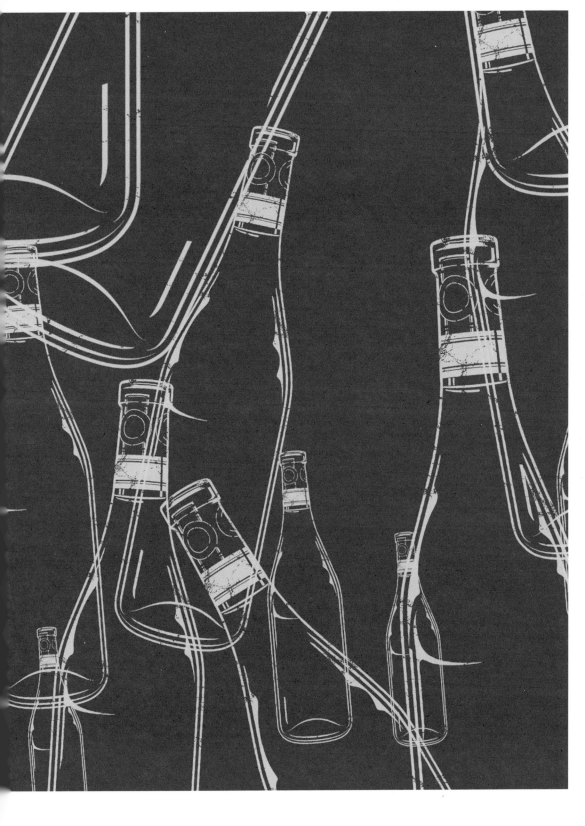

SOUTH AUSTRALIA

South Australia is the grape state. In no other jurisdiction does viticulture and winemaking impact on everyday life to such a degree. Well, not in Australia anyway. Enter South Australia and you're already reminded of the importance of horticulture when you have to dump your fruit at the airport or the border. Australia has a relatively young wine industry but compared to the other states, South Australia is ye olde worlde. Others may claim earlier dates of establishment and a longer history but this is a place where there are family-owned wine companies that date back to the very beginnings—wineries where a dynasty of six or seven generations has run the show uninterrupted since the mid 1800s. Old stone buildings are not there for the tourists to imagine what life was like in those days: they're still used, and there are plenty of gnarled old vines and surprisingly few gnarly locals.

This whole dominance and reliance on the wine industry is a boon for the cellar door traveller. It means that wine quality is high across the board, that the state government puts great importance on wine tourism and that the place is specifically set up for the cellar door adventurer. Travelling around South Australia's wine regions you learn a lot about our wine history, where we are now and what Australian wine really tastes like.

N

Clare Valley ●

Barossa Valley ●
ADELAIDE ● ● Eden Valley
McLaren Vale ● ● Adelaide Hills
● Langhorne Creek

● Padthaway

● Mount Benson

Coonawarra ●

BAROSSA VALLEY

WINERIES

1. Kaesler
Barossa Valley Way (Murray St), Nuriootpa
08 8562 4488

2. Whistler Wines
Seppeltsfield Rd, Marananga
08 8562 4942

3. Two Hands Wines
Neldner Rd, Marananga
08 8562 4566

4. Seppeltsfield
Seppeltsfield Rd, Seppeltsfield
08 8568 6217

5. Hentley Farm
cnr Jenke & Gerald Roberts Rds,
Seppeltsfield
08 8333 0241

6. Murray Street Vineyards
Lot 723 Murray St, Greenock
08 8562 8373

7. Langmeil Winery
cnr Para & Langmeil Rds, Tanunda
08 8563 2595

8. Turkey Flat
Bethany Rd, Tanunda
08 8563 2851

9. Bethany Wines
Bethany Rd, Bethany
08 8563 2086

10. St Hallett
St Hallett Rd, Tanunda
08 8563 7000

11. Villa Tinto
Krondorf Rd, Tanunda
08 8563 3044

12. Charles Melton
Krondorf Rd, Tanunda
08 8563 3606

13. Rockford
Krondorf Rd, Tanunda
08 8563 2720

14. Cimicky Wines
Hermann Thumm Dr, Lyndoch
08 8524 4025

15. Gomersal Wines
Lyndoch Rd, Gomersal
08 8563 3611

WHERE TO EAT

A. Kaesler Restaurant
Barossa Valley Way (Murray St), Nuriootpa
08 8562 2711

B. 1918 Bistro and Grill
94 Murray St, Tanunda
08 8563 0405

C. Krondorf Road Cafe
Krondorf Rd, Krondorf
08 8563 0889

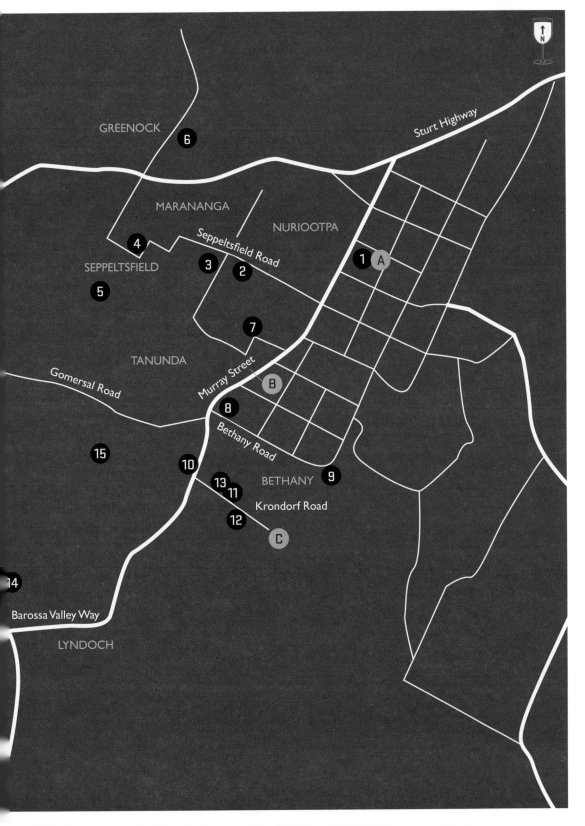

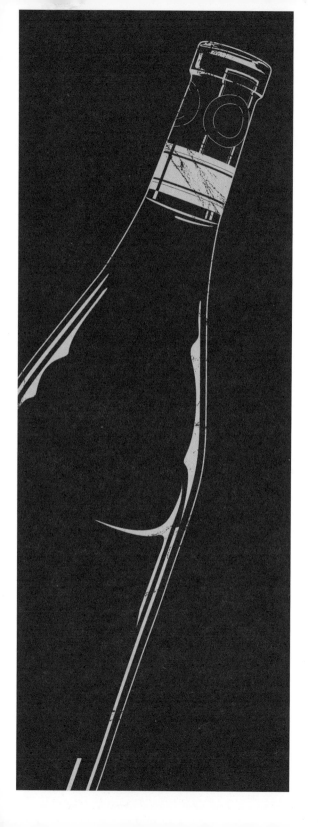

Snapshot

There are two things that make the Barossa a unique wine region. The first is its Germanic heritage and the second is its shiraz. The two are an odd pairing but in the Barossa they seem quite compatible. Both came as accidental immigrants to South Australia but have given the Barossa a unique flavour. The Lutheran past isn't overly apparent—there are no themed restaurants or lederhosen—but you might find a grape grower with a German name, or a butcher selling local mettwurst, or some semi-Teutonic architecture. This is against the background of some of the biggest, richest red wine produced in the world from vines that date back to the 1800s.

The background

Colonial William Light named the 'Barrossa' with a double 'r' in 1837. He named the valley after a battle fought near the 'Hill of Roses' in the sherry country of Spain during the Napoleonic wars. The Barossa has had a host of misspellings over the years. One 'r' and double 's' finally stuck and the Barrossa became the Barossa. The land was described as the 'real cream of South Australia' and the first vineyards duly appeared in the 1840s. By the 1870s, famous brands such as Gramps, Henschke and Seppelt were going concerns.

The Germanic influence can be sheeted home to George Fife Angas, who is now immortalised in the Barossa town of Angaston. The legend goes that he needed workers and financed the immigration of three shiploads of German Lutheran farmers from Silesia, who were being oppressed by King Frederick III. The result of those three shiploads of Lutherans is that now in a place with an Aboriginal name like Nuriootpa you can get a range of German smallgoods that you can't get in a big city.

As for the reason that shiraz is such a big part of the Barossa, it's simple—that was what was available. In 1832 James Busby took a dozen shiraz/syrah cuttings from the Hill of Hermitage in the Rhône Valley. They were propagated and soon spread through the Barossa. The oldest existing shiraz in the Barossa is at Langmeil and was planted in 1843. From then until the present the Barossa has been victim to a series of booms and busts as demand for its product ebbed and flowed. The most recent bust was the notorious 'Vine Pull' scheme of the 1980s. It's almost too horrific to contemplate but grape growers were paid a bounty on ripping out old shiraz (and other) grapevines. How ridiculous fashion can be—now those old shiraz vines are gold.

The wines

It is a land of shiraz, big shiraz, bigger shiraz and biggest shiraz. There are other varieties but they are bit players. The Barossa produces very good cabernet, grenache, mourvèdre (which used to be called mataro), even semillon and riesling, but if you don't like tasting shiraz you're not going to get much out of the Barossa.

The prices

It used to be one of the most inexpensive places to buy wine, but well-heeled American wine drinkers have discovered the Barossa and the prices show it. Expect lesser ranges to sell for about $18 and iconic shiraz to go anywhere from $40 to infinity.

The layout

When you're on the ground in Nuriootpa it's a bit hard to understand the Barossa as a valley. The hills don't cradle it in the same way as you imagine they should in something called a valley. The truth is, it's a very broad, long valley that runs roughly north-east/south-west between the towns of Lyndoch and Nuriootpa and is bounded to the north-west by Greenock and to the east by Angaston by way of the Barossa ranges. On the valley floor it's about 250 metres above sea level (not very high) but in the Barossa ranges it goes to

600 metres. There are more than 70 cellar doors so unless you're a very keen taster, a plan of attack is essential. For an overview of the valley, one of the best vantage points is to head up to the Menglers Hill Lookout. From there, looking north-west, you can see it all spread before you and with a map in hand the subregions of Gomersal, Lyndoch and Greenock begin to make sense.

A suggested route

Nuriootpa is the first big town you reach from the Sturt Highway coming from Adelaide. Heading out from Nuri towards Tanunda on your left is **Kaesler** (Barossa Valley Way (Murray St), Nuriootpa; open Mon–Sat 10 am–5 pm, Sun & public holidays 11.30 am–4 pm; 08 8562 4488; www.kaesler.com.au), a winery in the old Barossa sense with a name that sounds like a German sausage and an old stone building.

Silesian immigrants originally founded Kaesler in 1893. The old vines and Germanic touches remain but there's nothing olde worlde about the winemaking, as the funky, wild-yeast viognier demonstrates. There's also a bit of Aussie humour. One of the top shirazes is called 'Bogan' after the winemaker who once wore a mullet. It's very popular with the American cognoscenti who, unaware of Aussie slang, pronounce

Bogan in a semi-French way as you would Rodin. The same company also has the Nashwauk label made from McLaren Vale fruit and also available for tasting.

Head down Barossa Valley Way till you get to Seppeltsfield Road and turn right. Down this road is the corrugated-iron tasting room of **Whistler Wines** (Seppeltsfield Rd, Marananga; open daily 10.30 am–5 pm; 08 8562 4942; www.whistlerwines.com), a relative newcomer (the vines were planted in 1994) that is making a bit of a splash. The wines are made by one of the new breed of top Barossa winemakers, Troy Kalleske. Highlights are the cabernet sauvignon and the bargain is the Hubert Irving Red Blend at $17.

Keep driving up the road, turn left into Neldner Road and you'll get to the restored stone building that houses the cellar door of **Two Hands Wines** (Neldner Rd, Marananga; open daily 10 am–5 pm; 08 8562 4566; www.twohandswines.com). This is a very Barossan winery in that it is dedicated to shiraz—and not necessarily Barossa shiraz, either. It's all very 'designed'. Even the spittoons are set into the tasting benches with the contents hidden so when they get a bit full they don't spit second-hand shiraz back at you.

At Two Hands you can taste and compare wines from Australia's renowned shiraz regions—Heathcote and McLaren Vale as well as the Barossa. It's a good exercise in showing how versatile our favourite red grape is.

Get back onto Seppeltsfield Road and head for **Seppeltsfield** (Seppeltsfield Rd, Seppeltsfield; open daily 10.30 am–5 pm; 08 8568 6217; www.seppeltsfield.com.au). You'll know you're getting close when you see the huge date palms that were planted by Benno Seppelt during the Great Depression. Rather than lay his employees off, he had them plant palms and groom the grounds of Seppeltfield. Benno was a man of big dreams as a look around the buildings and the Seppelt family mausoleum shows. Apparently he used to ride around on horseback directing his workers and inspecting vineyards with a violin and dressed in clothes he designed himself. Needless to say, the wine industry (if not the world) needs more Bennos.

Seppeltsfield has been purchased by the Kilkanoon group and has had a rev-up. Fortified-wine legend James Godfrey is still in charge of the barrels of magic fortifieds going back to the 1800s. There are different tours and tastings you can take and they cost money, but given that you're tasting the best fortified wine in Australia dating back more than 100 years, it's pretty good value.

Nearby is **Hentley Farm** (cnr Jenke & Gerald Roberts Rds, Seppeltsfield; open daily 10 am–5 pm; 08 8333 0241; www. hentleyfarm.com.au), a newcomer with a classic stone-built cellar door, a good range of wines and a special line in zinfandel. The Fools Bay range is really well priced.

From Seppeltsfield, head towards Greenock and there you'll find **Murray Street Vineyards** (Lot 723 Murray St, Greenock; open daily 10 am–4.30 pm; 08 8562 8373; www.murraystreet.com.au). Winemaker Andrew Seppelt is a dynastic extension of Benno and is doing the family name proud. The tasting room is stone and looks out over the vineyards that creep towards the main street. It's a sit-down-on-the-couch-and-get-the-spiel-with-a-plate-of-food scenario, which makes a nice change. Prices aren't cheap but the wines are top-notch. The shiraz is a speciality with a Greenock and Gomersal version of the variety.

Head back towards Tanunda and up Para Road and you'll come to the historic-looking **Langmeil Winery** (cnr Para & Langmeil Rds, Tanunda; open daily 10.30 am–4.30 pm; 08 8563 2595; www.langmeilwinery.com.au), which still has the oldest-living block of vines in Australia. There's plenty of great old-vine shiraz here but the Blacksmith Barossa Cabernet Sauvignon is worth tasting, too.

Heading towards Lyndoch, take a detour up Bethany Road and you'll come to **Turkey Flat** (Bethany Rd, Tanunda; open daily 11 am–5 pm; 08 8563 2851; www.turkeyflat.com.au). The sparkling shiraz is one of the Barossa's best, there's an intriguing pedro ximenez, the rosé is a classic and the Butchers Block Shiraz Grenache Mourvèdre is often the pick of the reds.

At the top of the road and up the hill is **Bethany Wines** (Bethany Rd, Bethany; open Mon–Sat 10 am–5 pm, Sun 1 pm–5pm; 08 8563 2086; www.bethany.com.au). The cellar door is a well-cared-for bluestone building nestled into the hill, there's a great riesling with a cellaring pedigree and some decent reds.

Head down Barossa Valley Way once more and you'll come to the famous Krondorf Road. Just opposite the turn-off is **St Hallett** (St Hallett Rd, Tanunda; open daily 10 am–5 pm; 08 8563 7000; www.sthallett.com.au), one of the original wineries to reap the rewards of big Barossa shiraz coming back into fashion. The Old Block Shiraz is the flagship but the Eden Valley Riesling is pretty good, too. Up Krondorf Road is a cellar door that is as close as you can get to the old Barossa, albeit with an Argentinean flavour.

The wines of **Villa Tinto** (Krondorf Rd, Tanunda; open daily 11 am–5 pm; 08 8563 3044; www.villatinto.com.au) might not be up to the standard of some of the big names but they have a handmade quality about them, they come in half-bottles, they're not expensive and you'll get a good welcome from the Di Palma family.

Charles Melton (Krondorf Rd, Tanunda; open daily 11 am–5 pm; 08 8563 3606; www.charlesmeltonwines.com.au) is a Barossa legend making cult wines for appreciative fans. His Nine Popes is always a beauty and the Rose of Virginia is one of the best pink wines in the country.

Across the road is **Rockford** (Krondorf Rd; Tanunda; open 11 am–5 pm; 08 8563 2720; www.rockfordwines.com.au). It looks like a film set for a winemaking movie set in 1886 and it is arguably South Australia's wine cognoscentes' favourite cellar door. The Black Shiraz sparkling red is mythic as are most of the reds. The riesling is the bargain.

Towards Lyndoch on Hermann Thumm Dr, you'll find the stately cellar door of **Cimicky Wines** (Hermann Thumm Dr, Lyndoch; open Tue–Sat 10.30 am–4.30 pm; 08 8524 4025; www.cimickywines.com.au). There's a good hierarchy of wines here and the Trumps Shiraz at $20 is a bargain.

Head up Lyndoch Road towards the subregion of Gomersal and on your right you'll eventually find the corrugated-ironclad facade of **Gomersal Wines** (Lyndoch Rd, Gomersal; open daily 10 am–5 pm; 08 8563 3611; www.gomersalwines.com.au) made by the winemaker gun-for-hire Ben Glaetzer. The range and prices are good— the $25 Gomersal Shiraz is the favourite.

Where to eat
On the outskirts of Nuriootpa is **Kaesler Restaurant** (Barossa Valley Way, Nuriootpa; open daily noon–2.30 pm for lunch, Thu–Sat 7 pm–9 pm for dinner; 08 8562 2711; www.krc.net.au). The food is wholesome and the wine list is huge.

In Tanunda is the institution known as **1918 Bistro and Grill** (94 Murray St, Tanunda; open Mon–Sat for lunch, weekends for dinner; 08 8563 0405; www.1918.com.au).

Krondorf Road Cafe (Krondorf Rd, Krondorf; open daily for lunch; 08 8563 0889; www.kabminye.com) is in the heart of the Barossa and offers a Barossan Germanic menu.

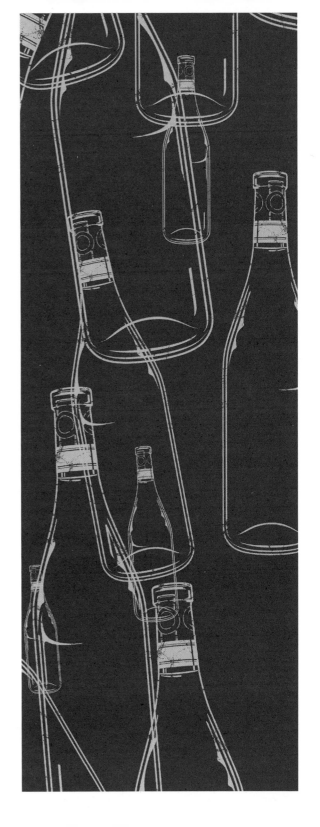

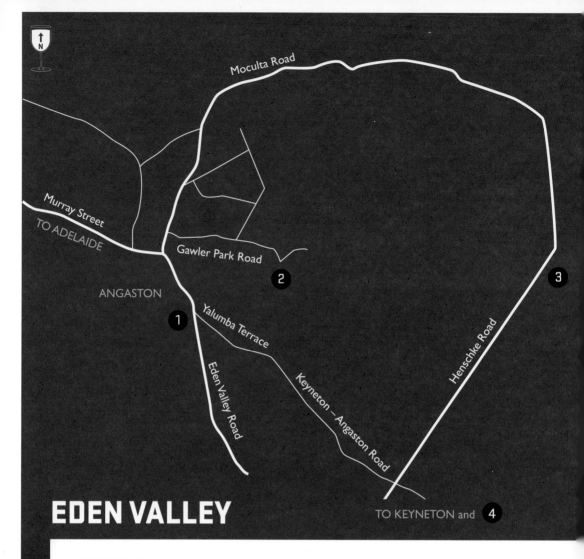

EDEN VALLEY

WINERIES

1. Yalumba
Eden Valley Rd, Angaston
08 8561 3200

2. Thorn-Clarke Wines
Gawler Park Rd, Angaston
08 8564 3036

3. Henschke
Henschke Rd, Keyneton
08 8564 8223

4. Peter Seppelt Wines
cnr R. Dewells & Laubes Rds, Springton
08 8568 2452

Snapshot

Where exactly is the Eden Valley? Driving around the Barossa it's hard to know where it begins and where it ends. You don't turn a corner and see Adam and Eve and the snake eating apples. But as you drive east from the Barossa it gets higher, the riesling gets better, the reds a tad more elegant and the cellar doors become less thick on the ground. You're in the Eden Valley. If you're visiting the Barossa it's not much of a detour and is well worth the effort.

The background

Although not as famous as its neighbour, the Eden Valley can claim considerable heritage and pedigree. Vines were planted where Pewsey Vale is now, in 1847, and the riesling soon had a good reputation, which it still has. Yalumba and Henschke are two of the oldies in the region. Yalumba or Yealumba (a local Aboriginal word for 'the land around') goes back to 1849 when Samuel Smith made his way to Angaston.

By 1861 he was claiming: 'With proper care and skillful management we believe it impossible to plant too many vines or to make too much wine in South Australia.' The Henschkes were grape growers up until 1952 when they decided to have a bash at making wine. They've done quite well at it. Henschke's Hill of Grace is the second most famous shiraz in the country after Grange. Despite that, the Eden Valley is not a household name and doesn't have the reputation or the fame it should.

The wines

Since Yalumba made the wise decision to grow riesling high in the Eden Valley rather than at the lower altitudes of the Barossa floor, the Eden Valley has cemented a reputation for the noble variety which is second only to the Clare Valley. Shiraz comes in second and because of its relative coolness in comparison with the Barossa, it means that the cabernets can be more elegant. Yalumba has also pioneered viognier and there's a fair bit of that variety at the cellar door.

The prices

Compared to its illustrious neighbour, Eden Valley has some bargains and there are quite a few very good wines at the $15 price point. At the other end of the scale, if you've got a spare $600 you can always buy a bottle of Hill of Grace.

The layout

The Eden Valley starts at Angaston in the west and goes to Truro in the north and Springton in the south and then merges into the Adelaide Hills. Most of the cellar doors are at the northern end.

A suggested route

As you drive out of the Barossa Valley you'll come to Angaston and the impressive old stone clock tower building that symbolises **Yalumba** (Eden Valley Rd, Angaston; open daily 10 am–5 pm; 08 8561 3200; www.yalumba.com). It's the oldest family-owned winery in Australia and Robert Hill-Smith is the great-great-grandson of the legendary Samuel Smith. It's home to the piquant Pewsey Vale rieslings and the best viognier in the country, Virgilius. In fact, the tasting room is a monument to viognier. There's even an eau de vie distilled from the variety.

From Yalumba, head north to **Thorn-Clarke Wines** (Gawler Park Rd, Angaston; open weekdays 9 am–5 pm; weekends noon–4 pm; 08 8564 3036; www.thornclarkewines.com.au). It's home to some very good wines at surprisingly low prices. The Shotfire Barossa Shiraz at $20 competes with wine triple the price. The Sandpiper Riesling is great value at $17 and there are some $15 beauties, too.

From there, make the pilgrimage to **Henschke** (Henschke Rd, Keyneton; open weekdays 9 am–4.30 pm, Sat 9 am–noon; 08 8564 8223; www.henschke.com.au).

Don't expect to rock up and taste Hill of Grace but there are some high-end Henschkes available to sample and some of Henschke's lesser-known whites are worth a look.

As you drive out of the Eden Valley towards the Adelaide Hills, you'll come to **Peter Seppelt Wines** (cnr R. Dewells & Laubes Rds, Springton; open Thu–Mon 10 am–5 pm; 08 8568 2452; www.peterseppeltwines.com.au). It's a memorable building that looks like it belongs in a fairytale and is set in picturesque grounds. There's excellent wood-fired pizza on weekends and an eclectic range of wines including a fino sherry. The picks are the riesling and the merlot.

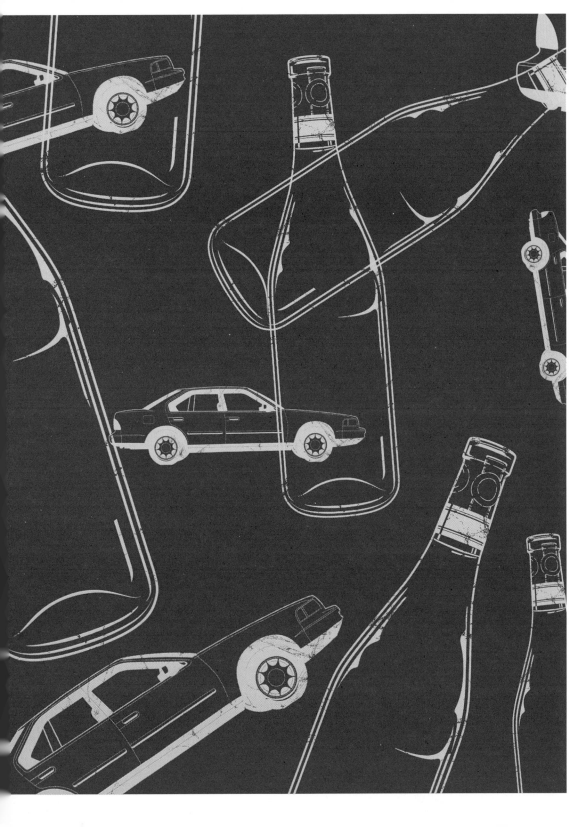

ADELAIDE HILLS

WINERIES

1. Bridgewater Mill
Mount Barker Rd, Bridgewater
08 8339 9222

2. Lloyd Brothers Wine and Olive Oil Company
94 Main St, Hahndorf
08 8388 1188

3. Hahndorf Hill Winery
Pains Rd, Hahndorf
08 8388 7512

4. Nepenthe
Jones Rd, Balhannah
08 8398 8888

5. Shaw and Smith
Lot 4 Jones Rd, Balhannah
08 8398 0500

6. Leabrook Estate
cnr Greenhill & Reserve Rds, Balhannah
08 8398 0421

7. Bird in Hand
cnr Bird in Hand & Pfeiffer Rds, Woodside
08 8389 9488

8. Ashton Hills Vineyard
Tregarthen Rd, Ashton
08 8390 1243

9. Lobethal Road
Lot 1 Lobethal Rd, Mount Torrens
08 8389 4595

10. Chain of Ponds
Adelaide Mannum Rd, Gumeracha
08 8389 1415

11. K1 by Geoff Hardy
Tynan Rd, Kuitpo
08 8388 3700

12. Longview Vineyard
Pound Rd, Macclesfield
08 8388 9694

WHERE TO EAT

A. Bridgewater Mill
Mount Barker Rd, Bridgewater
08 8339 9222

B. Hahndorf Hill
Lot 10 Pains Rd, Hahndorf
08 8388 7512

C. Chain of Ponds
Adelaide Mannum Rd, Gumeracha
08 8389 1415

Love Winery

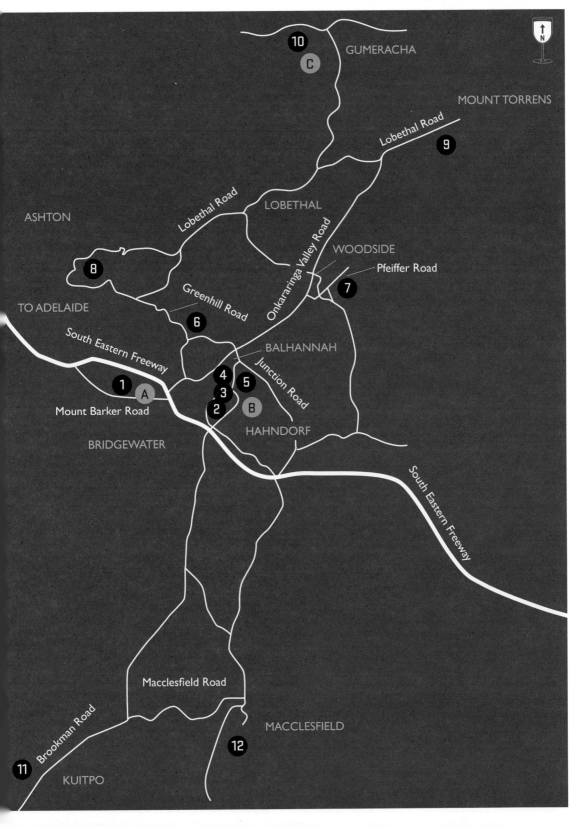

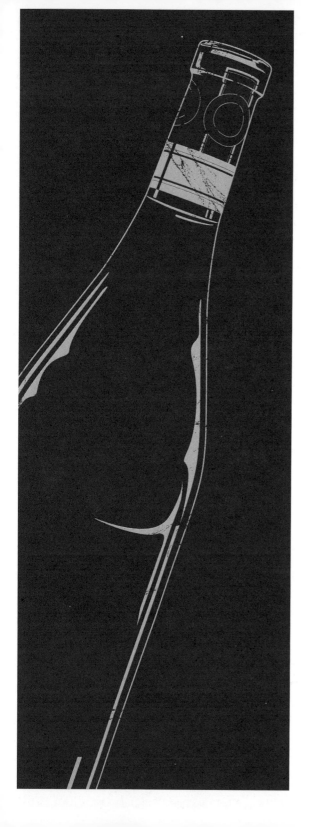

Snapshot

Driving up to the Adelaide Hills from Adelaide on a stinking-hot day is a little like going to a magic wonderland. In a seemingly short drive up the hill, you go from the baking tray that is Adelaide to a rolling, green, sometimes misty place that seems a million miles away from Rundle Street. It's quite an experience. If Adelaide—or South Australia, for that matter—didn't have the Adelaide Hills it would be a much poorer place. The hills average about 400 metres above sea level and go as high as 730 metres. It doesn't snow but it is cool and is producing some of the best chardonnay in this chardonnay-soaked land.

The background

The Adelaide Hills story is pretty similar to most of the wine regions in South Australia. Persecuted Silesians and Prussians settled in Hahndorf, Lobethal and Birdwood and gave them a Teutonic flavour. By the 1870s, after a mini gold rush, there were 530 hectares of vines, but like much of cool-climate viticulture of the era, the forces of fashion and phylloxera and the trend towards warm-climate fortified wines meant that the grapevines were removed. By World War II the Adelaide Hills was virtually vine free. It was Brian Croser (of Petaluma fame) who brought the Hills back to life when he kick-started the region again at Piccadilly in the 1970s.

The wines

The Adelaide Hills does most wine styles very well with a sort of understated aplomb. There's sparkling, riesling, chardonnay, pinot noir, shiraz, even cabernet sauvignon, and lest we forget the variety for which it is most famous, sauvignon blanc. I'd argue that the variety for which the Adelaide Hills will go down in wine history is chardonnay. Some of the best versions of the variety this country has ever produced come from the Hills.

The prices

Wines under $20 are rare in the Adelaide Hills. Most are around $20–$30. That said, Longview has some very decent products around the $15–$18 mark.

The layout

You can approach the Adelaide Hills from either end. The usual way is to go up the Princes Highway through the tunnel to Hahndorf and approach it south to north. You can also get at it from the scenic Gorge Road up to Gumeracha and Birdwood and go back the other way. There's also the option to approach it from the Barossa via the Eden Valley, which is a pretty good way to get a feel for how the Barossa heights merge into the Adelaide Hills.

A suggested route

On the way along the highway from Adelaide is a turn-off for Bridgewater and **Bridgewater Mill** (Mount Barker Rd, Bridgewater; open daily 10am–5pm; 08 8339 9222; www.bridgewatermill.com.au). Here you can taste the excellent Petaluma and Bridgewater Mill products; some from Adelaide Hills and some from Coonawarra fruit. The Petaluma Chardonnay is a beauty and the spot is legendary for lunch.

In the town of Hahndorf is **Lloyd Brothers Wine and Olive Oil Company** (94 Main St, Hahndorf; open Wed–Sun & public holidays 11am–5pm; 08 8388 1188; www.lloydbrothers.com.au). This is operated by the nephew of Mark Lloyd of Coriole fame. There are reds from both McLaren Vale and the Adelaide Hills and some tasty olive oil.

Not far away is **Hahndorf Hill Winery** (Pains Rd, Hahndorf; open daily 10am–5pm; 08 8388 7512; www.hahndorfhillwinery.com.au), a lively cellar door with a good range of wines. The rosé is the standout.

Next stop is **Nepenthe** (Jones Rd, Balhannah; open daily 10am–5pm; 08 8398 8888; www.nepenthe.com.au). It sits proudly on the brow of a hill and is the biggest producer in the Hills. The massive McGuigan Simeon group now owns it. The standout wine is the chardonnay.

Close by is **Shaw and Smith** (Lot 4 Jones Rd, Balhannah; open weekends & public holiday Mondays 11 am–4 pm; 08 8398 0500; www.shawandsmith.com), which is definitely worth a visit. From the grounds to the tasting room to the coolroom in the winery where the fruit is chilled before crushing, this is a perfectionist operation. Shaw and Smith has the best shiraz in the Hills and the M3 Chardonnay is the style most quality chardonnay producers model theirs on. The sauvignon blanc is the money-spinner and very good.

Also in Balhannah is **Leabrook Estate** (cnr Greenhill & Reserve rds, Balhannah; open weekends & public holidays 11 am–5 pm; 08 8398 0421; www.leabrookestate.com), a family-run operation with tasty chardonnay. The merlot isn't bad either.

Head back to the Onkaparinga Valley Road, follow it towards Woodside and off to the right is **Bird in Hand** (cnr Bird in Hand & Pfeiffer Rds, Woodside; open weekdays 10 am–5 pm, weekends & public holidays 11 am–5 pm; 08 8389 9488; www.birdinhand.com.au). In Adelaide Hills terms it's a big winery with both Adelaide

Hills and Clare Valley wines for sale. As with most wineries in the region, the chardonnay is the standout, especially the $60 Nest Egg Chardonnay. There's also a very good shiraz.

From here you can choose a different route back to Adelaide via Ashton and **Ashton Hills Vineyard** (Tregarthen Rd, Ashton; open weekends & public holidays 11 am–5.30 pm; 08 8390 1243), a cult winery with some really stylish wines. Check out the riesling and pinot noir, in particular.

Keep heading towards Lobethal and you'll arrive at **Lobethal Road** (Lot 1 Lobethal Rd, Mount Torrens; open Thu–Sun & public holidays 11 am–5 pm; 08 8389 4595; www.lobethalroad.com), a friendly cellar door with a standout shiraz.

At the northern end of the region is **Chain of Ponds** (Adelaide Mannum Rd, Gumeracha; open weekdays 9.30 am–4.30 pm, weekends & public holidays 10.30 am–4.30 pm; 08 8389 1415; www.chainofponds.com.au), a vineyard and winery that has pioneered Italian varieties in the region. The cabernet and chardonnay are very good but so is the Novello range of Italian blends—bargains at $15.

There are two other wineries worth visiting in the region that are a little out of the way. Twenty kilometres from Willunga in McLaren Vale is **Kuitpo** and **K1** by Geoff

Hardy (Tynan Rd, Kuitpo; open weekends & public holidays 11 am–5 pm; 08 8388 3700; www.k1.com.au), a legendary vineyard that looks like a landscaped garden with an impressive building overlooking the dam. The shiraz, cabernet sauvignon and chardonnay are beauties.

15 kilometres from Strathalbyn on the way to Langhorne Creek is **Longview Vineyard** (Point Rd, Macclesfield; open daily 11 am–5 pm; 08 8388 9694), home to the tasty Yakka Shiraz and Devil's Elbow Cabernet Sauvignon. The $15 cabernet shiraz is worth buying by the case.

Where to eat

Bridgewater Mill (Mount Barker Rd, Bridgewater; open Thu–Mon for lunch; 08 8339 9222; www.bridgewatermill.com.au) is a legendary spot for elongated Sunday luncheons.

Hahndorf Hill (Lot 10 Pains Rd, Hahndorf; open weekends for lunch; 08 8388 7512; www.hahndorfhillwinery.com.au) is a good spot for a glass of rosé and a bite.

Chain of Ponds (Adelaide Mannum Rd, Gumeracha; open Mon–Sat for lunch; 08 8389 1415; www.chainofponds.com.au) has a panoramic outlook and serves antipasto and cheese mid-week and a full Italian-style menu at other times.

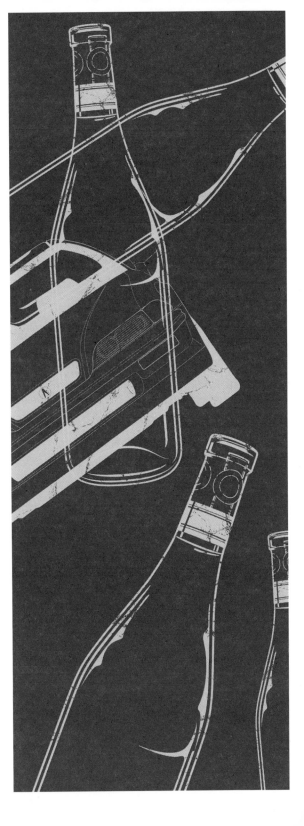

McLAREN VALE

WINERIES

1. d'Arenberg
Osborn Rd, McLaren Vale
08 8329 4888

2. Coriole
Chaffeys Rd, McLaren Vale
08 8323 8305

3. Chapel Hill
Chapel Hill Rd, McLaren Vale
08 8323 8429

4. Woodstock
Douglas Gully Rd, McLaren Flat
08 8383 0156

5. Kangarilla Road
Kangarilla Rd, McLaren Vale
08 8383 0533

6. The Salopian Inn
cnr McMurtrie & Main Rds,
McLaren Vale
08 8323 8769

7. Gemtree
184 Main Rd, McLaren Vale
08 8323 8199

8. Wirra Wirra
McMurtrie Rd, McLaren Vale
08 8323 8414

9. Fox Creek
Malpas Rd, McLaren Vale
08 8556 2403

WHERE TO EAT

A. The Salopian Inn
cnr McMurtrie & Main Rds, McLaren Vale
08 8323 8769

B. d'Arry's Verandah Restaurant
Osborn Rd, McLaren Vale
08 8329 4848

C. The Kitchen Door
Penny's Hill and Mr Riggs cellars,
Main Road, McLaren Vale
08 8556 4460

D. Star of Greece I
The Esplanade, Port Willunga
08 8557 7420

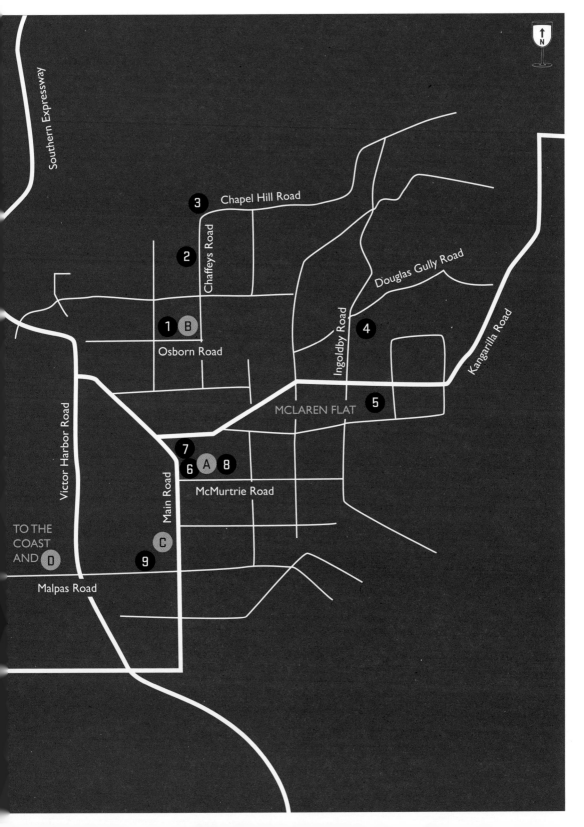

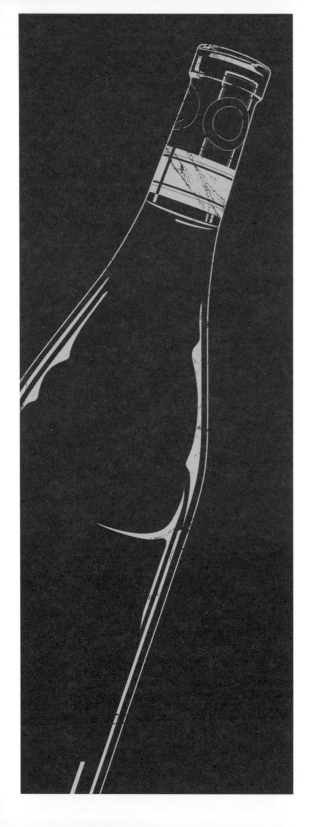

Snapshot

If you're in Adelaide and only have a short time, don't do what most do and head north for the Barossa, go south to McLaren Vale. It's closer (only 35 kilometres), easier to navigate, contains loads of fantastic wineries, a wider choice of wine styles and plenty of South Australian flavour to savour.

The background

The difference between McLaren Vale and its South Australian equivalents is that there is no Germanic influence. It was pork pies not mettwurst that fed the intrepid first vignerons. The Anglican heritage is reflected in fine British surnames synonymous with the region such as Hardy and Reynell. By 1900 McLaren Vale was producing 3 million litres of wine in wineries that still exist in some form or other today: Pirramimma, Wirra Wirra, Tatachilla et al.

Big reds were the stock in trade and this was the first Australian wine to be exported in reasonable quantities. Since then, McLaren Vale's fashionability has ebbed and flowed with the fortunes of the warm-climate red. Big reds are now modish and McLaren Vale is as dynamic as it ever was.

The wines

McLaren Vale is red country, most notably shiraz, cabernet sauvignon, grenache and mourvèdre (mataro). It is here that the notorious but rarely spotted 'bush grenache vine' can be seen in the wild. It's difficult to make a weedy red here and if you like your wines big and gushy with plenty of flavour, it will be heaven. There are also some decent whites and some handy Italian varietals, too.

The prices

Most of the larger wineries have a hierarchy of brands so you can go from $15 all the way up to $100. The value lies around the $20–$25 mark.

The layout

Most of McLaren Vale lies between the Onkaparinga River and Hill Range Road. The region starts at Reynella, which has been swamped by suburbs. The region itself is quite closely concentrated and most wineries are within a 10-kilometre radius.

A suggested route

Coming from Adelaide you get on the Southern Expressway or if you've got time you can go the scenic coast way along A15 past Port Noarlunga. Before you get to McLaren Vale township itself, follow the signs to **d'Arenberg** (Osborn Rd, McLaren Vale; open daily 10 am–5 pm; 08 8329 4888; www.darenberg.com.au),

one of the granddaddies of the region and still at the top of its game. The wines are very good, particularly the reds, but don't forget to taste the Adelaide Hills Chardonnay. Beware, the range is huge and if you try to taste everything you'll be there all day and they'll have to carry you out.

Further up the road is **Coriole** (Chaffeys Rd, McLaren Vale; open weekdays 10 am–5 pm, weekends 11 am–5 pm; 08 8323 8305; www.coriole.com). The cellar door occupies a picturesque spot on the top of the hill. The shiraz is very good and should be tasted but owner Mark Lloyd has also pioneered the growing and making of Italian varietals. The Coriole Sangiovese is one of the best in the country and Coriole also champions Fiano, which is an ancient white variety dating back to Roman times. Try it.

Chapel Hill (Chapel Hill Rd, McLaren Vale; open daily noon–5 pm; 08 8323 8429; www.chapelhillwine.com.au) should be on your tasting list. The arrival of ex-Tatachilla winemaker Michael Fragos has seen the entire range get a quality and style boost. The cabernet sauvignon is a favourite, the rosé is great and it's hard to find a bad product in the range.

Follow Chapel Hill road until Blewitt Springs Road, turn right and head back down the hill till you get to Douglas Gully

Road and there you'll find **Woodstock** (Douglas Gully Rd, McLaren Flat; open daily 10 am–5 pm; 08 8383 0156; www. woodstockwine.com.au). Here are some typically generous McLaren Vale reds and a friendly cellar door (the cellar door manager is a star).

Down Ingoldby Road is **Kangarilla Road** (Kangarilla Rd, McLaren Vale; open weekdays 9 am–5 pm, weekends 11 am–5 pm; 08 8383 0533; www.kangarillaroad. com.au). Winemaker Kevin O'Brien has a special touch and the entire range has a stylishness about it. The shiraz is excellent but try the Italian variety, primitivo, as well.

From there it's a short drive to the best luncheon destination in the Vale, **The Salopian Inn** (cnr McMurtrie & Main rds, McLaren Vale; open Wed–Sun for lunch, Thu–Sat for dinner; 08 8323 8769; www. mvbeer.com/the-salopian-inn.html). It's the spot where you can taste one of the up-and-comers of McLaren Vale, **Gemtree** (184 Main Rd, McLaren Vale, open daily 10 am–5 pm; 08 8323 8199; www.gemtree vineyards.com.au).

The viticulture is biodynamic and you can taste the care given to the vines and the winemaking. The Citrine Chardonnay is one of the best chardys to come from McLaren Vale and the White Lees Shiraz absolutely rocks.

Wirra Wirra (McMurtrie Rd, McLaren Vale; open Mon–Sat 10 am–5 pm, Sun & public holidays 11 am–5 pm; 08 8323 8414; www.wirrawirra.com) is up there with d'Arenberg as one of the big companies in the region with a big profile and a huge range. The cellar door is well tended and the range goes from the affordable Scrubby Rise range all the way up to the Chook Block Shiraz at $130. It's hard to find a dud wine.

Fox Creek (Malpas Rd, McLaren Vale; open daily 10 am–5 pm; 08 8556 2403; www.foxtreewines.com) is out on its own off Victor Harbor Road heading south and is home to big, ballsy McLaren Vale reds in a pretty setting. Check out the affordable Shadows Run wines named after Fox Creek's legendary border collie, Shadow.

Where to eat

Make a booking at the **The Salopian Inn** (cnr McMurtrie & Main Rds, McLaren Vale; open Wed–Sun for lunch, Thu–Sat for dinner; 08 8323 8769; www.mvbeer.com/ the-salopian-inn.html) if you fancy a long lunch, with an extensive range of wines or a glass of Vale Ale.

d'Arry's Verandah Restaurant (Osborn Rd, McLaren Vale; open daily from noon; 08 8329 4848; www.darenberg. com.au), is a closed-in verandah looking down the hill towards the sea with a menu well matched to the wine range.

The Kitchen Door at Penny's Hill and Mr Riggs cellars (Main Road, McLaren Vale; open daily for lunch; 08 8556 4460; www.pennyshill.com.au) has good food—sit-down or tapas—to go with the wide range of wines. Don't miss out on the Coffin Bay oysters.

Star of Greece I (The Esplanade, Port Willunga; open for lunch Wed–Sun 12 pm–3 pm and dinner Fri–Sat from 5.30 pm, kiosk open daily weather permitting; 08 8557 7420). Don't expect souvlaki, the place gets it name from an old cargo ship wrecked on the beach below in 1888. Perched on a cliff overlooking the sea, it's part café, part kiosk, part restaurant and bar. There's a wine list that features highlights from Australia's smaller wineries and some excellent international beverages. Sipping one on the deck as the sun goes down is one of South Australia's great experiences.

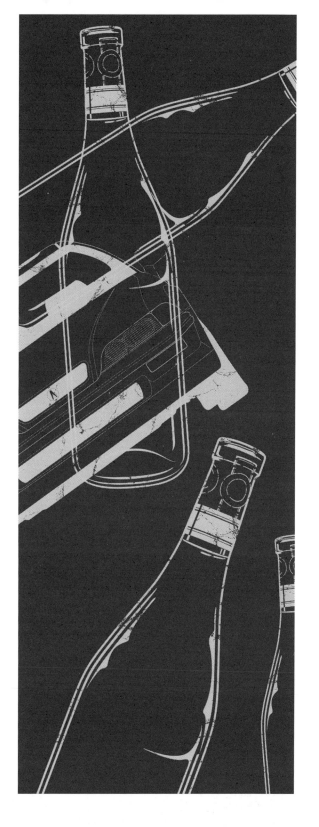

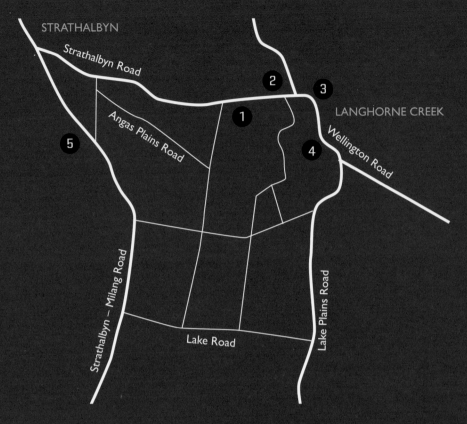

STRATHALBYN

Strathalbyn Road

LANGHORNE CREEK

Angas Plains Road

Wellington Road

Strathalbyn – Milang Road

Lake Plains Road

Lake Road

LANGHORNE CREEK

WINERIES

1. Zonte's Footstep
Strathalbyn Rd, Langhorne Creek
08 8537 3334

2. Bremerton Wines
Strathalbyn Rd, Langhorne Creek
08 8537 3093

3. Ben Potts Wines
Wellington Rd, Langhorne Creek
08 8537 3029

4. Bleasdale Vineyards
Wellington Rd, Langhorne Creek
08 8537 3001

5. Temple Bruer
Strathalbyn–Milang Rd, Strathalbyn
08 8537 0203

Snapshot

Langhorne Creek the wine region is like those songwriters who write the hits for the singers and never get the recognition. Umpteen Jimmy Watson winners contained Langhorne Creek fruit while Coonawarra and Barossa got the fame. It has produced some of the most luscious red wines this country has known yet is probably the least familiar region. It adjoins Lake Alexandrina, which is where the Murray finishes its journey. Langhorne Creek's future is tied up with the health of the Murray. Problems with water are an issue for Langhorne Creek, but while the region survives it is producing remarkably good wine.

The background

The region is named after Alfred Langhorne, who drove a mob of cattle from Sydney all the way down the Murray to the mouth—it's one of those Burke and Willsian deeds that isn't more famous because it didn't end in tragedy. Frank Potts was the first vigneron in the region. He planted shiraz and verdelho and his ancestors still run Bleasdale. Potts invented a system of flood irrigation that worked well back in the nineteenth century but wouldn't be allowed in these water-conscious times. The old history still abounds in Langhorne

Creek and there is a planting of shiraz and cabernet sauvignon at a place called Metala (which still features on Saltram Metala labels), which dates back to 1892.

The wines

With 85 per cent red varieties, it's a red wine lover's paradise. You won't find steely chardonnays or flinty rieslings; the white variety for which the place has received the most praise is verdelho.

The prices

Good news here, Langhorne Creek has some of the best value at the cellar door and most of them are at Bleasedale. It's a place where you can get a sub $10 red.

The layout

It's a detour off the M1 through Strathalbyn but once you're there the distances aren't that great—most wineries are within a five-kilometre radius.

A suggested route

Coming from Strathalbyn, the first winery you get to is **Zonte's Footstep** (Strathalbyn Rd, Langhorne Creek; open daily 10 am–5 pm; 08 8537 3334; www.zontesfootstep.com.au). It's yet another label connected to the indefatigable Ben Riggs, who just can't stop making wine. The range is vast and the quality good. Check out the Lake Doctor Shiraz Viognier and the malbec.

Up the road is **Bremerton Wines** (Strathalbyn Rd, Langhorne Creek; open daily 10 am–5 pm; 08 8537 3093; www.bremerton.com.au), one of the must-visits of the district. Run by sisters Rebecca and Lucy Wilson, the wines are top quality throughout the range and very good value, especially the cabernet shiraz malbec merlot blend known as Tamblyn.

Ben Potts Wines (Wellington Rd, Langhorne Creek; open daily 10 am–5 pm; 08 8537 3029; www.benpottswines.com.au) is a label run by Ben Potts who is a descendant of the famous Frank. The wines are named after the Potts dynasty and the Fiddles Block Langhorne Creek Shiraz, named after his great-grandfather, is a beauty.

Further down Wellington Road is **Bleasdale Vineyards** (Wellington Rd, Langhorne Creek; open daily 10 am–5 pm; 08 8537 3001; www.bleasdale.com.au). History freaks will love it. You can still see some of the redwood winemaking gear they made and still used until quite recently. In those days if you couldn't get it, you built it. Apparently old man Potts even made a piano out of local redwood because he couldn't get hold of a proper one.

The top-of-the-range wines are good but the bargains are too good to be true. The Second Innings Malbec is a favourite at $15, the Mulberry Tree Cabernet Sauvignon at $18 should be tasted and the Langhorne Crossing Red at $9 is a price from another era.

There is one more cellar door to the south-east. **Temple Bruer** (Strathalbyn–Milang Rd, Strathalbyn; open weekdays 9.30 am–4.30 pm; 08 8537 0203; www.templebruer.com.au) is one of the Australian pioneers of organic viticulture. Beloved by wine drinkers susceptible to sulphur dioxide, Temple Bruer specialises in high-quality preservative-free wines.

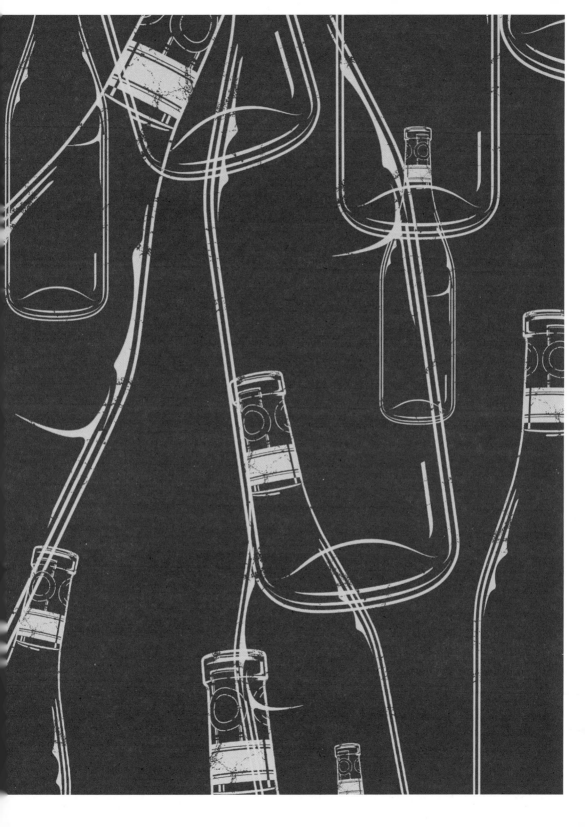

CLARE VALLEY

WINERIES

1. Mount Horrocks
The Old Railway Station, Curling St,
Auburn
08 8849 2243

2. Grosset
King St, Auburn
08 8849 2175

3. Taylors Wines
Taylors Rd, Auburn
08 8849 1111

4. Annie's Lane
Quelltaler Rd, Watervale
08 8843 0003

5. Kilikanoon
Penna Ln, Penwortham
08 8843 4206

6. Penna Lane Wines
Lot 51 Penna Ln, Penwortham
08 8843 4364

7. Mitchell Wines
Hughes Park Rd, Sevenhill
08 8843 4258

8. Jeanneret
Jeanneret Rd, Sevenhill
08 8843 4308

9. Sevenhill Cellars
College Rd, Sevenhill
08 8843 4222

10. Neagles Rock
Main North Rd, Clare
08 8843 4020

11. Jim Barry Wines
Craig's Hill Rd, Clare
08 8842 2261

WHERE TO EAT

A. Skillogalee Winery Restaurant
Trevarrick Rd, Sevenhill
08 8843 4311

B. The Station Cafe
The Old Railway Station at Mount
Horrocks, Curling St, Auburn
08 8849 2202

C. The Rising Sun Hotel
Main North Road, Auburn
08 8849 2015

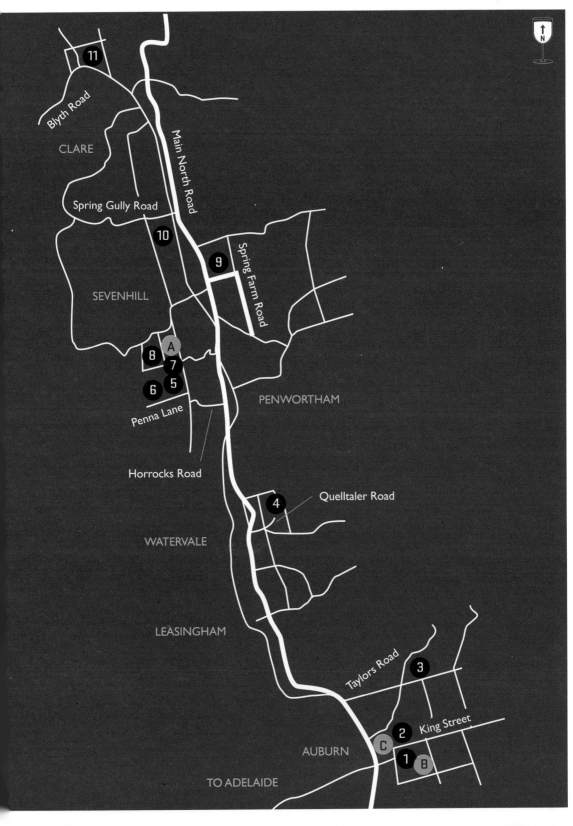

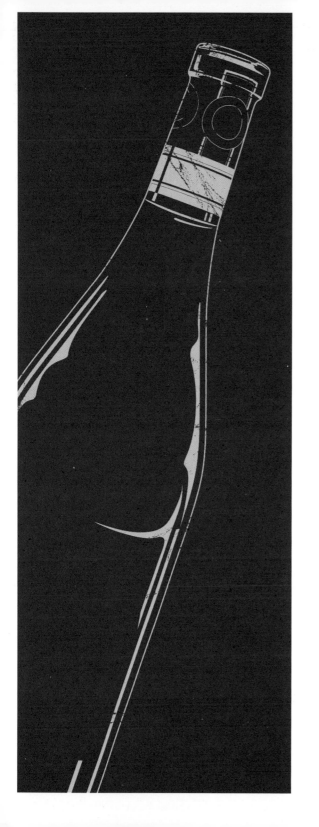

Snapshot

If the Clare Valley were on the coast I'd probably be living there. It's as quaint as wine regions get without getting chintzy, and is packed with fantastic wines and cosy cellar doors. It's all contained in an easily drivable or pushbikable 20-kilometre strip and is full of the stuff that makes visitors to South Australia get excited: stone buildings, lovely pubs and friendly locals. It produces arguably Australia's most unique wine style, Clare Valley riesling, but if you prefer reds you won't be disappointed. The shiraz and cabernet sauvignon have a distinct 'Clare' character about them.

The background

Like most wine regions, the Clare Valley was settled by intrepid pastoralists. In this case it was a bloke called John Horrocks in 1840. It is he who is credited with planting the first vines, and the Mount Horrocks winery now bears his name. A homesick Irishman from County Clare, Edmund Burton Gleeson, founded Clare, or Clareville as it was known. He planted 500 or so vines but the thing that put a rocket into Clare viticulture was the discovery of copper at Burra, a town just to the north.

Following the copper, there was a wheat boom and then the slate of Mintaro was quarried (hence all the gorgeous stone buildings) and by the end of the 1900s there were more than 500 hectares of vineyards in the valley and names such as The Stanley Wine Company (which is now saved only for wine casks), Quelltaler (which is now Annie's Lane), Wendouree and Sevenhill were going strong. The fortunes of Clare have suffered from the effects of wine fashion ever since, and would be a lot more famous if the riesling got the recognition it deserves.

The wines

Riesling is Clare's speciality. Clare defies all the climatic data in that it appears to be a hot region yet produces wines that taste like they come from a cooler climate. That and some of the stony ground up on Polish Hill is one of the reasons the riesling is so good. But Clare is far from a one-trick pony. The shiraz is powerful, fragrant and seems to inherit a little bit of a eucalypt character from the local trees, as does the cabernet sauvignon, which is notoriously gutsy and powerful.

The prices

As befits a big wine region, prices can go from $15 to $50, depending on where you are and what you're buying. The best advice is to ignore the icon wines (unless you're into that sort of thing) and purchase the reds and whites that sit around the $18–$25 mark.

The layout

Clare is north of all of the rest of the South Australian wine regions on the cusp of where South Australia changes from fertile land to the semi-desert. When you arrive from Morgan through Burra to Clare it is amazing how quickly and dramatically the landscape changes. Coming from Adelaide you enter Clare at Auburn and finish at Clare.

A suggested route

Assuming you're coming from Adelaide, the first town you hit is Auburn and in Auburn there are a couple of gems. **Mount Horrocks** (The Old Railway Station, Curling St, Auburn; open weekends & public holidays 10 am–5 pm; 08 8849 2243; www.mounthorrocks.com) is in an old railway station that has been remodelled into a well-run cellar door. The riesling, the legendary sticky—the Cordon Cut Riesling—and the shiraz are particularly good.

Next on your list should be **Grosset** (King St, Auburn; open Wed–Sun 10 am–5 pm from September or until stocks last; 08 8849 2175; www.grosset.com.au). Note the 'until stocks last' comment. Grosset is a cult winery and the Polish Hill and Watervale Rieslings are justly revered. Don't neglect to taste the cabernet blend known as Gaia.

Further north you'll find the turn-off to **Taylors Wines** (Taylors Rd, Auburn; open weekdays 9 am–5 pm, Sat & public holidays 10 am–5 pm, Sun 10 am–4 pm; 08 8849 1111; www.taylorswines.com.au). Founded in 1969, this company is still a dynamo in the area. It's big (more than half a million cases of wine) but has a commitment to the Clare Valley and the wines reflect Clare character. Check out the standard riesling, cabernet sauvignon and shiraz but also the premium Jarraman range.

Up the road in the town of Watervale is **Annie's Lane** (Quelltaler Rd, Watervale; open weekdays 8.30 am–5 pm, weekends 11 am–4 pm; 08 8843 0003; www.annieslane.com.au). It's owned by one of the mega wine companies but is a historic spot, which still has some of the relics on show. The wines are good, too.

In the subregion of Sevenhill are some of the most memorable cellar doors. Turn left at Penwortham and travel up and into the next valley and you'll come to **Kilikanoon** (Penna Ln, Penwortham; open Thu–Sun & public holidays 11 am–5 pm; 08 8843 4206). The Mort's Riesling is regularly one of the best in the valley.

Up the hill a bit is **Penna Lane Wines** (Lot 51 Penna Ln, Penwortham; open Thu–Sun & public holidays 11 am–5 pm; 08 8843 4364; www.pennalanewines.com.au), one of the new generation of Clare wineries with good wines and atmosphere. I recommend you check out the riesling and shiraz, in particular.

Mitchell Wines (Hughes Park Rd, Sevenhill; open daily 10 am–4 pm; 08 8843 4258; www.mitchellwines.com) is a legend of the region, famous for its riesling, shiraz and a very good semillon.

Jeanneret (Jeanneret Rd, Sevenhill; open weekdays 9 am–5 pm, weekends & public holidays 10 am–5 pm; 08 8843 4308; www.jeanneretwines.com) is one winery you probably won't have heard of, but the cave-like cellar door is worth a visit for the riesling, the shiraz and the cat.

Back on the Main North Road heading north, turn right up College Road and you'll come to the historic **Sevenhill Cellars** (College Rd, Sevenhill; open weekdays 9 am–5 pm, weekends & public holidays 10 am–5 pm; 08 8843 4222; www.sevenhill.com.au). It's a Jesuit operation that dates back to 1851 and looks it. The wines are increasingly modern despite the Benedictine patina, and the Inigo range at $19 offers very good value for money, particularly the merlot.

Neagles Rock (Main North Rd, Clare; Mon–Sat 10 am–5 pm, Sun 11 am–4 pm; 08 8843 4020; www.neaglesrock.com) got its name from the local Lover's (Neagles) Rock where Clare adolescents would go to pash. Run by Jane Willson and until recently a large black labrador named Bob, this relative newcomer (1997) has leapt to the top of the heap with a wide range of varietals, the highlights being the sangiovese, riesling and the Mr Duncan Cabernet Shiraz.

Last on the list is **Jim Barry Wines** (Craig's Hill Rd, Clare; open weekdays 9 am–5 pm, weekends & public holidays 9 am–4 pm; 08 8842 2261; www.jimbarry.com), a large, family-owned winery with some historic vineyards in the region. The Florita Riesling from a famous old vineyard is regularly brilliant and the Lodge Shiraz is always worth a taste.

Where to eat

Skillogalee Winery Restaurant (Trevarrick Rd, Sevenhill; open for lunch; 08 8843 4311; www.skillogalee.com.au) pretty much sums up what the Clare Valley is all about—low-ceilinged stone buildings, long lunches and a glass or two of delicious riesling.

The **Station Cafe at Mount Horrocks** (The Old Railway Station, Curling St, Auburn; open weekends & public holidays for lunch; 08 8849 2202; www.mounthorrocks.com) is the nicest railway station you'll ever have lunch in.

The **Rising Sun Hotel,** (Main North Rd, Auburn; 08 8849 2015) is an old stone pub right in the heart of quaint Auburn. It has decent accommodation. The food can be good, the Clare dominated wine list is excellent and the Coopers on tap is fantastic.

COONAWARRA

WINERIES

1. Punters Corner
Riddoch Hwy, Coonawarra
08 8737 2007

2. Balnaves
Riddoch Hwy, Coonawarra
08 8737 2946

3. Katnook
Riddoch Hwy, Coonawarra
08 8737 2394

4. Majella
Lynn Rd, Coonawarra
08 8736 3055

5. Zema Estate
Riddoch Hwy, Coonawarra
08 8736 3219

6. Wynns Coonawarra Estate
Memorial Dr, Coonawarra
08 8736 2225

7. Rymill
Riddoch Hwy, Coonawarra
08 8736 5001

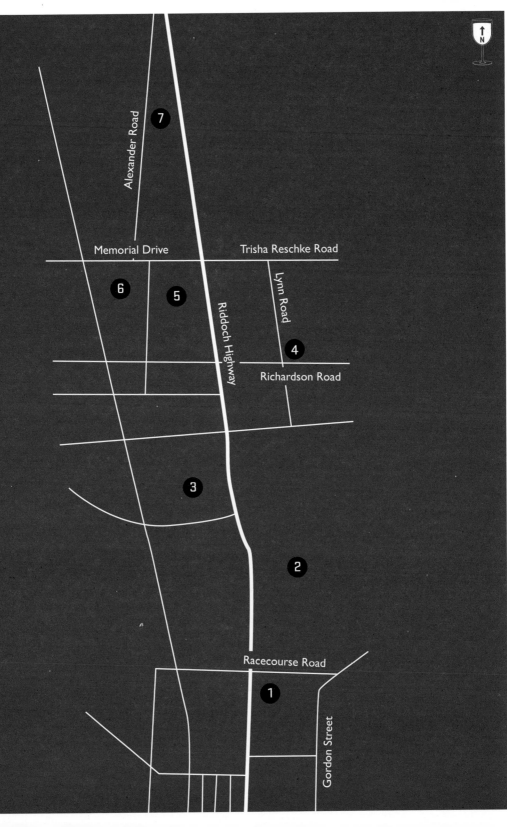

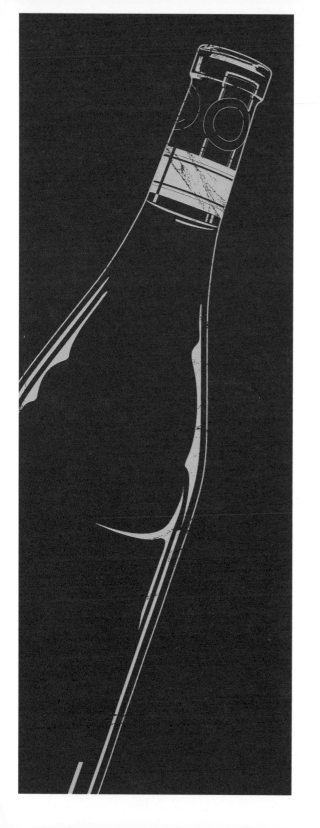

Snapshot

Coonawarra offers the interesting conundrum in that it is probably one of the least-blessed wine regions in terms of scenery and the most blessed in terms of dirt. To put it bluntly, Coonawarra is not much to look at. It's an excellent place to ride a pushbike with no gears, which is a rather polite way of saying it's as flat as a pancake.

Hot in summer and freezing in winter, to be fair there are probably some gorgeous mornings in spring and some lovely afternoons in autumn but that doesn't stop Coonawarra feeling like it is in the middle of nowhere. However if, like me, you have a penchant for Coonawarra reds, a pilgrimage to the red dirt should be on the cards.

The background

Coonawarra was settled for its dirt. It was pretty much left to itself until 1844 when a squatter named Alexander Cameron stopped there. In 1861 John Riddoch (a name immortalised in Coonawarra nomenclature) arrived and bought a lease for vast amounts of land. He then created what we now know as Coonawarra. He also organised a road from Mount Gambier and helped get the rail line from Naracoorte up and running.

The most important thing from a wine point of view was the establishment of the Penola Fruit Company. He subdivided and sold his land to potential farmers with the guarantee that he would buy their grapes to make wine. The winery that is still standing and appears on the Wynns label was built in 1890 just as the depression of that era hit. Things didn't go to well for Coonawarra for some time. In the 1930s the first of the Australian vine-pull schemes was tried. The state government offered Coonawarra farmers money to pull out their vines and turn to dairying. Many chose the udder option and Redman is the only name to survive from the Penola Fruit Company.

The revival began in 1951 when the dynamic David Wynn (the man responsible for the Wynns wine cask) bought the old Riddoch winery and the vineyard and brought the Coonawarra name to the attention of the small but enthusiastic red-wine-drinking audience. It's been growth ever since with peaks in the 1980s followed by a decline in wine quality in the 1990s. New blood arriving to the region at that time has turbo charged the region and the wine has never been better.

The wines

The undoubted King of Coonawarra is cabernet sauvignon; perhaps nowhere else in Australia, barring Margaret River, does the noble cabernet grape express itself so articulately. Depth, structure and longevity are all characteristics of Coonawarra cab. That said, don't leave shiraz off your tasting list: it's great. Of the whites, chardonnay can be OK and the riesling can't be ignored.

The prices

For such a legendary wine region, prices aren't too bad. You can pay about $25 for a top-notch red that you can stick in your cellar and the whites are cheaper still. There are plenty of $50–$100 iconic wines if that sort of thing takes your fancy.

The layout

Coonawarra is 500 kilometres from Melbourne and 375 kilometres from Adelaide and a very long way from Sydney. It's not a region you nip off to on a whim but can be bundled in with some of the lesser-visited and more recently established regions in the general district, such as Robe, Mount Benson and Padthaway. Coonawarra itself is laid out in a strip north to south on the Riddoch Highway. It's very hard to get lost.

A suggested route

From Melbourne, the first winery you should visit is **Punters Corner** (Riddoch Hwy,

Hwy, Coonawarra; open daily 10 am–5 pm; 08 8737 2007; www.punterscorner.com.au). It's not Ricky Ponting's winery—it's one of the recent arrivals which, with the help of the winemaking crew at Balnaves (up the road), produces some excellent wine—the reds especially.

Next on the hit list should be **Balnaves** (Riddoch Hwy, Coonawarra; open weekdays 9 am–5 pm, weekends noon–5 pm; 08 8737 2946). It's one of the up-and-comers in Coonawarra. Wine quality and style is spot-on and it's surprisingly inexpensive. The sub $20 'blend' is a great wine for the money. Balnaves wines are available by the glass for $5 if you want to have a picnic by the pond.

Katnook (Riddoch Hwy, Coonawarra; open Mon–Sat 10 am–5 pm, Sun 11 am–4 pm; 08 8737 2394; www.katnookestate.com.au) is one of the bigger players with a cellar door reconstructed from what used to be John Riddoch's office during the Penola Fruit Colony era. The range of wines stretches from $100 or so for the ominously named 'Odyssey' and 'Prodigy' to the $20-odd Founder's Block wines. These are excellent value, particularly the cabernet and the shiraz.

From Katnook head up the Riddoch Highway to **Majella** (Lynn Rd, Coonawarra; open daily 10 am–4.30 pm; 08 8736 3055; www.majellawines.com.au), a grape grower with a wine label most others would envy. The shiraz and cabernet are great and the blend of the two, named The Musician, is one of Coonawarra's bargains. There's also a good sparkling red.

Next stop is **Zema Estate** (Riddoch Hwy, Coonawarra; open daily 9 am–5 pm; 08 8736 3219; www.zema.com.au), one of the livelier cellar doors in the region and one with a Calabrian influence. The Zemas were Italians growing grapes before they were winemakers. The standard $25 reds are excellent value for money—the cabernet can be fantastic—and a worthy addition to any cellar.

Check in at **Wynns Coonawarra Estate** (Memorial Dr, Coonawarra; open daily 10 am–5 pm; 08 8736 2225; www.wynns.com.au). It's part of the vast Foster's wine company now but Wynns wines are still typical Coonawarra and the old vineyards and buildings are worth a look.

The rearing horse statue tells you that you've arrived at **Rymill** (Riddoch Hwy, Coonawarra; open daily 10 am–5 pm; 08 8736 5001; www.rymill.com.au). Very good fruit and clever winemaking has meant Rymill is making sophisticated products. The MC2 is a favourite.

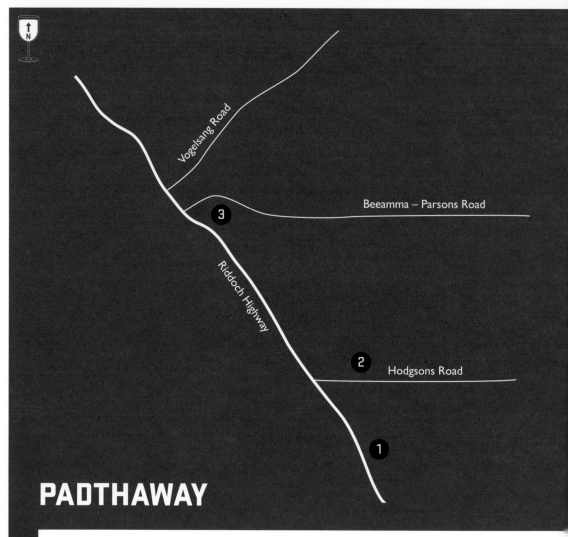

PADTHAWAY

WINERIES

1. Stonehaven
Riddoch Hwy, Padthaway
08 8765 6166

2. Henry's Drive
Hodgson's Rd, Padthaway
08 8765 5251

3. Padthaway Estate
Riddoch Hwy, Padthaway
08 8765 5505

Snapshot

Padthaway is one of the least-loved wine regions. It's not surprising. It was never meant to be anything other than a vast vineyard to supply the thirsty needs of the big wine companies when Australia's wine boom was in full swing. It was identified in the early 1960s as a likely spot; the climate was cool, the land was cheap and the dirt had a bit of the terra rossa about it.

It is still a big wine factory and quaint cellar doors are not that common. Definitely not worth a special drive—it's out in the middle of nowhere—but if you're in the area and want to put a picture to what you taste, it's worth a visit.

The background

Padthaway is almost 50 years old (which is young for a wine region) and was always targeted as a fruit supply for the big brands. What surprised the experts was how good the fruit was. The trouble with the branding was that Hardys called the region Keppoch after the sheep station, Lindemans called it Padthaway after the town to the north and when the average wine drinker saw either Keppoch or Padthaway on a wine label they didn't have a clue where it was. Padthaway eventually stuck.

The wines

When it was planted, it was meant as a red-producing region but to many people's surprise it produced very good chardonnay, and it was Padthaway chardonnay, in particular the Lindemans model of the 1980s, that first put the name to the front of drinkers' cerebellums. Now it is primarily shiraz, cabernet sauvignon and chardonnay.

The prices

Costs of production are low and wine quality is high which means more bang for the buck for the cellar door traveller. It's a long way to go for a bargain, though …

The layout

Padthaway runs in a strip from Naracoorte north of Coonawarra up towards the town of Keith. If you're touring the Limestone Coast it can easily be put into the driving plan.

A suggested route

From Naracoorte head north. You go past Keppoch and the first stop is **Stonehaven** (Riddoch Hwy, Padthaway; open daily 10 am–4 pm; 08 8765 6166; www.stonehavenvineyards.com.au). It's a big winery but with some very well priced wines. At the time of writing, Stonehaven is for sale by the multi national mega company that owns it and the future is anyone's guess.

Up the road a bit further is **Henry's Drive** (Hodgson's Rd, Padthaway; open daily 10 am–4 pm; 08 8765 5251; www.henrysdrive.com), a nice cellar door with some of the best bargains in the state. The Pillar Box Red at $18 is a beauty.

Padthaway Estate (Riddoch Hwy, Padthaway; open daily 10 am–4 pm; 08 8765 5505; www.padthawayestate.com) is home to the oldest, grandest building in Padthaway and provides accommodation. There is also more affordable housing in the renovated shearers' quarters. There are surprisingly good sparklings, a decent shiraz and a fruity olive oil.

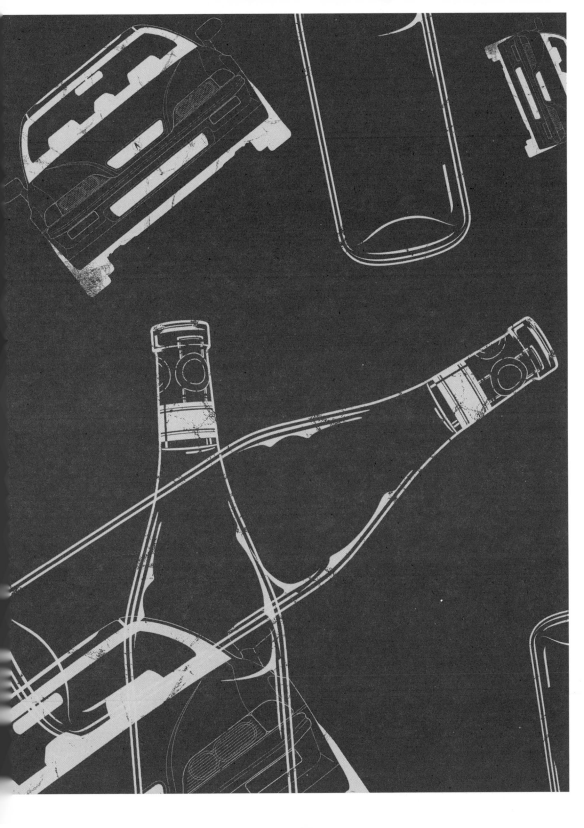

MOUNT BENSON

WINERIES

1. Wehl's Mount Benson Vineyards
Wrights Bay Rd, Mount Benson
08 8768 6251

2. Murdup Wines
Southern Ports Hwy, Mount Benson
08 8768 6190

3. Wangolina Station
cnr Southern Ports Hwy & Limestone
Coast Rd, Mount Benson
08 8768 6187

4. Norfolk Rise
Limestone Coast Rd, Mount Benson
08 8768 5080

5. Ralph Fowler Wines
Limestone Coast Rd, Mount Benson
08 8768 5000

6. Cape Jaffa
Limestone Coast Rd, Mount Benson
08 8768 5053

Snapshot

South Australia's Margaret River? Not quite, but Mount Benson does have some of what it takes—surf coast, a unique chunk of land and some very good wines. It hasn't yet got the tourists or the hype but that can be a good thing. Situated north of the town of Robe between Boatswain Point and Cape Jaffa, it's one of the newest wine regions.

The wine business dates from the 1990s but much of the action occurred after the turn of this millennium. There's not much to see apart from the surf, the pretty town of Robe and the wines but that's enough, isn't it? The region has its own vibe and the wines are great.

The background

The difference between Mount Benson and most newish wine regions is that dabblers didn't pioneer this one. First up were Peter and Leah Wehl in 1989 who started off as grape growers selling large quantities of quality fruit to big wine companies, then came Cape Jaffa in 1993. The region got the French stamp of approval when Chapoutier planted a vineyard in 1998. The Belgian tanning company known as Kreglinger (which also owns Pipers Brook and Ninth Island in Tasmania) arrived in 2000 and established Norfolk Rise. Mount Benson doesn't have a huge profile but the wines are getting out there and getting respect.

The wines

It's mostly red and mostly shiraz. That seems to be the strength and that's certainly what attracted the Rhône Valley shiraz producer, Chapoutier. There's some chardonnay, merlot, sauvignon blanc, pinot gris and various other bits and pieces as well.

The prices

It's a bit pricier than Padthaway up the road but not over the top.

The layout

The region is 320 kilometres south of Adelaide and 120 kilometres from Coonawarra. It's an easy place to get around and while there is a lot of viticultural activity, not all of the players—especially the foreign ones—have their doors open to the public, which is a shame. Most of the action is clustered around Limestone Coast Road.

A suggested route

Starting from Robe, head north on the Southern Ports Highway, take a left down Wrights Bay Road and you'll come to **Wehl's Mount Benson Vineyards** (Wrights Bay Rd, Mount Benson; open

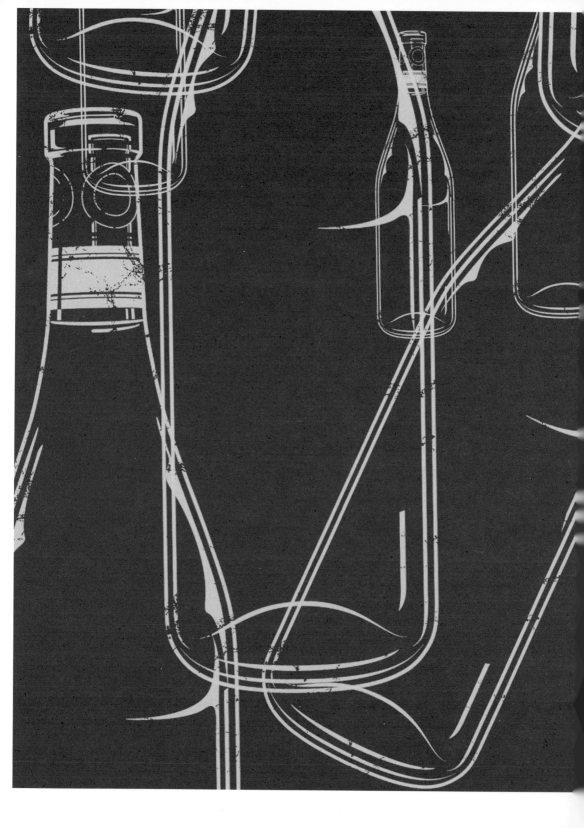

daily 10 am–4 pm; 08 8768 6251; www. wehlsmtbensonvineyards.com.au). This is primarily a grape-growing operation but there are some good wines, particularly the reds. Check out the cabernet sauvignon, in particular.

Back on the main road you come to **Murdup Wines** (Southern Ports Hwy, Mount Benson; phone ahead for opening times; 08 8768 6190). It was planted in 1997 and is small compared to many, with a quaint cellar door and some decent reds.

Head down the main drag till you come to Limestone Coast Road and turn left. On the corner is **Wangolina Station** (cnr Southern Ports Hwy & Limestone Coast Rd, Mount Benson; open daily 10 am–5 pm; 08 8768 6187; www.wangolina.com.au). As the name suggests, it's been a grazing property in the same family since 1923 until winemaker Anita Goode went down the grape track. Wine quality is high in both reds and whites (there's a very good barrel-fermented semillon) and prices are affordable.

Further down Limestone Coast Road is **Norfolk Rise** (Limestone Coast Rd, Mount Benson; open weekdays 9 am–5 pm; 08 8768 5080; www.kreglingerwineestates.com). It's run by the aforementioned Kreglinger mob and is one of the biggest organisations in the district with an 85,000-case production. It does have a bit of a corporate feel but the wines are pretty good.

Off to the right is **Ralph Fowler Wines** (Limestone Coast Rd, Mount Benson; open daily 10 am–4 pm; 08 8768 5000; www.ralphfowlerwines.com.au). Ralph used to be a high-flying big-company winemaker before settling down at Mount Benson. The wines are very good, particularly the riesling and the shiraz viognier, and prices are $20 and below.

Opposite Ralph Fowler is one of the not-to-miss spots, **Cape Jaffa** (Limestone Coast Rd, Mount Benson; open daily 10 am–5 pm; 08 8768 5053; www.capejaffawines.com.au). It's biodynamic and the wines are really stylish and arguably the best in the region. There are cheese platters and even emu mettwurst at the cellar door.

WESTERN AUSTRALIA

Looking for an ideal wine region? A spot uniquely Australian but with wines that overseas people with European tastes can understand? A place with kangaroos, surf, bush and sun and, most importantly, world-killing wine products? Problem solved, here it is. Western Australia is arguably Australia's most marketable wine state. Western Australia does have a problem, though. Whenever the conversation turns to wine and Western Australia, a giant elephant appears in the room known as Margaret River. The problem is that Margaret River is just too good, too scenic, too tasty and too damned enjoyable to travel around in that it overshadows everything else in Western Australia. But take heed, Western Australia is not a one-stop wine shop. There are lots of other winey areas in Western Australia well worth your travelling time and your palate. Explore.

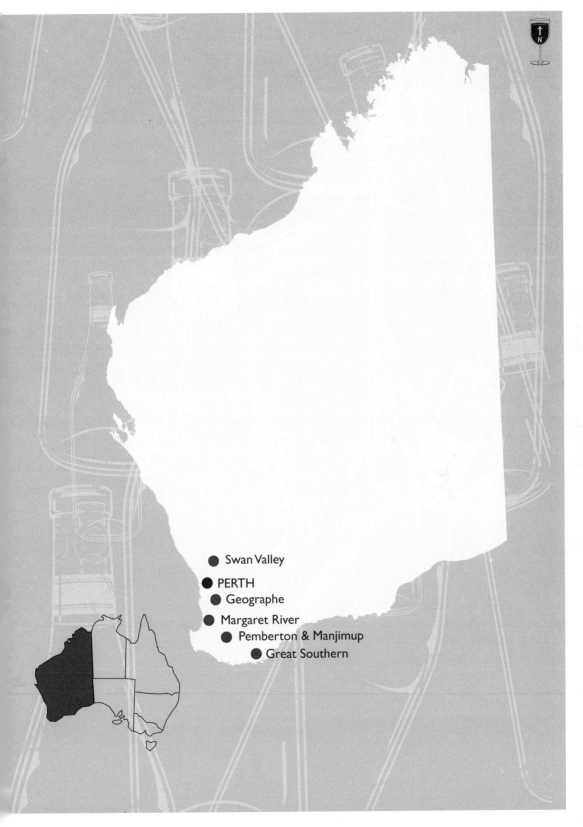

MARGARET RIVER

WINERIES

1. Wise Wine
Eagle Bay Rd, Dunsborough
08 9756 8627

2. Amberley
Thornton Rd, Yallingup
08 9750 1113

3. Clairault
Caves Rd, Wilyabrup
08 9755 6225

4. Brookland Valley
Caves Rd, Wilyabrup
08 9755 6042

5. Pierro
Caves Rd, Wilyabrup
08 9755 6220

6. Cullen Wines
Caves Rd, Cowaramup
08 9755 5277

7. Vasse Felix
cnr Caves Road and Harmans
Road South, Cowaramup
08 9756 5000

8. Juniper Estate
Harmans Road South, Cowaramup
08 9755 9000

9. Howard Park
Miamup Rd, Cowaramup
08 9756 5200

10. Cape Mentelle
Wallcliffe Rd, Margaret River
08 9757 0888

11. Voyager Estate
Lot 1 Stevens Rd, Margaret River
08 9757 6354

12. Leeuwin Estate
Stevens Rd, Margaret River
08 9759 0000

13. Redgate
Boodjidup Rd, Margaret River
08 9757 6488

WHERE TO EAT

A. Wise Vineyard Restaurant
Eagle Bay Rd, Dunsborough
08 9755 3331

B. Vasse Felix
cnr Caves Road & Harmans Road South,
Cowaramup
08 9756 5000

C. Cullen Wines
Caves Rd, Cowaramup
08 9755 5656

D. Voyager Estate
Lot 1 Stevens Rd, Margaret River
08 9757 6354

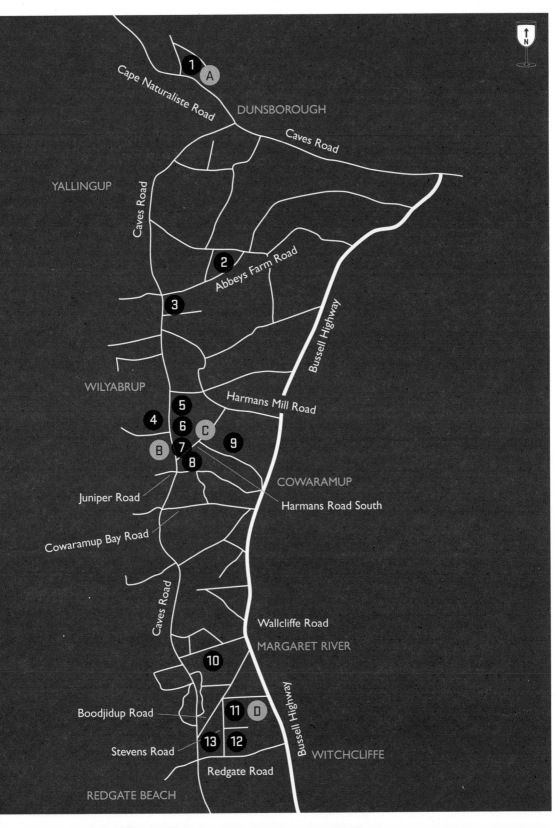

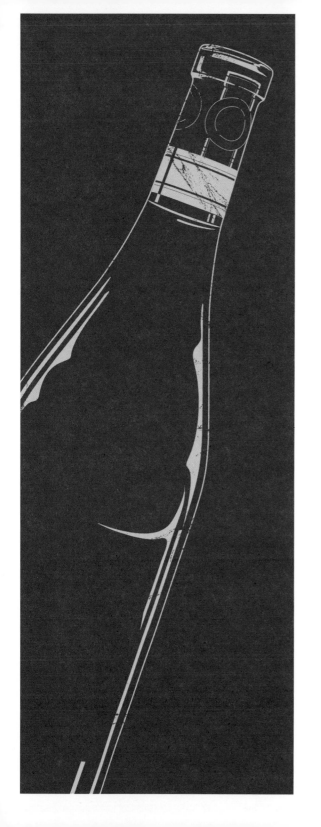

Snapshot

If you were God and you could design a wine region from scratch you'd probably come up with something that looks, tastes and feels like Margaret River. The knob of land that sticks out into the Indian Ocean known as the Leeuwin Peninsula has proved perfect for grape growing and particularly for chardonnay and cabernet sauvignon. If you are a dedicated cellar door traveller it's an absolute must. Cellar doors are an art form here both in their design and operation. True, it's pricey, but this is world-class stuff. A must-visit.

The background

When it comes to Australia's 170-year wine history, Margaret River is relatively recent. There were vines planted in Bunbury in the late nineteenth century by Vanya Cullen's great-grandfather and a report by one of the instigators of Western Australian viticulture, Dr Gladstone, marked Margaret River out as a virtual paradise for grapes. His studies led to the establishment of Vasse Felix in 1967 followed by Cullen. It was the swinging sixties and the wine business was small and run by environmentally conscious doctors/surfers who cared for the natural beauty of the place and didn't bulldoze the Karris. It was one of the first wine regions that didn't go in for the look of

European chateaus, instead opting for corrugated iron and rammed earth. With money and fame things have changed a bit but it is still cellar door nirvana—easy distances, a beautiful coastline, great surf and fantastic wine.

The wines

One of the great debates among wine tossers is 'What grape variety does Margaret River do best?' Chardonnay immediately comes to mind. Leeuwin, Pierro, Mosswood and Cullen models are all justly famous, then there's the semillon/sauvignon blend, which is Margaret River's bread and butter, but my vote would go to cabernet sauvignon. There's something classic about the dusty, leafy cabernets Margaret River produces that makes it so memorable.

The prices

Margaret River wine is not cheap. Generally there's a link between land prices and the cost of grapes and that's certainly the case here. Add demand, world fame and brand recognition to the equation and you're not going to walk out of a cellar door with a bottle of wine and much change from a $20 note. Standard ranges are from $18 to $25; premium ranges anything from $35 up.

The layout

The Leeuwin Peninsula sticks out from the coast of Western Australia like an anvil on its side running from Cape Naturaliste at the northern tip to Cape Leeuwin on the southern tip below Augusta. The wineries run pretty much north to south along Caves Road and the Bussell Highway. As far as cellar door travel, it needs two or three days to cover everything and it's probably best to do the northern part of the region one day and the southern the next.

A suggested route

Starting at the top there's a winery worth visiting for the views of Geographe Bay alone. **Wise Wine** (Eagle Bay Rd, Dunsborough; open daily 10 am–5 pm; 08 9756 8627; www.wisewine.com.au) has a special piece of real estate. The chardonnay and semillon sauvignon blanc are good and it's a nice spot for lunch.

Amberley (Thornton Rd, Yallingup; open daily 10 am–4.30 pm; 08 9750 1113; www.amberleyestate.com.au) is one of the more understated cellar doors with an excellent semillon sauvignon blanc and a pretty good cabernet merlot.

Clairault (Caves Rd, Wilyabrup; open daily 10 am–5 pm; 08 9755 6225; www.clairaultwines.com.au) is in a beautiful spot and has particularly good whites. The Holy Land as far as Margaret River vineyard land goes is situated around the junction of Metricup and Caves Roads.

Here you'll find going north to south **Brookland Valley** (Caves Rd, Wilyabrup; open daily 10 am–5 pm; 08 9755 6042; www.brooklandvalley.com.au), which is owned by Hardys (Constellation Wines). But don't let that worry you: the wines are fantastic and the site is pretty special, too. The cabernet merlot and chardonnay are some of the best.

Pierro (Caves Rd, Wilyabrup; open daily 10 am–5 pm; 08 9755 6220; www.pierro.com.au) isn't a memorable cellar door but the chardonnay is.

Cullen Wines (Caves Rd, Cowaramup; open daily 10 am–4 pm; 08 9755 5277; www.cullenwines.com.au) is biodynamic and organic. The chardonnay is fantastic, the semillon sauvignon blanc is legendary and the Margan red blend is well worth investigating.

Further south is **Vasse Felix** (cnr Caves Road and Harmans Road South, Cowaramup; open daily 10 am–5 pm; 08 9756 5000; www.vassefelix.com.au), the oldest winery in Margaret River, and a very good spot for lunch. Both the grounds and the wines are well groomed. The cabernet is a favourite.

Close by is **Juniper Estate** (Harmans Road South, Cowaramup; open daily 10 am–5 pm; 08 9755 9000; www.juniperestate.com.au). It's not as fancy as most Margaret cellar doors but is home to good wines and some of the best value.

Howard Park (Miamup Rd, Cowaramup; open daily 10 am–5 pm; 08 9756 5200; www.howardparkwines.com.au) is a spectacular modern building with polished-concrete floors and very polished wines. Both the Howard Park range and more affordable Madfish range are available for tasting here.

Closer to the town of Margaret River towards the coast is **Cape Mentelle** (Wallcliffe Rd, Margaret River; open daily 10 am–4.30 pm; 08 9757 0888; www.capementelle.com.au), which dates back to 1970 and despite its fame and fortune still looks a bit seventies. The cabernet is famous and the semillon sauvignon blanc is one of the wines that sets the standard.

Voyager Estate (Lot 1 Stevens Rd, Margaret River; open daily 10 am–5 pm; 08 9757 6354; www.voyagerestate.com.au) should be visited just for the Cape Dutch architecture, roses and dogs. The wines are pretty smart, too. The 'Girt by Sea' range is affordable—the cabernet merlot is a favourite—and the top-of-the-line chardonnay is brilliant.

Leeuwin Estate (Stevens Rd, Margaret River; open daily 10 am–5 pm; 08 9759 0000; www.leeuwinestate.com.au) is a bit further south and features one of the best driveways in the business. The tasting experience can be a little snooty—this was one of the first wineries with the gall to charge $90 for a chardonnay—and bargains are not to be had, but it's worth a visit just to say you've been there.

Redgate (Boodjidup Rd, Margaret River; open daily 10 am–5 pm; 08 9757 6488; www.redgatewines.com.au) is in a great spot, close to Redgate Beach. Both winery and beach got their name from a nearby farm, which (you guessed it) used to have a red gate. It's been around since the late 1970s and has some of the best value in Margaret River. There's the odd bargain only available at the cellar door, and the cabernet blend, Bin 588 Cabernet at $23, can be brilliant.

Where to eat

In the north, the **Wise Vineyard Restaurant** (Eagle Bay Rd, Dunsborough; open daily for lunch, Fri & Sat for dinner; 08 9755 3331; www.wisefood.com) is worth stopping for lunch just for the view. The food isn't bad, either.

Vasse Felix (cnr Caves Rd & Harmans Road South, Cowaramup; open daily for lunch; 08 9756 5000; www.vassefelix. com.au) is one of the established dining spots and still offers some of the best food. Ambience is good, too.

Cullen Wines (Caves Rd, Cowaramup; open daily 10 am–4 pm; 08 9755 5656; www.cullenwines.com.au) is simple food with great flavour and, like the wines, is biodynamic and organic.

Down south, **Voyager Estate** (Lot 1 Stevens Rd, Margaret River; open daily 10 am–5 pm; 08 9757 6354; www. voyagerestate.com.au) is a little like visiting a winery in South Africa and has a kids' menu if you've got the crew in tow.

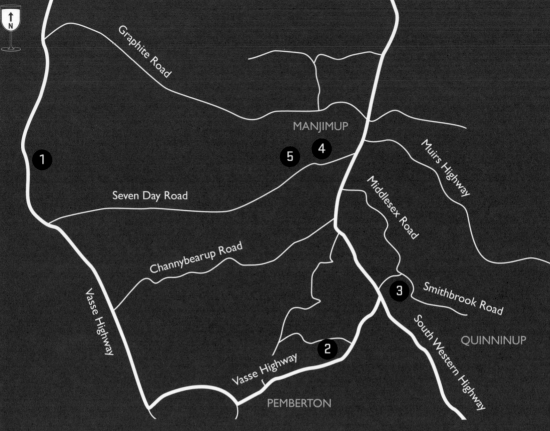

PEMBERTON & MANJIMUP

WINERIES

1. Donnelly River Wines
Lot 159 Vasse Hwy, Pemberton
08 9776 2052

2. Salitage
Vasse Hwy, Pemberton
08 9776 1195

3. Smithbrook
Smithbrook Rd, Pemberton
08 9772 3557

4. Fonty's Pool
Seven Day Rd, Manjimup
08 9777 0777

5. The Wine & Truffle Co
Seven Day Rd, Manjimup
08 9777 2474

Snapshot

Long before I'd ever been there, I remember a highly respected winemaker saying to me that Pemberton would be the most exciting wine region Australia had yet seen. That was in the early 1990s. It hasn't quite happened that way but the region is producing some magnificent wine. It's God's own country, the rural jewel in WA. Undulating, with good rainfall and soil, and about as far removed from the Western Australia William Dampier had a look at and rejected as it is possible to get.

The background

Where vines are concerned the history is very short. Pemberton and Manjimup are timber country, as the amount of chainsaw shops in Manjimup attests. The first vines went in at Pemberton in the same year that the Sex Pistols released 'Never Mind the Bollocks'. Like Frankland River it was a spot that was used to grow grapes rather than pursue any serious cellar door trade. But its tourist potential has been growing. It's a pretty place to drive around and has some stunning wines.

The wines

It's almost half/half red and white with chardonnay and pinot ruling the roost. Pemberton produces excellent cabernet sauvignon, shiraz and sauvignon blanc as well.

The prices

Not cheap. If you can find anything under $20 you're doing well.

The layout

The best way to approach this region is in a larger exploration of Margaret River or Margaret River through to Great Southern. It's about four hours from Perth, about two hours from Margaret River and about three hours' drive from Albany.

A suggested route

Arriving from the Margaret River side, you'll get to **Donnelly River Wines** (Lot 159 Vasse Hwy, Pemberton; open daily 9.30 am–4.30 pm; 08 9776 2052; www. donnellyriverwines.com.au), the first winery in the district. Tasting highlights tend to be the chardonnay and the cabernet sauvignon.

From there, head into Pemberton through town and you'll get to **Salitage** (Vasse Hwy, Pemberton; open daily 10 am– 4 pm; 08 9776 1195; www.salitage.com.au), a handsome estate and not surprisingly because owner John Horgan is the brother of Dennis of Leeuwin Estate fame. It's the chardonnay that has garnered most of the fame but check out the pinot, too.

At the junction of the Vasse and South Western Highways is **Smithbrook** (Smithbrook Rd, Pemberton; open weekdays 9 am–4 pm; 08 9772 3557; www.smithbrook.com.au), arguably Pemberton's most widely distributed label. The quality through the range is very good, in particular the Yilgarn Red Blend and the sauvignon blanc.

North-west on the Southwestern Highway brings you to **Fonty's Pool** (Seven Day Rd, Manjimup; open daily noon–4 pm; 08 9777 0777; www.fontyspoolwines.com.au), a famous spot in Pemberton history because of Archie Fontanini and the large dam he built, which became known as 'Fonty's Pool'. This is a cooler part of the region and the pinot and chardonnay are particularly good.

A little further up the road is the highly entrepreneurial **The Wine & Truffle Co** (Seven Day Rd, Manjimup; open daily 10 am–4.30 pm; 08 9777 2474; www.wineandtruffle.com.au). It's a truffle venture that is actually producing the goods and it may be your first opportunity to taste real fresh truffles. The wines aren't bad, either— the shiraz and riesling, in particular.

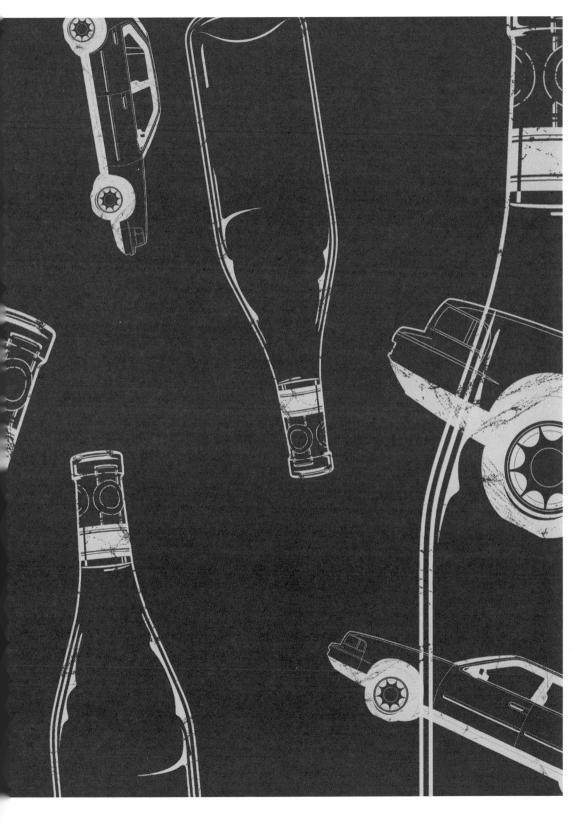

GREAT SOUTHERN

WINERIES

1. Ferngrove
276 Ferngrove Rd, Frankland River
08 9855 2378

2. Alkoomi
Wingebellup Rd, Frankland River
08 9855 2229

3. Frankland Estate
Frankland Rd, Frankland
08 9855 1544

4. Forest Hill Vineyard
South Coast Hwy, Denmark
08 9848 2199

5. Howard Park
Scotsdale Rd, Denmark
08 9848 2345

6. Harewood Estate
Scotsdale Rd, Denmark
08 9840 9078

7. West Cape Howe
678 South Coast Hwy, Denmark
08 9848 2959

8. Wignalls Wines
Highway 1, Albany
08 9841 2848

9. Plantagenet
Albany Hwy, Mount Barker
08 9851 3131

10. Gilberts
RMB 438 Albany Hwy, Kendenup
08 9851 4028

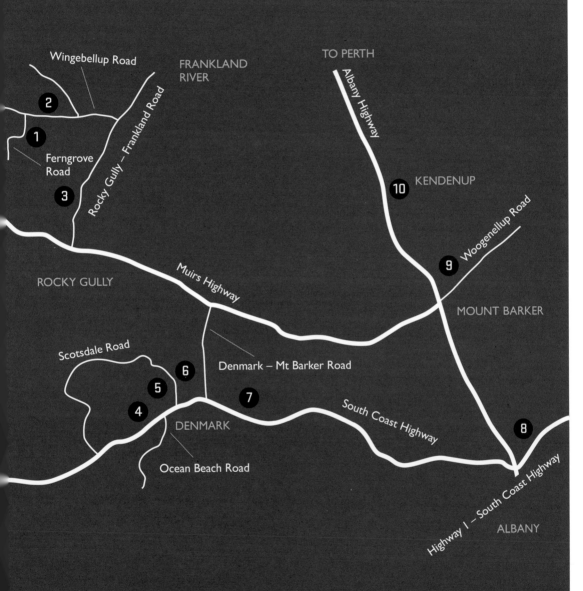

N

Wingebellup Road

FRANKLAND RIVER

TO PERTH

Albany Highway

2

1

Ferngrove Road

Rocky Gully – Frankland Road

3

10 KENDENUP

Woogenellup Road

9

Muirs Highway

ROCKY GULLY

MOUNT BARKER

Scotsdale Road

6

Denmark – Mt Barker Road

5

7

South Coast Highway

4

DENMARK

8

Ocean Beach Road

Highway 1 – South Coast Highway

ALBANY

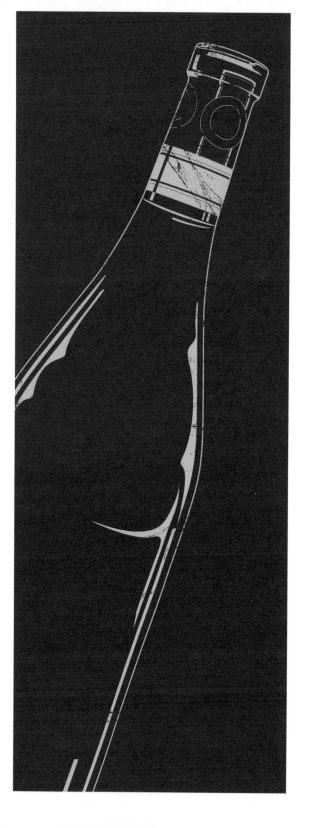

Snapshot

If you like driving; if you like to experience the vastness of Australia, the idea of the road stretching out as far as your tank of juice lasts and you also happen to enjoy a tangy riesling or a big red, then this corner of Western Australia is for you. It's vast but it's not all the same. Karris give way to banksias, which give way to rugged bush. There are untrodden beaches and a spectacular coastline. With dimensions of about 150 kilometres west to east and 100 kilometres north to south, it's a far cry from dinky wine regions that can be traversed on a pushbike.

The evocatively named 'Great Southern' includes the regions of Frankland River, Mount Barker, Denmark, Albany and Porongurup. In recent years it's been booming and we've been seeing many more wines from Great Southern 'over East' as they say in the West. The wines are pretty damn good, too. Distances are vast but the rewards for the cellar door traveller are great.

The background

While a couple of winemaking legends, Jack Mann (who visited the area playing cricket) and Maurice O'Shea, had shown enthusiasm about the climate, it took Professor Harold Olmo (now remembered by the Frankland

River's Olmo's Reward), who was in the pay of the WA government, to do something about it. A vineyard was established at Forest Hill in 1965 and others followed such as Plantagenet and Goundrey. In the past 15 years as the quality of the riesling and reds has become apparent, the place has boomed. The cost of land (by comparison with Margaret River) is not prohibitive and larger companies have been investing in the place as a fruit source and to increase the quality of their mass-market wines.

The wines

It's riesling that Great Southern is most renowned for among the wine snobs. Along with the Clare and Eden Valleys it rates as one of the top regions for the variety. Shiraz and cabernet sauvignon also do very well. There's also chardonnay, sauvignon blanc and the odd malbec.

The prices

For Western Australia, the prices are pretty good. Most of the large wineries have a two-tiered wine range with the first tier less than $20 and the top tier above.

The layout

Touring Great Southern is probably best joined to a large holiday that includes Margaret River. You can do a circuit that goes from Margaret River to Pemberton to Frankland River to Denmark to Albany to Mount Barker and back up the highway to Perth.

A suggested route

Starting at Frankland River, first up is **Ferngrove** (276 Ferngrove Rd, Frankland River; open weekdays 10 am–4 pm; 08 9855 2378; www.ferngrove.com.au). It's a relatively new operation—established in 1997—but is making a big splash. Winemaker Kim Horton has some very good fruit to make wine from and produces a wide range of really good wines at pretty good prices. It starts with the Symbols range at about $16 and ends with the shiraz/cab sauvignon Stirlings at $50. The King Malbec and Majestic Cabernet Sauvignon are particularly good.

Travel a little way down the road and you'll arrive at **Alkoomi** (Wingebellup Rd, Frankland River; open daily 10 am–5 pm; 08 9855 2229; www.alkoomiwines.com.au). Alkoomi is one of the pioneers, having been planted in 1971 by the irrepressible Merv Lange. In a style different from so many modern places the winery looks like those houses that keep getting bits tacked on them as the family keeps growing. That's the way the business has gone and now it's almost a 100,000-case winery.

The Blackbutt Red Blend has long been a Western Australian classic and there's a good riesling. The range is huge and prices go down to $15.

Frankland Estate (Frankland Rd, Frankland; open weekdays 10 am–4 pm; 08 9855 1544; www.franklandestate.com) is a label that is improving the reputation of Great Southern. The range of rieslings from different vineyards is interesting to taste—the Poison Hill is a favourite, the Olmo's Reward Red Blend is a beauty and the Rocky Gully range is affordable.

Head along Muirs Highway and take a right towards Denmark. On the western side of town is **Forest Hill Vineyard** (South Coast Hwy, Denmark; 08 9848 2199; open daily 10 am–5 pm; www.foresthillwines.com.au). It's the cellar door and winery for the vineyard that can proudly claim the first vines in the region in 1965. French winemaker Celine Haselgrove is doing great things. The cabernet sauvignon and riesling are standouts. The Great Southern Cabernet Sauvignon is a bargain at $25 and the Boobook range at $19 is good value. The restaurant attached to the cellar door is also one of one of the best in the region.

Head back into the delightful town of Denmark, turn left up Scotsdale Road and you'll get to **Howard Park** (Scotsdale Rd, Denmark; open daily 10 am–4 pm; 08 9848 2345; www.howardparkwines.com.au), the secondary cellar door for the brand (the big one is in Margaret River). It's a brand that has been built steadily and is exceptionally good, from the Madfish range through to the single-vineyard Scotsdale Great Southern Cabernet Sauvignon. It's hard to find a dud wine at Howard Park.

Nearby is **Harewood Estate** (Scotsdale Rd, Denmark; open daily 10 am–4 pm; 08 9840 9078; www.harewoodestate.com.au) run by an ex-winemaker from Howard Park who has put his money behind the region. Quality is excellent especially the riesling, and the prices for the quality of the wine (less than $20) is hard to beat. Check out the Great Southern Shiraz Cabernet blend.

Back in Denmark if you head towards Albany you'll come to **West Cape Howe** (678 South Coast Hwy, Denmark; open daily 10 am–5 pm; 08 9848 2959; www.westcapehowewines.com.au), a growing brand whose winemaker Gavin Berry used to work at Plantagenet, has his own place, Mount Trio, and shows a real understanding of the local fruit. The Styx Gully Chardonnay and a cabernet merlot are particular favourites.

Albany is a strange place—'full of retired wheat farmers', as one local put it—with an incredible beauty and a bloody past (whaling only came to an end here in 1978). The most famous local winery is **Wignalls Wines** (Highway 1, Albany; open daily 11 am–4 pm; 08 9841 2848; www.wignallswines.com.au), which was famous in the pinot-obsessed 1980s and not surprisingly is the variety for which the place is most renowned. The collective wisdom now says that Great Southern is not a great place for pinot but Wignalls isn't listening and still makes a stunning one. Don't forget to taste the chardonnay and the shiraz, either.

Heading towards Perth you arrive at Mount Barker and **Plantagenet** (Albany Hwy, Mount Barker; open daily 9 am–5 pm; 08 9851 3131; www.plantagenetwines.com). This is one of the early wineries that showed the potential of the region. The cellar door is an ex-apple shed, the winemaker is ex-Cape Mentelle and the range of wines is still stunning. It's hard to pick a winner but as is usual for the area the riesling is fantastic and the cabernet equally brilliant. The more affordable Hazard Hill range at $12 is great value.

Back on the highway to Perth, nearly halfway between Mount Barker and the next town of Cranbook, is **Gilberts** (RMB 438 Albany Hwy, Kendenup; open Wed–Mon 10 am–5 pm; 08 9851 4028; www.gilbertwines.com.au), a small, friendly, family-run business with a killer of a riesling for $18, a very affordable chardonnay and some decent reds.

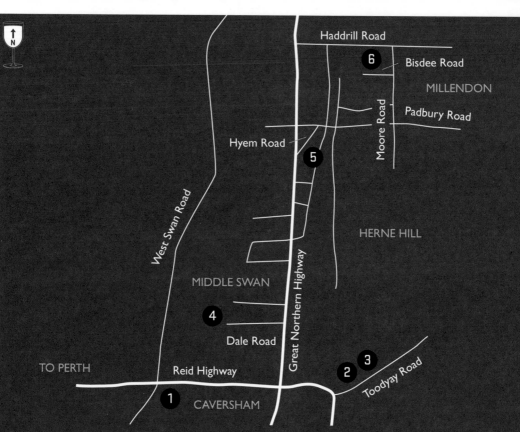

SWAN VALLEY

WINERIES

1. Sandalford
West Swan Rd, Caversham
08 9374 9374

2. Garbin Estate
209 Toodyay Rd, Middle Swan
08 9274 1747

3. Jane Brook
229 Toodyay Rd, Middle Swan
08 9274 1432

4. Houghton
Dale Rd, Middle Swan
08 9274 9540

5. Talijanich
26 Hyem Rd, Herne Hill
08 9296 4289

6. Lamont's
85 Bisdee Rd, Millendon
08 9296 4485

Snapshot

The Swan Valley once had everything going for it. It was an easy drive from Perth and made very good fortified wines, but trends, fashions and the development of something called Margaret River further south caused it to fall from favour. It has a big advantage being close to Perth for the visitors but a disadvantage being close to Perth for the grapes—the climate. It's stinking-hot. As a fine-wine region this is a little bit limiting. But winemakers and vineyards all have ways of adapting and overcoming the obstacles and the Swan Valley is not only home to Western Australia's wine history, it's having a mini rebirth.

The background

Where would we be without immigration? While the Barossa had the Lutherans, the Swan Valley had Yugoslavs. But it didn't start that way. Settlement of the valley occurred in 1829 and two men named Houghton and Sandalford (famous WA wine names) got land grants about 20 years later and planted vineyards. With immigration during the early 1900s, Yugoslavs and Dalmations, who didn't mind a bit of hard work and heat, increasingly populated the valley. It became famous for the export of table grapes, drying grapes and fortified wines and for the immigrants coming on weekends from Perth to fill up their containers at the wineries. With the decline in popularity of the fortifieds, the emergence of cool-climate fashion and Margaret River, the Swan fell from favour but it remains an interesting place to visit for cellar door enthusiasts.

The wines

No other wine region can claim it but the Swan Valley's main grape is chenin blanc, the pour cousin to sauvignon blanc. The Swan makes one of the better Australian versions. There's also a fair bit of verdelho (Swan Valley put the variety on the map), there's some shiraz and a smattering of the rest. Fortifed wine is still a strong point—I know a bloke who raves about a white port he tasted on a trip to the Swan Valley.

The prices

As you'd expect, it's not a name region and prices reflect that. Swan Valley wine is very affordable.

The layout

If you're in Perth or arriving at Perth it's pretty easy to get to. Just 10 minutes from the airport and 25 minutes from the centre of Perth, it's a region that can be done on a whim.

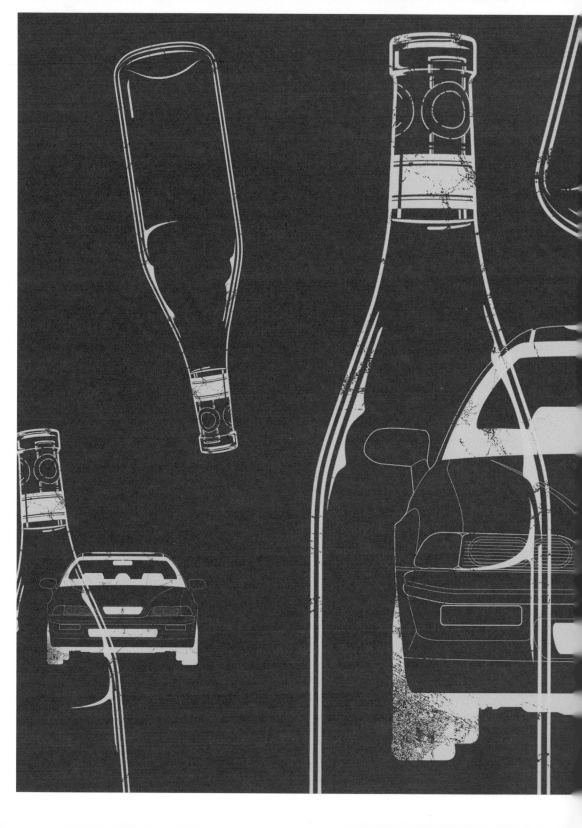

A suggested route

Coming from Perth along the Reid Highway, the first winery you get to is **Sandalford** (West Swan Rd, Caversham; open daily 10 am–5 pm; 08 9374 9374; www. sandalford.com). It's a large, 100,000-case winery whose quality has come ahead in leaps and bounds in the past five years. It has its interests spread between the Swan Valley and Margaret River. The range is all very good and the Margaret River reds and the chardonnay are excellent.

Follow the Reid Highway through the traffic lights till you get to Toodyay Road and **Garbin Estate** (209 Toodyay Rd, Middle Swan; open Tue–Sun 10.30 am–5.30 pm; 08 9274 1747; www.garbinestatewines. com.au). This is the classic Swan Valley story of a fisherman from Dalmatia buying land in the 1950s. His son is now modernising things yet it retains the traditional character. The chenin blanc and merlot are particularly good value.

Jane Brook (229 Toodyay Rd, Middle Swan; open daily 10 am–5 pm; 08 9274 1432; www.janebrook.com.au) is next door. One of the best of the Swan cellar doors to hang in, like many Swan Valley producers Jane Brook is supplementing its range with wine made from Margaret River fruit. The locally made Back Block Shiraz can be good and there's a surprisingly good sparkling.

Head back and turn right onto the Great Northern Highway, turn off at Dale Road and you'll come to **Houghton** (Dale Rd, Middle Swan; open daily 10 am–5 pm; 08 9274 9540; www.houghton-wines. com.au). It's a vast winemaking factory with wines made from fruit from all over the state but it is home to some pretty smart products that are all available for tasting. The Museum Sparkling Shiraz is good for a taste as is the Museum White Classic (previously called White Burgundy).

Further along the Great Northern Highway is something completely different. **Talijanich** (26 Hyem Rd, Herne Hill; open Wed–Mon 10.30 am–4.30 pm; 08 9296 4289) is one of the authentic Yugoslav family-run wineries. It makes a good verdelho and very good fortified wine including a liqueur muscat and a liqueur verdelho. It's also biodynamic.

North-east of Talijanich is **Lamont's** (85 Bisdee Rd, Millendon; open weekends & public holidays 10 am–5 pm; 08 9296 4485; www.lamonts.com.au), a business with several cellar door/restaurants throughout the state. The wines are from fruit from a variety of places and there's plenty to taste. Check out the Black Monster Malbec and White Monster Chardonnay for something a bit different.

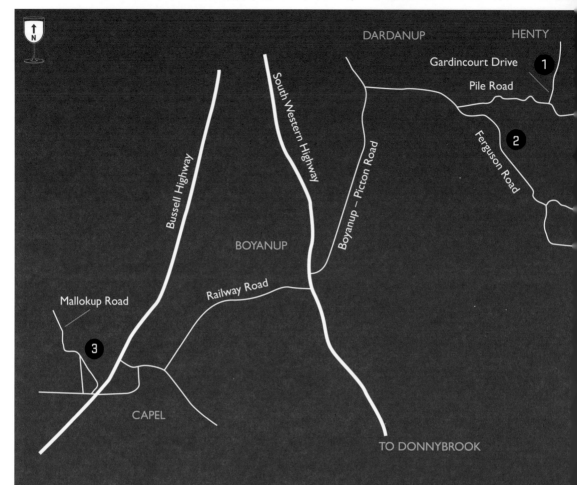

GEOGRAPHE

WINERIES

1. Willow Bridge Estate
Gardincourt Dr, Henty
08 9728 0055

2. Hackersley Estate
Ferguson Rd, Dardanup
08 9384 6247

3. Capel Vale
Mallokup Rd
08 9727 1986

Snapshot

Geographe is one of those wine regions that is a bit of a one-man band. Capel Vale dominates. More of a thoroughfare than a destination—on the way from Perth to Margaret River—it's a good way to break up the trip.

The background

Geographe would probably not exist were it not for Capel Vale, which was established in the tiny town of Capel by radiologist Dr Peter Pratten way back when Skyhooks and Sherbet were on *Countdown*. In the 1980s the wines made a big splash but it wasn't until the late 1990s that the region received a big growth spurt.

The wines

Shiraz and cabernet sauvignon, the odd good merlot, and, white-wise, chardonnay and sauvignon blanc.

The prices

Not too bad. Capel Vale has some absolute bargains and at most wineries it is easy to find a wine for less than $20.

The layout

Most of the wineries lie between Harvey (a place renowned for its beef cattle) and Busselton.

A suggested route

East of Bunbury is **Willow Bridge Estate** (Gardincourt Dr, Henty; open daily 11 am–5 pm; 08 9728 0055; www.willowbridge.com.au). It has a good tempranillo and the Black Dog Shiraz is expensive but often worth it.

Hackersley Estate (Ferguson Rd, Dardanup; open Fri–Sun 10 am–4 pm; 08 9384 6247; www.hackersley.com.au) is worth visiting for the merlot and the sauvignon blanc.

Capel Vale (Mallokup Rd, Capel; open daily 10 am–4 pm; 08 9727 1986; www.capelvale.com) has a huge range of wines from all of the name regions in Western Australia and the quality is top-notch. The Debut range offers particularly good value, especially the merlot and the cabernet sauvignon. Capel Vale is also a good spot for lunch.

TASMANIA

Tassie is a unique place to travel within. It's not just that you have to go by boat or plane that changes things, or the fact that everyone who lives in Tassie refers to the rest of the country as the mainland; it's that Tasmania is like a mini country with a north and a south and distinct cultural differences in each. Launceston has *The Examiner* and Hobart has *The Mercury* and the papers play up to the north/south rivalry. Footy culture, beer culture and local mores make Deloraine different from Margate. The north–south border isn't actually defined but exists on the Midlands Highway around the town of Ross when the Boag's runs out and the Cascade begins.

Tasmania is girt by sea and that has trapped it in time—a little bit. Head off the beaten track—or at least off the tourist track—and you'll find things the way they were in the 1970s.

It wasn't gold or immigration that spread the vine through Tasmania. Tasmania was the vine nursery for the mainland during the early history of Australian winemaking. The rootlings and cuttings that were planted in Victoria and South Australia came from the Apple Isle. By 1865 commercial nurseries in Tassie were offering 45 different varieties! Ironically, it was the gold rush that put an end to the venture as the workforce departed Tassie for the goldfields.

It took the cool-climate madness of the 1980s for Tasmania to be included on the Australian wine map. In the search for finesse, elegance and decent pinot noir, intrepid grape growers planted in Tasmania. So Heemskerk and Pipers Brook were established.

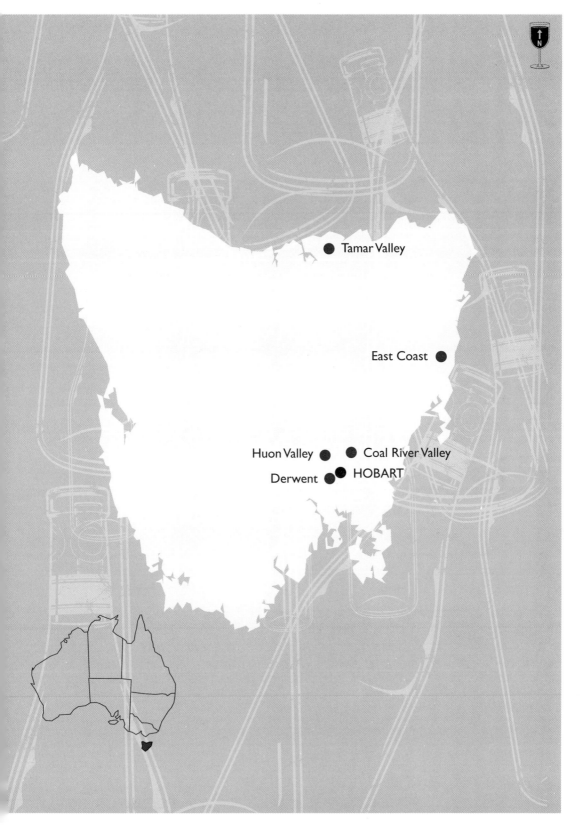

TAMAR VALLEY

WINERIES

1. Clover Hill
Clover Hill Rd, Lebrina
03 6395 6114

2. Jansz
Pipers Brook Rd, Pipers Brook
03 6382 7066

3. Kreglinger
Pipers Brook Rd, Pipers Brook
03 6382 7527

4. Delamere Vineyards
Bridport Rd, Pipers Brook
03 6382 7190

5. Bay of Fires
40 Baxters Rd, Pipers River
03 6382 7622

6. Rosevears Estate/Pirie
1a Waldhorn Dr, Rosevears
03 6330 0300

7. Stoney Rise
Hendersons Ln, Gravelly Beach
03 6394 3678

8. Goaty Hill Wines
Auburn Rd, Kayena
03 6391 9090

9. Tamar Ridge
Auburn Rd, Kayena
03 6394 1111

WHERE TO EAT

A. Estelle Restaurant
Rosevears Vineyard, 1a Waldhorn Dr,
Rosevears
03 6330 0300

B. Daniel Alps at Strathlynn
Ninth Island Vineyard, 95 Rosevears Dr,
Rosevears
03 6330 2388

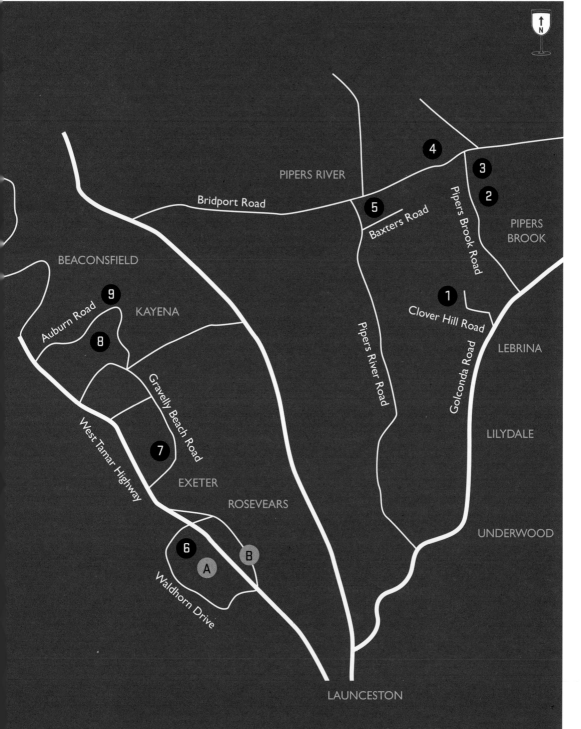

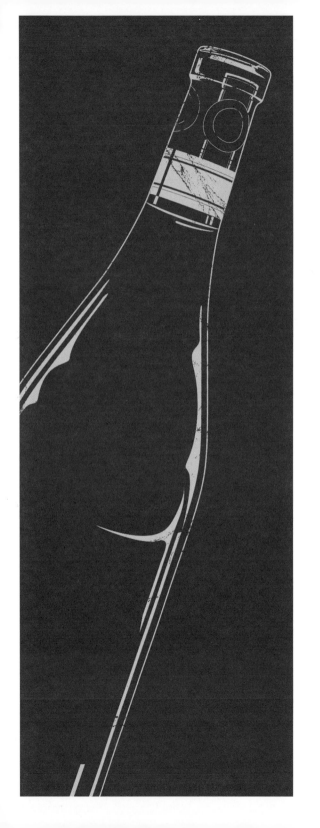

Snapshot

The Tamar is Tasmania's oldest, most established and most cellar door-rich wine region on the Apple Isle. It accounts for just over half of the total grape production of the state. Many of the big names you recognise from mainland bottle shops such as Pipers Brook, Tamar Ridge, Ninth Island, Clover Hill and Jansz are located here, and while it produces just about every wine style it is increasingly gaining a reputation for sparkling wine—the Reims or Epernay of Australia, you might say—such is the quality of the fizz. It's all to do with the climate: those cool summers, long autumns and slow ripenings.

The background

A Frenchman called Jean Miguet, who worked for the Hydro Electric Commission planted a vineyard in 1956 called, optimistically, La Providence. But the man who really turned the Tamar into a viable viticultural paradise was Andrew Pirie. Dr Pirie famously did Australia's first PhD on viticulture and used the knowledge gained in the process to find the ideal place for planting grapes. He decided on the area to the north-east of Launceston known as Pipers Brook and planted a vineyard there in the 1970s. Graham Wiltshire was also a pioneer and planted an experimental vineyard at Heemskerk in 1966, which he expanded in the 1980s. Heemskerk only exists now as a label but back in the 1980s was one of the biggest producers. Heemskerk hooked up with Louis Roederer and that begat Jansz, which is still producing some of Tassie's best sparkling wines.

The wines

Sparkling leads the pack followed by pinot noir and chardonnay. There is also some very good riesling and pinot gris, the odd sauvignon blanc and, on the warm sites on the banks of the Tamar River, the occasional good cabernet sauvignon is a pleasant surprise.

The prices

Expensive. Cool-climate viticulture, even when done on a large scale, costs much more than the warm-climate equivalent. For the smaller producer, variable seasons and dodgy summers can make it a heartbreaking pursuit. Wines above $20 are the norm rather than the exception.

The layout

The region is basically split between the Pipers Brook area on the eastern side of the Tamar and the wineries on the western bank of the Tamar. It differs considerably: the countryside on the east being more undulating and bushy and that on the west being more open and pastoral. It is a region that can be covered in a day but to do it in comfort and have a relaxing long lunch, two days is advised.

A suggested route

Starting from Launceston head up the East Tamar Highway and on to Lilydale Road via the Newnhams Link. You'll drive by the Boag's Centre for Beer Lovers—pop in if that interests you. Head up Lilydale Road which becomes Golconda Road—you'll go past the little towns of Underwood and Lilydale—keep driving and you'll arrive at Lebrina and **Clover Hill** (Clover Hill Rd, Lebrina; open daily 10 am–5 pm; 03 6395 6114; www.cloverhill.com.au), an excellent spot for a glass of bubbly. Clover Hill's delicate vintage fizz is regularly one of the best in the region (if not the country) and the still wines known as Lalla Gully are pretty good too, particularly the riesling.

Further north is **Jansz** (Pipers Brook Rd, Pipers Brook; open daily 10 am–5 pm; 03 6382 7066; www.jansz.com.au). The wine room here is a pretty good place to sample the wide range of Jansz fizzy products, from the late-disgorged to the non-vintage rosé and to learn about the methode.

The neighbour is **Kreglinger**, known beforehand as Pipers Brook (Pipers Brook Rd, Pipers Brook; open daily 10 am–5 pm; 03 6382 7527; www.kreglingerwineestates. com), which is home to Pipers Brook and Ninth Island labels, and despite the departure of founder Andrew Pirie is still doing very good stuff. The Ninth Island products are some of the best value for money on the island and Kreglinger is a very good sparkling wine. The tasting room has a pleasant outlook and also has a cafe.

Delamere Vineyards (Bridport Rd, Pipers Brook; open daily 10 am–5 pm; 03 6382 7190; www.delamerevineyards. com.au) has a very good chardy and in the good years the pinot is excellent.

Turn left at Pipers River Road then left up Baxters Road and you'll come to **Bay of Fires** (40 Baxters Rd, Pipers River; open daily 10 am–5 pm, winter 11 am–4 pm; 03 6382 7622; www.bayoffireswines. com.au), one of the larger brands on the island and home to some very good wines from all over Tasmania. The sparklings are excellent and the riesling and gewürztraminer are worth a try, too.

On the other side of the Tamar, head north up the West Tamar Highway until you come to **Rosevears Estate/Pirie** (1a Waldhorn Dr, Rosevears; open daily 10 am–5 pm; 03 6330 0300; www.rosevears.

com.au). This spectacular spot overlooking the Tamar is home to lots of wine to taste. There are the excellent products from Pirie, the second label South, Coombend from the East Coast and Tamar Ridge from up the road. If you can't find a Tasmanian wine here to like then you are very hard to please. Estelle Restaurant is an excellent spot for lunch, too.

Head towards Exeter, take a right-hand turn into Hendersons Lane to **Stoney Rise** (Hendersons Ln, Gravelly Beach; open Thu–Mon 11 am–5 pm; 03 6394 3678; www. stoneyrise.com). This is the old Rotherhythe vineyard restored and improved. The wines are cunningly made by Joe Holyman, who also brags the largest planting of the German variety, grüner veltliner, in the country (1000 vines). The pinot noir especially is absolutely top-notch.

Goaty Hill Wines (Auburn Rd, Kayena; open daily 10 am–5 pm August–May; 03 6391 9090; www.goatyhill.com) is a relatively new (established 1998) brand on the scene doing good things. The wines are skilfully made by Fran Austin of Bay of Fires. The chardonnay and pinot noir are standouts.

Turn right at Beaconsfield and you'll come to one of the biggies of the region, **Tamar Ridge** (Auburn Rd, Kayena; open daily 10 am–5 pm; 03 6394 1111; www.

tamarridgewines.com.au). With an 80,000-case production, this isn't the typical boutique Tasmanian winery. Andrew Pirie heads the winemaking team and the wines are very good across the board. The Devil's Corner range at $18 offers some of the best value on the island. As usual in Tassie, the pinot noir and chardonnay are the picks. There's also a very good botrytised riesling.

Where to eat

Estelle Restaurant (Rosevears Vineyard, 1a Waldhorn Dr, Rosevears; open daily for lunch, dinner Fri & Sat in summer; 03 6330 0300; www.rosevears.com.au) has spectacular views over the Tamar and food that is designed to make the wines of Tamar Ridge and assorted brands shine.

Daniel Alps at Strathlynn (Ninth Island Vineyard, 95 Rosevears Dr, Rosevears; open daily for lunch from 10 am, closed in August; 03 6330 2388; www. kreglingerwineestates.com) is one of Tasmania's institutions and famous for its use of Tasmanian produce.

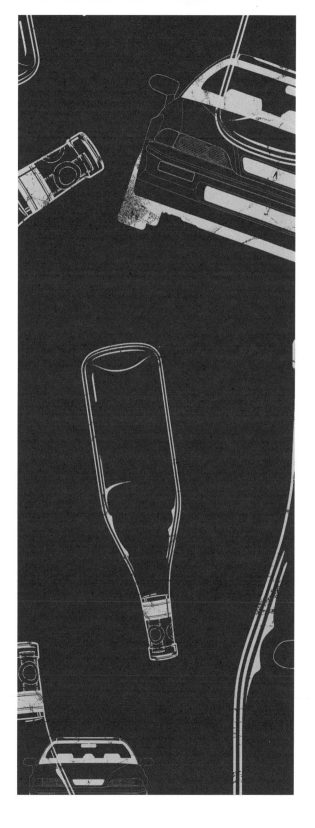

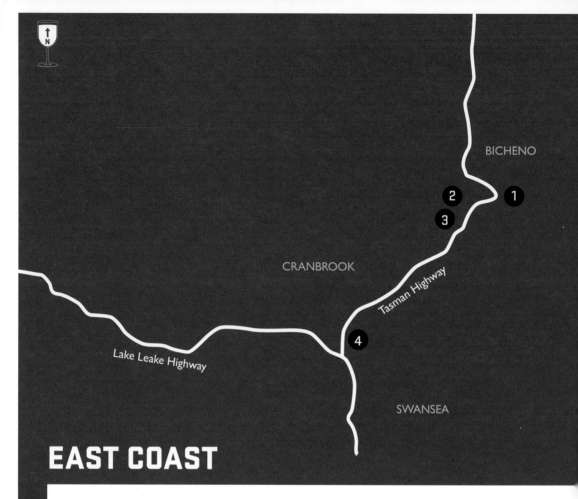

EAST COAST

WINERIES

1. The Apsley Gorge Vineyard
The Gulch, Bicheno
03 6375 1221

2. Coombend Estate
16017 Tasman Hwy, Bicheno
03 6257 8881

3. Freycinet Vineyard
15919 Tasman Hwy, Bicheno
03 6257 8574

4. Spring Vale Vineyards
130 Spring Vale Rd, Cranbrook
03 6257 8208

Snapshot

The East Coast, which runs from St Helens to Triabunna, is one of the areas Tasmanians go for their beach holidays and although it might not be what a mainland Australian might think of as typical beach, with its frigid water and weird weather, it has a particular beauty that can be addictive. The smell of the bush on the Freycinet Peninsula, the colour of the water in Wine Glass Bay, the rusty tinge to the rocks at Bicheno all stick in the memory. Oh, and there are some excellent wines, too.

The background

One of the nurseries that provided cuttings for the mainland was located in the strangely beautiful seaside village of Falmouth. The most famous historical grape planting in Tasmania occurred on Maria Island, off the coast of Triabunna. An Italian, Diego Bernacchi, got some cabernet sauvignon cuttings from St Huberts in the Yarra Valley and planted a vineyard on the island in the late 1800s. It was an entrepreneurial dream that lasted just 10 years. There's a story that Signor Bernacchi attached bunches of grapes to his vines in an effort to make the vineyard look good for potential investors. By all accounts they weren't fooled.

Diego needed an abalone licence. Good abalone divers who are prepared to brave the White Pointers make a lot of money, and one of the East Coast's viticultural pioneers, Stuart Bull, planted Freycinet Vineyard in 1980 on abalone money. It's a well-chosen site in a natural amphitheatre/heat trap close by Coles Bay. The quality of those wines has seen the establishment of several other East Coast producers but not as many as you might think.

The wines

Like most of Tasmania, it is pinot noir and chardonnay that dominate with a few exceptions.

The prices

Expensive—the viticulture is labour intensive and the prices reflect that.

The layout

The few vineyards/cellar doors are close by the Tasman Highway from Bicheno to Swansea. One of the best ways to do the East Coast is on a trek either north to the Tamar River via Scotsdale and St Helens or North on the Esk Highway via Fingal and St Marys.

A suggested route

Coming from the north, the first opportunity for tasting is at Bicheno at **Apsley Gorge** (The Gulch, Bicheno; open daily

November–March, phone ahead for times; 03 6375 1221; www.apsleygorgevineyard. com.au). The Apsley Gorge Vineyard is further inland and the cellar door is an old shed on the coast—a great spot for lunch and to taste the excellent pinot noir and chardonnay. Winemaker Brian Franklin is a stickler for detail and it shows. Drive through the town and head for 'The Gulch', and when you are overlooking the sea, look out for a driveway to the left.

Further down the coast, just after the turn-off to Coles Bay, is **Coombend Estate** (16017 Tasman Hwy, Bicheno; open daily 10 am–5 pm; 03 6257 8881; www.coombend. com.au), which is at the entrance to Freycinet. Coombend Estate is one of the few Tassie wineries to produce a very good cabernet blend known as 'The Mail Run'; the winery has been recently purchased by the vast Tamar Ridge conglomerate and is set for expansion.

Freycinet Vineyard (15919 Tasman Hwy, Bicheno; open daily 9.30 am–4.30 pm; 03 6257 8574; www.freycinetvineyard. com.au) is just down the driveway. The wine is a family affair—charming winemaker Claudio Radenti is married to founder Stuart Bull's daughter, Lindy. Freycinet regularly produces ethereal pinot noir, but Claudio has a magic touch in the winery and the entire range is excellent. The Radenti

sparkling wine is well worth taking home. If you're after a cleansing ale, he also brews beer. The hearty Hazards Ale is available for tasting at the cellar door.

Down the highway another 15 or so kilometres brings you to **Spring Vale Vineyards** (130 Spring Vale Rd, Cranbrook; open daily 10 am–4 pm; 03 6257 8208; www.springvalewines.com), another family affair with the wines made by David Cush, husband of fellow winemaker Kristen Cush, daughter of the owner. There's a good gewürz here: suspend your prejudice and give it a taste. One of the other highlights is a very good lighter-style pinot noir/pinot meunier blend known as Melrose, which is a good drink slightly chilled.

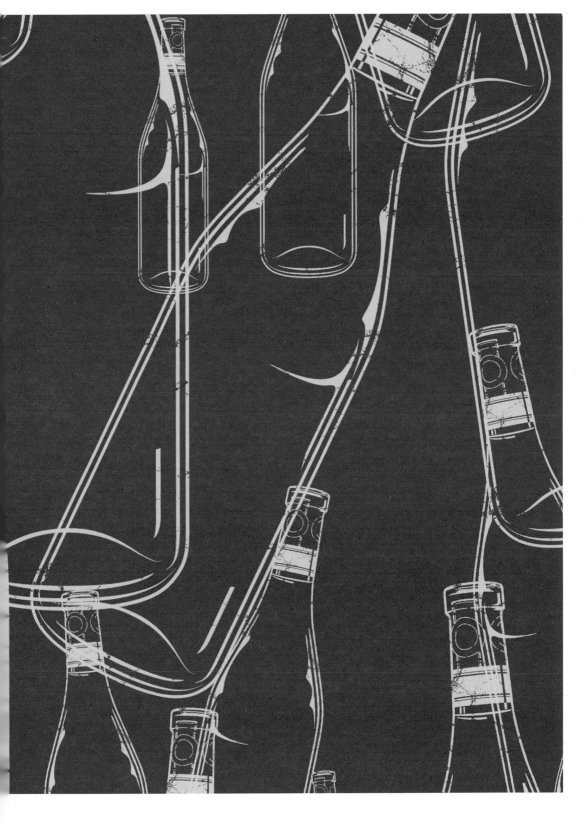

COAL RIVER VALLEY

WINERIES

1. Craigow
528 Richmond Rd, Cambridge
03 6248 5379

2. Frogmore Creek
20 Denholms Rd, Cambridge
03 6248 5844

3. Meadowbank
699 Richmond Rd, Cambridge
03 6248 4484

4. Puddleduck Vineyard
992 Richmond Rd, Richmond
03 6260 2301

5. Domaine A
Tea Tree Rd, Campania
03 6260 4174

WHERE TO EAT

A. Meadowbank Estate
699 Richmond Rd, Cambridge
03 6248 4484

Snapshot

Forget the name, there's not a lump of coal to be seen. But there are lots of vines. Bounded by the Tasman Highway and the Derwent River, it's an easy drive out of Hobart, it's almost a suburb and is very close to the airport. It produces some unique wine, has some good spots for lunch and is a pleasant daytrip from Hobart.

The background

Towards the end of 1803, a party explored eastwards from Hobart hunting kangaroo and emus when they discovered coal and named the river. In 1823, the erection of the Richmond Bridge enabled travel to the East Coast and the Tasman Peninsula over what is now Midway Point. In 1824 the township of Richmond was named, and in 1825 the first commercial vineyard was planted.

The modern era began in 1973 when a bloke called George Park who, like Jean Miguet before him, worked for the Hydro Electric Commission, planted a one-acre vineyard on his property near Campania. Wine was his hobby and by skill or luck or both, he had planted his vines in a heat trap—a sheltered place that was warmer and drier in summer and autumn. During the 1980s when Tasmanian cabernet sauvignon reeked of capsicum and was barely ripe, George was making cabernet and even

shiraz that was luscious. The quality of his wines led to others investigating the area, including viticulture gurus from the mainland. Since that promising start, the Coal River Valley has become one of Tassie's top wine regions and the fruit is now sought after by big, publicly owned wine companies—especially for pinot noir and chardonnay.

The wines

Given the cool climate, it's pinot noir and chardonnay that rule the roost but that's not the full story. There's a little sauvignon blanc and, in the warm spots, cabernet sauvignon can be very good.

The prices

Make sure your credit card is fully charged—sub $20 wines are hard to find.

The layout

From Hobart you head across the bridge along the Tasman Highway and turn off at Cambridge. It's only a half-hour drive and you can do a circuit going from the Coal River Valley to Tea Tree, to Bridgewater and back to the Derwent wineries (see Derwent chapter, page 178).

A suggested route

From the turn-off at Cambridge the first vineyard you arrive at is **Craigow**

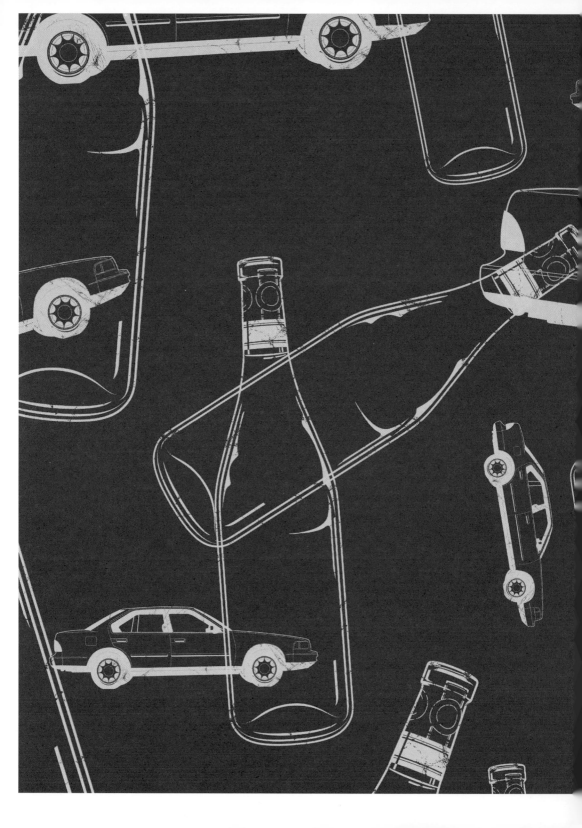

(528 Richmond Rd, Cambridge; open daily Christmas–Easter, phone ahead for times; 03 6248 5379; www.craigow.com.au), home to a very good pinot and some delicious riesling at a sub $20 price tag. The iced riesling sticky is also worth a look.

Four kilometres from the Cambridge turn-off and a right-hand turn off Richmond Road is what used to be Hood Wines and is now the cellar door for **Frogmore Creek** (20 Denholms Rd; Cambridge; open weekends 11 am–4 pm; 03 6248 5844; www.frogmorecreek.com.au). It's an international joint venture that has given Coal River wines a bigger presence in the marketplace. The vineyard is organic and the wines are fantastic.

The range of brands made at the winery includes Frogmore, 42 Degrees South and Wellington wines. Standout varietals are the riesling and chardonnay; the pinot is pretty good, too.

Back on the Richmond Road you'll come to **Meadowbank** (699 Richmond Rd, Cambridge; open daily 10 am–5 pm; 03 6248 4484; www.meadowbankwines.com.au), arguably the ritziest cellar door in the valley. With fruit that is mostly grown on a property at Glenora up the Derwent River, the wines are good and it's a nice spot for lunch. The riesling is a favourite and the chardonnay is particularly worth tasting.

Up the road is **Puddleduck Vineyard** (992 Richmond Rd, Richmond; open daily 10 am–5 pm; 03 6260 2301; www.puddleduckvineyard.com.au). It's a cottagey cellar door with a pretty good pinot noir and decent cabernet sauvignon.

Keep heading up Richmond Road and turn left at Richmond into Colebrook Road and then left again into Tea Tree Road and you come to **Domaine A** (Tea Tree Rd, Campania; open weekdays 9 am–4 pm; 03 6260 4174; www.domaine-a.com.au). This is what once was George Park's Stoney Vineyard. It has been expanded and a large winery has been built. Winemaker Peter Althaus is a perfectionist and the wines and vineyards reflect that. The cabernet sauvignon and pinot noir are expensive but fantastic and the Lady A Sauvignon Blanc is one of the best sav blancs in the region.

Where to eat

If you're thinking of lunch, **Meadowbank Estate** (699 Richmond Rd, Cambridge; open daily noon–3 pm; 03 6248 4484; www.meadowbankwines.com.au) is the spot. It's a stylish venue and the wines are well matched to the French-inspired food.

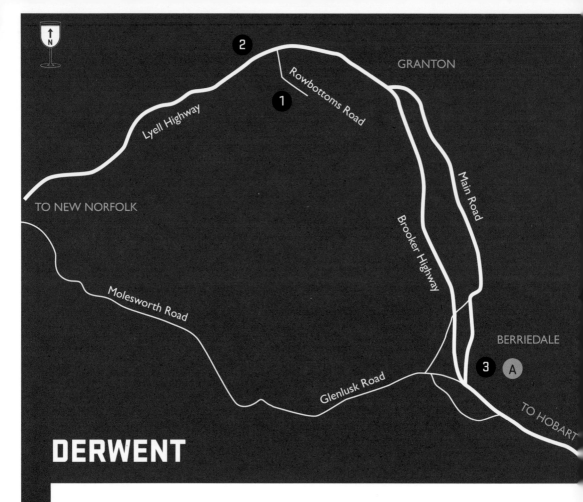

DERWENT

WINERIES

1. Stefano Lubiana
60 Rowbottoms Rd, Granton
03 6263 7457

2. Derwent Estate
329 Lyell Hwy, Granton
03 6263 5802

3. Moorilla Estate
655 Main Rd, Berriedale
03 6277 9900

WHERE TO EAT

A. The Source Restaurant
655 Main Rd, Berriedale
03 6277 9900

Snapshot

For the lack of a better name, this region, which sits on the banks of the Derwent, is called the Derwent. The wineries are almost in the suburbs of Hobart so you could call this wine region Hobart, but that might be confusing. It's an easy drive from town and if you're staying in Hobart, these are wineries that could even be visited on a whim.

The background

For such a small wine region this spot has a long history. One of Hobart's great patrons, Claudio Alcorso, planted an acre of vines on the banks of the Derwent way back in 1958. Years of problems followed. Most thought it a rich man's folly and professional help was limited. This was cool-climate viticulture in its infancy. But the grapevine is a tough plant and Claudio's vines somehow survived, with the 1980s seeing some measure of success. I was one of the grape pickers at Moorilla for vintage 1984 and 1985 and was paid in the bottles of pinot noir—a slightly weedy but fragrant wine, I seem to remember, and nowhere near as good as what is being produced now. It was in the 1990s that the region really hit its straps, especially after the arrival of Stefano Lubiana down the road at Granton. These two wineries produce some of the best wine in Tasmania.

The wines

Pinot noir and chardonnay dominate, but Moorilla always had a fruit salad of varieties and retains quite a wide range of varietals. Riesling, pinot noir and chardonnay are the picks. Stefano Lubiana makes an excellent bubbly, too.

The prices

For Tassie, the prices are pretty good, especially at Moorilla. You can pay big for the reserve wines but both Stefano Lubiana and Moorilla have a good range of wines priced under the expensive stuff.

The layout

Head out of Hobart towards the northern suburbs and before you know it you'll be in Berriedale, an ugly suburb, but sitting on the hill overlooking a bend in the Derwent is Moorilla. Head further down towards New Norfolk and you'll get to Granton and, soon after, Stefano Lubiana and Derwent Estate.

A suggested route

Head from Hobart down to Granton first to **Stefano Lubiana** (60 Rowbottoms Rd, Granton; open Sun–Thu 11 am–3 pm; 03 6263 7457; www.slw.com.au). It's an ideal spot to calibrate your palate to the quality this region offers. Up on the hill is the cellar door and it hasn't had an architect anywhere near it. The money has gone into the wines and the vineyard, and as you drive up towards the cellar door you can get a look at the perspective of the vineyards and garner some understanding as to how Steve Lubiana gets so much flavour in his wine. Check out the pinot noir, the chardonnay, the bubbly and the pinot grigio in particular.

Further towards New Norfolk you come to **Derwent Estate** (329 Lyell Hwy, Granton; open daily 10 am–4 pm; 03 6263 5802; www.derwentestate.com.au). The wines are made by Julian Alcorso, son of Moorilla founder and now a winemaker for hire. The wines are good—especially the pinot noir and riesling.

Get back on the highway heading towards Hobart and you'll come to **Moorilla Estate** (655 Main Rd, Berriedale; open daily 10 am–5 pm; 03 6277 9900; www.moorilla.com.au). It's worth spending some time here. There's an unexpectedly fantastic museum, there's the Moo Brew microbrewery, which produces a range of excellent beers, and the new restaurant is worth checking out, too. As far as wines go, the pinot noir and chardonnay rule.

Where to eat

The Source Restaurant at Moorilla Estate (655 Main Rd, Berriedale; open daily noon–2.30 pm for lunch, dinner Tue–Sat from 6.30 pm; 03 6277 9900; www.moorilla.com.au) makes great use of Moorilla's riverside position and the seafood is particularly good, especially with Moorilla's delicious riesling.

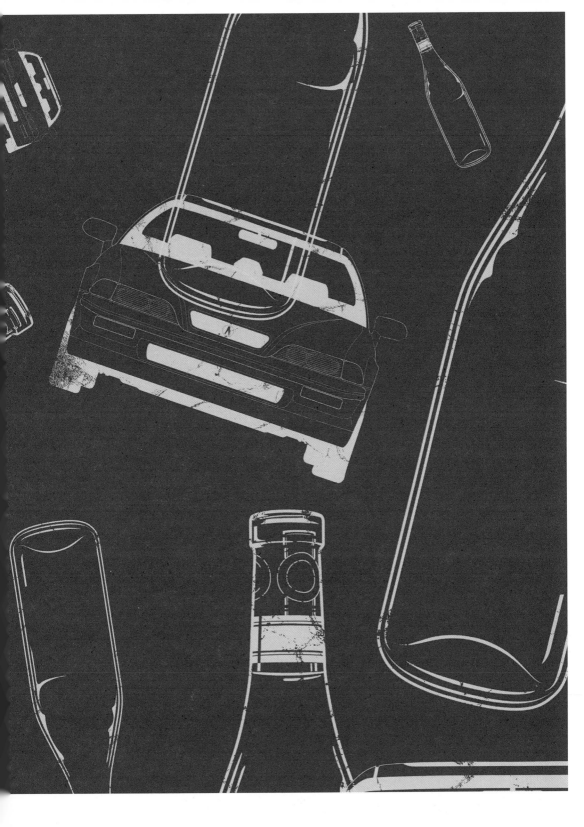

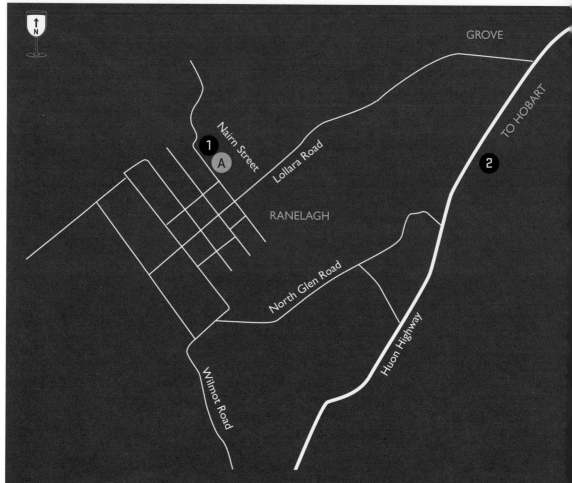

HUON VALLEY

WINERIES

1. Home Hill
38 Nairn St, Ranelagh
03 6264 1200

2. Panorama
The Apple Valley Teahouse,
2273 Huon Hwy, Grove
03 6266 3409

WHERE TO EAT

A. Home Hill
38 Nairn St, Ranelagh
03 6264 1200

Snapshot

Heading south from Hobart to the intricate waterways of the D'Entrecasteaux Channel is one of the highlights in a Tassie tour. The orchards, the fruit in the roadside stalls, the little towns—they are all exactly as you imagine Tasmania to be. There are not a lot of cellar doors but enough to punctuate the trip. Take a little extra time and get the ferry to Bruny Island. There's only one cellar door and, of course, the Bruny Island Cheese Company, but even without these it's worth a look. If you're into history, check out the Bruny Island History Room in the old courthouse at Alonnah.

The background

The first fruit trees in Australia were planted on Bruny Island, whose name comes from the French explorer Bruni D'Entrecasteaux. In the early 1980s, Eric and Jette Phillips planted a vineyard, Elsewhere, at Glaziers Bay where they had a flower farm. At the time it was the most southern wine region in the world. The Phillips produced decent pinot, which they sold at Salamanca Place on Saturday mornings along with their flowers.

The wines

It's mostly pinot noir and chardonnay but pinot gris and sparkling are at Home Hill.

The prices

Typical of Tasmania, under $20 is unusual.

The layout

First of all, check out the ferry timetable for Bruny Island. This will dictate your travelling plan.

A suggested route

Coming from Hobart, head down the Huon Highway and follow the signs to Huonville. There you'll find **Home Hill** (38 Nairn St, Ranelagh; open daily 10 am–5 pm; 03 6264 1200; www.homehillwines.com.au). It's architect-designed and impressive. The pinot noir and chardonnay are good and it's the best spot for lunch.

Close by is the cellar door for **Panorama** (The Apple Valley Teahouse, 2273 Huon Hwy, Grove; open Wed–Mon, phone ahead for times; 03 6266 3409; www.panoramavineyard.com.au). Chardonnay is the best suit but the 'Tom' Cabernet Sauvignon can be good in the warm years.

Where to eat

Home Hill (38 Nairn St Ranelagh; open daily from 12pm for lunch, Fri & Sat from 6 pm for dinner; 03 6264 1200; www.homehillwines.com.au) has a spacious restaurant. The menu uses local produce and the chef makes his own smallgoods.

NEW SOUTH WALES

For too long, two wine regions dominated the wine business in New South Wales: the Hunter Valley and Griffith. If you were a cynical type (or a Victorian) you might say that one is there because Sydney is so close and the other is there because it produces cheap grapes. There is some truth in this. The Hunter Valley has more cellar door customers than any other region but produces barely a few per cent of Australia's grape harvest. On the other hand Griffith has vineyards as big as suburbs and dams that are large enough to waterski on. It produces the most grapes in New South Wales with a smidgeon of the hype.

It was a rather unbalanced system and was far from fair. Because of the abundance of cellar door customers and inconsistent seasons, the Hunter Valley has for a long time boosted its production with grapes from other regions. Perfectly good New South Wales wine regions such as Mudgee and Orange were providing fruit to stock the shelves of Hunter Valley cellar doors and appearing on the label in small print if at all. Thankfully that situation has changed. The Hunter Valley is still a shopfront for a host of other wine regions but at least it's not hiding the fact … as much. With the growing fame of Orange, the recognition of Mudgee, the wines coming out of Canberra, the Hilltops and the cool heights of Tumbarumba, New South Wales can now claim a bit more diversity. It's in better shape than it ever was and while it doesn't have the variety and diversity of Victoria or South Australia, these days it is certainly a worthwhile destination for the wine traveller.

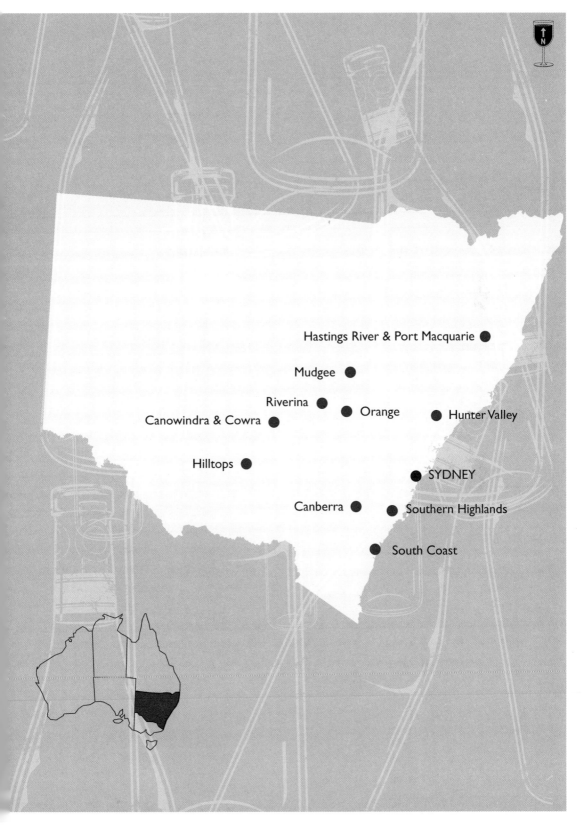

HUNTER VALLEY

WINERIES

1. Capercaillie
Londons Rd, Lovedale
02 4990 2904

2. Lake's Folly
Broke Rd, Pokolbin
02 4998 7507

3. Tower Estate
cnr Broke and Hall Rds, Pokolbin
02 4998 7989

4. Bimbadgen Estate
790 McDonalds Rd, Pokolbin
02 4998 7585

5. Marsh Estate
Deasys Rd, Pokolbin
02 4998 7587

6. Keith Tulloch Wine
Hunter Ridge, Hermitage Rd, Pokolbin
02 4998 7500

7. Tyrrell's
Broke Rd, Pokolbin
02 4993 7000

8. Small Winemakers Centre
McDonalds Rd, Pokolbin
02 4998 7668

9. Brokenwood
401 McDonalds Rd, Pokolbin
02 4998 7559

10. Margan Family Winegrowers
1238 Milbrodale Rd, Broke
02 6579 1372

11. Krinklewood
712 Wollombi Rd, Broke
02 6579 1322

WHERE TO EAT

A. Roberts
Tower Estate, Halls Rd, Pokolbin
02 4998 7330

B. Esca Bimbadgen
Bimbadgen Estate, 790 McDonalds Rd,
Pokolbin
02 4998 4666

C. Rock Restaurant
Pooles Rock Wines, De Beyers Rd,
Pokolbin
02 4998 6968

D. Margan Restaurant
Margan Family Winegrowers,
1238 Milbrodale Rd, Broke
02 6579 1372

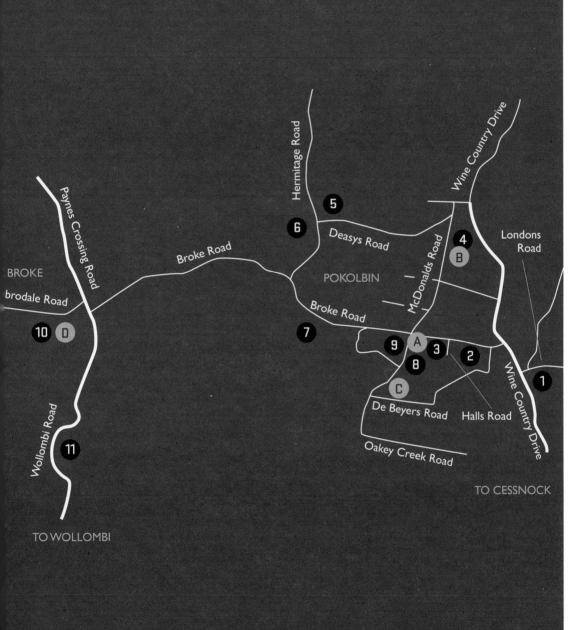

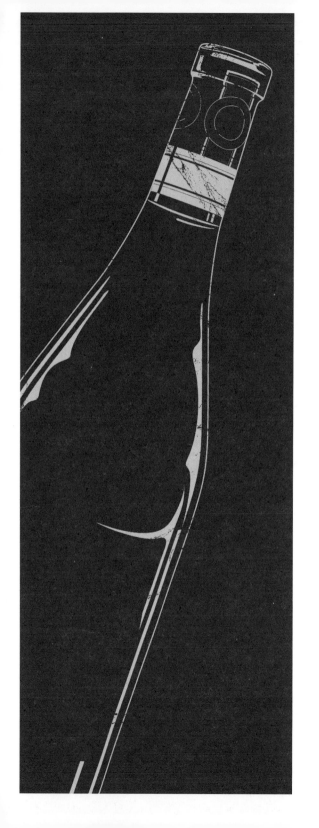

Snapshot

Hunter-haters love to poke fun at it. They site climatic data and argue that the Hunter is a bad place to grow grapes and it wouldn't be there if Sydney wasn't just down the road. It's all envy. The Hunter Valley has more cellar door customers than any other wine region. Less-visited wine regions hate that fact. There is a small amount of truth in what the Hunter-haters say though.

If you searched the world for the ideal place to grow wine grapes, you would never choose the Hunter Valley. It rains at the wrong time, it's humid when the grapes are hanging on the vine and all that encourages the grape's worst enemy, mould. But the Hunter has been around long enough to evolve to its conditions. Human ingenuity has worked out how to make decent wine within the climatic constraints and the result is truly unique wine styles that can only be reproduced in the weird and unsuitable weather of the Hunter Valley. I'm referring, of course, to Hunter Valley semillon and to a lesser extent, Hunter Valley shiraz, the region's two trump cards.

The background

The Hunter has the most publicised history in Australian wine because the old characters have been used in so much wine marketing—Dr Lindeman, George

Wyndham, Benjamin Ean (sorry, that last one was a joke). It began with James Busby, the bloke who was the first to show any genuine interest in making wine in the newly established colony. By 1834, James' brother-in-law had four hectares in the Hunter and other famous names soon followed: George Wyndham and Dr Henry Lindeman. The Draytons and Tyrrells soon showed up and by 1864 the original Rosemount in the upper Hunter was established. But the bank crashes of the 1890s and various World Wars impeded its prosperity even though the Hunter was still producing very good wine. Like a great artist among philistines, the legendary Maurice O'Shea was making killer wines for a very small audience in the 1930s and 1940s.

The real renaissance began at the beginning of what's known as the red-wine boom in the 1960s when Australians began to once again get a taste for red wine. Max Lake planted his Lake's Folly cabernet vineyard in the early 1960s. The lawyers planted Brokenwood in the early 1970s and the modern era of the Hunter was born.

The wines

Semillon and shiraz dominate, but the weird climate also produces very good chardonnay, cabernet sauvignon and those dabbling in Italian varietals are also producing decent results.

The prices

It's hard to find a bargain in the Hunter but if you hunt around there are sub $20 wines worth taking home.

The layout

At the intersection of McDonalds and Broke Roads, you're in the grand junction of Pokolbin and it's a good spot to have a look at a map, get your bearings and make a plan biting off how much you want to chew, or spit—as the case may be. There are a lot of cellar doors so a plan is crucial. Some of the subregions are well worth a visit, too.

A suggested route

As you head up towards Pokolbin on Wine Country Drive from Cessnock, on your right is **Capercaillie** (Londons Rd, Lovedale; open Mon–Sat 9 am–5 pm, Sun 10 am–5 pm; 02 4990 2904; www.capercailliewine.com.au). The cellar door has an interesting gallery and some very handy semillon.

Turn into Broke Road and on your left on top of the hill is the legendary **Lake's Folly** (Broke Rd, Pokolbin; open daily 10 am–4 pm; 02 4998 7507; www.lakesfolly.

com.au). The Lakes no longer own it but the chardonnay and cabernet still set a standard for the valley. It's not cheap, though.

Further on up the road you can't miss **Tower Estate** (cnr Broke and Hall Rds, Pokolbin; open daily 10 am–5 pm; 02 4998 7989; www.towerestatewines.com.au), a monument to yet another Hunter legend, Len Evans. It's a winery and cellar door that is a shopfront for Australia's great combos of grapes and regions. You'll find a Tower Estate Barossa Valley Shiraz, a Coonawarra Cabernet Sauvignon, a Hunter Semillon and a host of other grape/region matches all of very high quality.

Hang a right into McDonalds Road, drive another three or four kilometres and you'll come to another monumental building, **Bimbadgen Estate** (790 McDonalds Rd, Pokolbin; open daily 10 am–5 pm; 02 4998 7585; www.bimbadgen.com.au). Esca Bimbadgen is a good restaurant and the wines are well made, particularly the semillon and shiraz.

The polar opposite of Bimbadgen is a left-hand turn down Deasys Road. **Marsh Estate** (Deasys Rd, Pokolbin; open Mon–Fri 10 am–4.30 pm, weekends 10 am–5 pm; 02 4998 7587; www.marshestate.com.au) is a family-run affair with the showiness dial turned down low. There's something about understated surroundings and very

good wines that makes you feel like you've discovered something fantastic. The shiraz is great.

A little further up the road, at the junction of Hermitage and Deasys Road, is **Keith Tulloch Wine** (Hunter Ridge, Hermitage Rd, Pokolbin; open Wed–Sun 10 am–4 pm, Sat 10 am–5 pm; 02 4998 7500; www.keithtullochwine.com.au), a scenic, comfy spot to taste Keith's well-made wines. They're not cheap but they're very good, particularly the shiraz.

Head south on Hermitage Road, take a left at the intersection and you'll arrive back on Broke Road and at **Tyrrell's** (Broke Rd, Pokolbin; open daily 8.30 am–5 pm; 02 4993 7000; www.tyrrells.com.au). Tyrrell's is still family owned—despite no small amount of takeover offers. It's a dynamo of a wine company that shows no sign of slowing down. The wines are excellent across the board and the cellar door still looks like it would have in the old days. The Tyrrell's Vat 1 Semillon is one of the world's great white wines.

Next stop is the **Small Winemakers Centre** (McDonalds Rd, Pokolbin; open daily 10 am–5 pm; 02 4998 7668; www.smallwinemakerscentre.com.au). Here you can taste the product of talented winemaker Andrew Thomas. He concentrates on the Hunter's strengths, semillon and shiraz, and regularly produces some of the best in the valley.

Now head for nearby **Brokenwood** (401 McDonalds Rd, Pokolbin; open daily 9.30 am–5 pm; 02 4998 7559; www.broken wood.com.au). From humble beginnings, Brokenwood has grown and prospered and now features a huge range with fruit from many regions. The Hunter wines are still the pick of the bunch, particularly the shiraz and semillon.

If you are up for travelling further afield, head out towards Broke and **Margan Family Winegrowers** (1238 Milbrodale Rd, Broke; open daily 10 am–5 pm; 02 6579 1372; www.margan.com.au). There's a vast range of cleverly made wines in a fancy cellar door/restaurant and some tasty Italian varietals, notably the barbera. The rosé is one of the best in the Hunter and don't neglect the shiraz.

Down Crossing Road is **Krinklewood** (712 Wollombi Rd, Broke; open weekends 10 am–5 pm; 02 6579 1322; www.krinkle wood.com), a picturesque spot with biodynamic wines and a worthy chardonnay and shiraz.

Where to eat

Roberts (Tower Estate, Halls Rd, Pokolbin; open daily for lunch and dinner; 02 4998 7330; www.robertsrestaurant.com) is in an old settler's cottage and has loads of atmosphere. It's named after Robert Moline who is a Hunter legend. Prices aren't cheap but the food is very good.

Esca Bimbadgen (Bimbadgen Estate, 790 McDonalds Rd, Pokolbin; open daily for lunch; 02 4998 4666; www.bimbadgen. com.au) serves fusion food done well.

Rock Restaurant (Pooles Rock Wines, DeBeyers Rd, Pokolbin; open Thu–Sat for dinner; 02 4998 6968; www.rockrestaurant. com.au) has won quite a few awards and has wine-friendly French-style food.

Margan Restaurant (Margan Family Winegrowers, 1238 Milbrodale Rd, Broke; open Fri & Sat for lunch and dinner, Sun for breakfast and lunch; 02 6579 1372; www. margan.com.au) has excellent food to match the stylish wines.

MUDGEE

WINERIES

1. Logan
Castlereagh Hwy, Apple Tree Flat, Mudgee
02 6373 1333

2. Andrew Harris Vineyards
Sydney Rd, Mudgee
02 6373 1477

3. Frog Rock Wines
Edgell Ln, Mudgee
02 6372 2408

4. Huntington Estate
Cassilis Rd, Mudgee
02 6373 3825

5. Robert Stein
Pipeclay Ln, Mudgee
02 6373 3991

6. Robert Oatley Wines
Craigmoor Rd, Mudgee
02 6372 2208

7. Botobolar
89 Botobolar Rd, Mudgee
02 6373 3850

8. Thistle Hill
74 McDonalds Rd, Mudgee
02 6373 3546

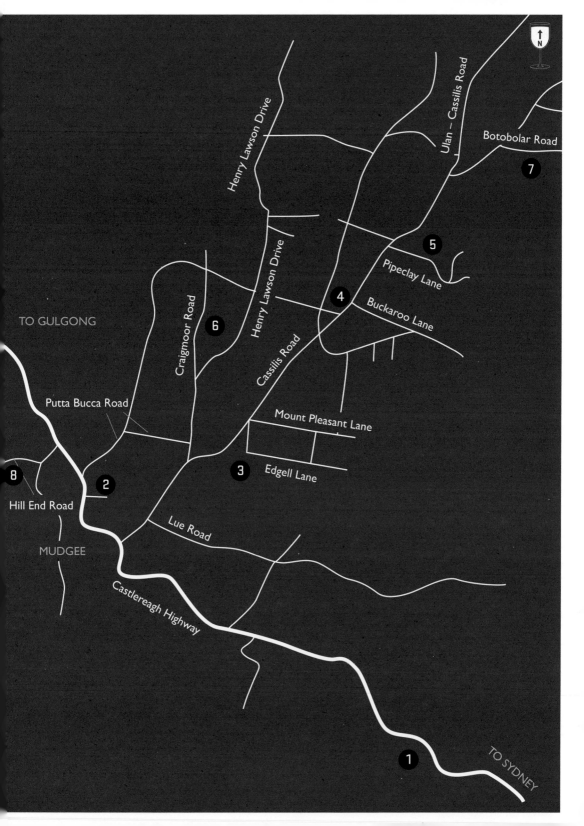

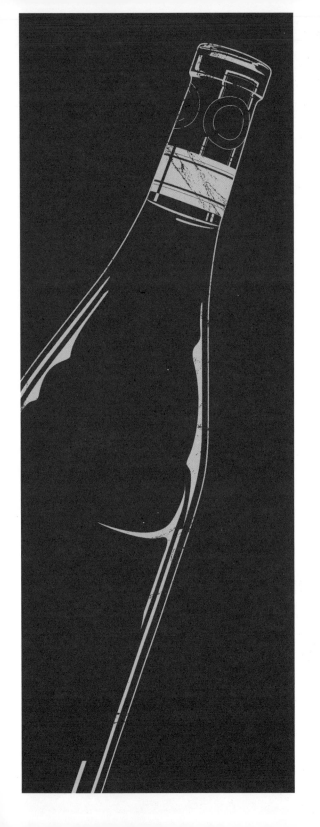

Snapshot

'Mudgee mud.' That was the first thing I remember associating with Mudgee wine. It was the 1970s, I was not of drinking age yet but that didn't stop a little scholarly tasting. My parents had been to Mudgee as a part of some larger exploration and returned with a boot full of Mudgee reds. After a little careful ageing—they were stuck in apple boxes underneath the house—the reds were duly consumed and I can still remember the gritty sludge at the bottom of the glass: Mudgee mud. I know now that this was not a fault but just the result of chunky wines made in small wineries with barely any filtration, but the name stuck.

Mudgee actually means 'nest in the hills' and on arrival one can see what they're talking about—rolling hills, bush-bounded paddocks—and it's pleasant on the eye. Wine quality has definitely improved in recent years, Mudgee's rusticity has been tempered and there are sophisticated products emerging. Elegance will never be a strong point; leave that to cooler regions. This is a land of hearty reds and the occasional great white and it is one of New South Wales' cellar door gems.

The background

Unlike most New South Wales wine regions, Mudgee has a history more akin to South Australian and Victorian models. Early German settlers planted vines in the 1850s and gold was discovered in 1872, which gave the wine business a boost. It all fell from favour and only a couple of wineries survived until the 1970s when the interest in table wine started the wine presses again. One of the significant things to happen was the arrival of Carlo Corino in the 1970s, who was the winemaker at Montrose. Piedmontese by birth, the charismatic Carlo was one of the first to plant and produce Italian varietals such as barbera, sangiovese and nebbiolo.

The wines

It's shiraz and cabernet country, with a bit of chardonnay and merlot on the side and a smattering of Italian varietals. The semillon can be pretty good and occasionally someone pops out a very good riesling. There's also Botobolar, which is organic and makes preservative-free wines.

The prices

Prices are great. This is one of the few wine regions where sub $20 wine is the norm not the exception.

The layout

Mudgee feels a lot bigger than it is. Most of it is in a 10-kilometre radius of the town and with good signage it's pretty easy to find your way around.

A suggested route

As you come in from Sydney the first winery on the agenda is **Logan** (Castlereagh Hwy, Apple Tree Flat, Mudgee; open daily 10 am–5 pm; 02 6373 1333; www.logan wines.com.au). This is a large, well-run, family-owned concern that makes wine from both Orange and Mudgee fruit. Winemaker Peter Logan claims that 'good wine should not be wasted on the wealthy' and his wines live up to the maxim. There's a great range from good sparklings through to great reds. Check out the Apple Tree Flat range at $11 for value.

The next stop here is **Andrew Harris Vineyards** (Sydney Rd, Mudgee; open daily 9 am–5 pm; 02 6373 1477; www. andrewharris.com.au). Andrew Harris burst onto the scene in the early 1990s, planting a huge vineyard on the outskirts of Mudgee. Tastings are in a restored shearing shed and there's a large range of decent-quality wines at different price points.

Head from there to Mudgee itself, past the clock tower then turn right past the racecourse up Cassilis Road and you'll find **Frog Rock Wines** (Edgell Ln, Mudgee; open daily 10 am–5 pm; 02 6372 2408; www.frogrockwines.com). Frog Rock has an affordable range of wines; the petit verdot is particularly worthy of mention.

A little bit further up the road is **Huntington Estate** (Cassilis Rd, Mudgee; open Mon–Sat 10 am–5 pm, Sun & public holidays 10 am–4 pm; 02 6373 3825; www.huntingtonestate. com.au). Huntington Estate is the legendary vineyard that used to be run by Bob Roberts and became famous for its classical music in the barrel hall and the fact that it managed to sell 20,000 cases of wine through the cellar door and a mailing list. It's been sold recently but the new owner and winemaker is a fan of the Huntington style and vows it won't change. It is home to some worthy cellaring reds.

Robert Stein (Pipeclay Ln, Mudgee; open daily 10 am–4.30 pm; 02 6373 3991; www.robertstein.com.au) is a cellar door with a specky view from the verandah, some good shiraz and one of the better rieslings in the valley.

Take Eurunderee Road and you'll get to Craigmoor Road and the new home of **Robert Oatley Wines** (Craigmoor Rd, Mudgee; open daily 10 am–4 pm; 02 6372 2208; www.robertoatley.com.au). This is a very historic place. It was the winery that kept the flame burning when winemaking in Mudgee had all but stopped and was one of the first vineyards to grow chardonnay.

Craigmoor has had an up-and-down life and not so long ago was called Poet's Corner. The Oatleys of Rosemount Estate fame have made it their cellar door. There is a host of wines made from Mudgee and fruit from all over Australia and all are well made. The Wild Oats, Robert Oatley Wines and Tick Tock brands precisely meet their price points and the Montrose wines are made from the old vines planted by Carlo Corino some 30 years ago.

Heading out of town, follow signs off to the right to **Botobolar** (89 Botobolar Rd, Mudgee; open Mon–Sat 10 am–5 pm, Sun 10 am–3 pm; 02 6373 3850; www. botobolar.com), one of the iconic wineries of Mudgee and one of the first organic vineyards in Australia. With its high-quality preservative-free reds, it's a special favourite with asthmatics.

Back on the highway on your left is **Thistle Hill** (74 McDonalds Rd, Mudgee; open Mon–Sat 9.30 am–4.30 pm, Sun & public holidays 9.30 am–4 pm; 02 6373 3546; www.thistlehill.com.au), another organic vineyard with a highly sought-after riesling.

ORANGE

WINERIES

1. Canobolas-Smith
Boree Ln, off Cargo Rd, Orange
02 6365 6113

2. Borenore Store
595 Borenore Lane, Borenore
02 6365 2261

3. Orange Mountain Wines
cnr Forbes Rd & Radnedge Ln, Orange
02 6365 2626

4. Philip Shaw Wines
Caldwell Ln, Orange
02 6365 2334

5. Bloodwood
Griffin Rd, Orange
02 6362 5631

6. Brangayne of Orange
837 Pinnacle Rd, Orange
02 6365 3229

7. Printhie
Yuranigh Rd, Molong
02 6366 8422

8. Mayfield
Icely Rd, Orange
02 6365 9292

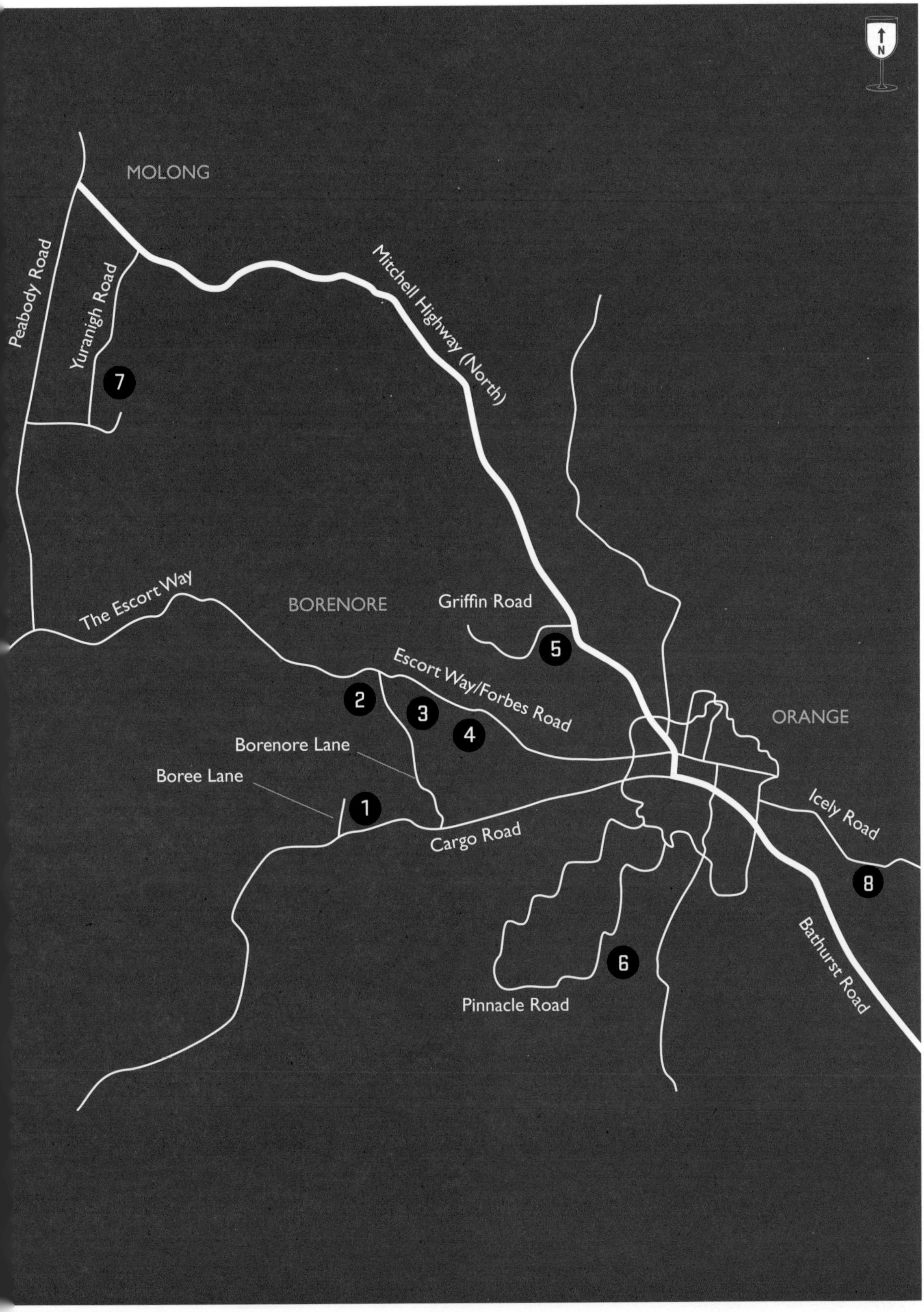

MOLONG

Peabody Road

Yuranigh Road

7

Mitchell Highway (North)

The Escort Way

BORENORE

Griffin Road

Escort Way/Forbes Road

5

2

3

4

Borenore Lane

Boree Lane

1

Cargo Road

ORANGE

Icely Road

8

6

Pinnacle Road

Bathurst Road

N

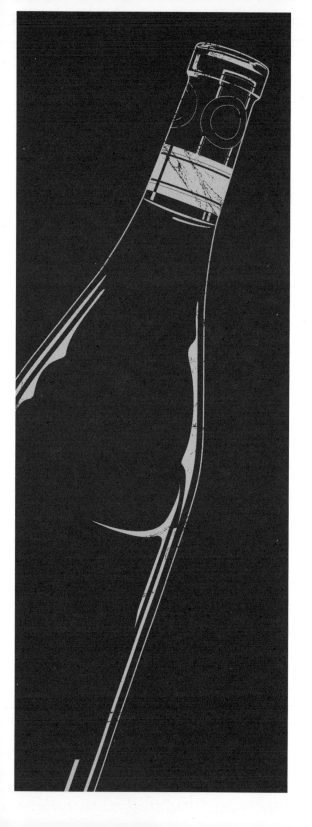

Snapshot

Orange appears to the driver coming from Cowra or Bathurst like an oasis—and not only because it's a bit greener. It's an oasis in terms of gastronomy. You arrive from a land of pies and chips and watery cappuccinos to a kingdom of ristrettos and risottos and waiting staff who can pronounce the word viognier with aplomb. It's civilised.

For New South Welsh people, Orange is the place that makes the news whenever a big winter cold front hits the state. Orange gets a dusting of snow and looks as pretty as a picture. It is unique in the vast west because of its height and everything hangs off Mount Canobolas—the highest point going west until you get to South Africa. The mountain is the secret to the success of the viticulture. The foothills and slopes have not only altitude but aspect—all good things for cool-climate grape growing. Unfortunately, Telstra, Optus et al. and their ugly mobile phone towers have defaced Canobolas.

Everything higher 600 metres above sea level in the district is 'Orange'; everything below isn't. With its snow, its height and its brightly flavoured wines, it is New South Wales' prettiest, tastiest cool-climate region.

The background

The Surveyor General of New South Wales named Orange in 1828 after Prince

William of Orange. At one stage Orange was favoured as a site for the national capital but was ruled out because of a lack of water. Like most places it had its gold rush—that was in 1851—but when the gold ran out Orange settled down to agrarian pursuits and excelled in apples and stone fruit. The old adage is that if you can grow decent apples, apricots and peaches that ripen slowly and have a lot of flavour you'll grow very good grapes and that's certainly true of Orange.

The wines

From a strictly wine-tasting point of view, Orange has more cards up its sleeve than any other region in New South Wales. It can make anything from sparkling wine through to fantastic reds and that's because of the variety of altitudes. This utility is both a boon and a curse. Wine marketing requires simple messages and Orange does so many wines so well it can't decide which variety to hang its hat on.

Some opt for sauvignon blanc, which Orange does very well (but so do a lot of other regions); the chardonnay and merlot are very good, too; and don't forget the cabernet … In fact, it's probably easier to list what Orange can't do well. The best advice is to taste everything and make up your own mind.

The prices

Orange is not too expensive by cool-climate wine-region standards. A really good bottle of wine can still be found for less than $20 and there are some really stunning wines that don't yet bear icon price tags.

The layout

From a driving point of view Orange is three-sided. There is the Cargo Road side that comes from Cowra, there's the Bathurst side on the Mitchell Highway and there's the Molong side. Biting off wineries in each sector is the way to go rather than crisscrossing the region.

A suggested route

On the Cowra side you enter Orange via the Cargo Road and first up is **Canobolas-Smith** (Boree Ln, off Cargo Rd, Orange; open weekends & public holidays 11 am–5 pm; 02 6365 6113; www.canobolassmithwines.com.au), a winery typical of the way Orange operations used to be, with a tiny production and a do-everything winemaker. Chardonnay is the thing here. Winemaker Murray Smith has a real knack with the variety, the reds are a bit more up and down but occasionally there's a killer of a pinot.

Turn left at Dindima and you'll find the Borenore Lane, which takes you a back way to the Escort Way into Orange. You'll go past the **Borenore Store** (595 Borenore Rd, Borenore; 02 6365 2261), an interesting place with a unique licence. It's a post office/general store that has a wide range of local wine, good coffee and the licence allows you to imbibe a glass of the local product!

Turn left onto the Escort Way/Forbes Road and you'll soon come to **Orange Mountain Wines** (cnr Forbes Rd & Radnedge Ln, Orange; open weekends & public holidays 9 am–5 pm; 02 6365 2626; www.orangemountain.com.au). Self-taught winemaker Terry Dolle is friendly, enthusiastic and unconstrained by convention. He makes wine from fruit grown within the Orange GI and from the lower altitude of Manildra. The shiraz viognier is the pick of the bunch but there's also an interesting viognier made as a sticky by freezing the grapes to concentrate the sugar.

Further down Forbes Road is **Philip Shaw Wines** (Caldwell Ln, Orange; open weekends noon–5 pm or by appointment; 02 6365 2334; www.philipshaw.com.au). It's unique in that the cellar door is actually the Shaws' house. Indeed, the kitchen bench is the tasting bench. Philip Shaw is the talented winemaker who helped make Rosemount famous and is a huge fan of

Orange's viticultural potential. His entire range shows a deft touch and the elegance and brightness of Orange fruit. It's difficult to pick a winner but the chardonnay and cabernets are regularly favourites.

Out along the Mitchell Highway on the way to Molong is **Bloodwood** (Griffin Rd, Orange; open by appointment; 02 6362 5631; www.bloodwood.com.au), one of the pioneers of Orange. Bloodwood is about vision and originality. The Bloodwood newsletter is legendary and most of the wines are sold via it. The picks are the Schubert Chardonnay, which is a beauty, but there are also some very nice reds, too.

Out of Orange along the Pinnacle Road are three wineries in the shadow of Mount Canobolas. The pick of them is **Brangayne of Orange** (837 Pinnacle Rd, Orange; open weekdays 11 am–4 pm, weekends 10 am–5 pm; 02 6365 3229; www.brangayne.com). The height of the vineyard means that the whites are particularly good, especially the chardonnay and sauvignon blanc.

Further out of Orange towards Molong is one of the larger operations: **Printhie** (Yuranigh Rd, Molong; open Mon–Sat 10 am–4 pm; 02 6366 8422; www.printhiewines.com.au). This is a label you are going to see a lot more of. Run by brothers David and Ed Swift and with wines stylishly made by Drew Tuckwell, the quality for the money you pay is excellent. The wines are fantastic across the range but the reds are the pick and are at sub $20 prices.

Another winery worth a visit is **Mayfield** (Icely Rd, Orange; open weekends 10 am–5 pm; 02 6365 9292; www.mayfieldvineyard.com) on the southeast of the town. With a wide range of wines all of good quality, this is a winery that shows that Orange can also make a good riesling.

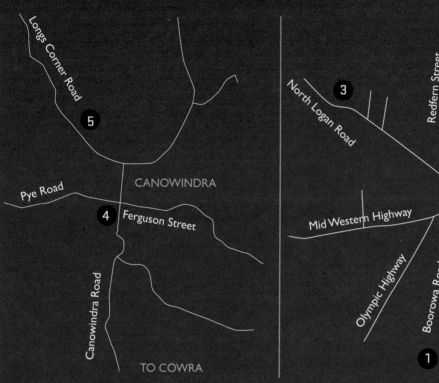

CANOWINDRA & COWRA

WINERIES

1. Cowra Estate
Boorowa Rd, Cowra
02 6342 1136

2. Windowrie Estate
Tastings at The Mill, Vaux St, Cowra
02 6344 3234

3. Mulyan
North Logan Rd, Cowra
02 6342 1336

4. Taste Canowindra
2 Ferguson St, Canowindra;
02 6344 2332

5. Hamiltons Bluff
Longs Corner Rd, Canowindra
02 6344 2079

Snapshot

When John Howard was Prime Minister of Australia he bought wine to put in his cellar for his guests at Kirribilli House. As a result of those purchases, rumours sped around the wine industry that Cowra chardonnay was his favourite wine. This caused no small amount of supercilious snickering from the cognoscente. At the time it seemed to me one of those statements like his declaration that his favourite musician was Bob Dylan except—and I paraphrase—'just for the music not the lyrics'. Now, I'm certainly not suggesting that Cowra chardonnay is as dissonant as Lord Dylan's harmonica but it is certainly not this country's best chardonnay product. It is a little like the music behind Bobby Dylan's lyrics—it serves the purpose.

The background

This is a place that has done very nicely on cropping and grazing. Vines were first planted in 1973 mainly for the purpose of bolstering the big brands as the chardonnay boom hit in the 1980s. Cowra chardonnay found its way into a multitude of mass-market chardys. The boom is over and many of the wineries established then are trying to diversify into other varieties.

The wines

Chardonnay, shardonnay and kardonnay. There are other varieties to break the monotony. Mulyan has a good shiraz, there's the odd decent cabernet and Hamiltons Bluff has had lots of success with sangiovese.

The prices

Fairly affordable; this is a spot where a $15 wine is not unusual.

The layout

The region clusters around Cowra in the south on the Lachlan River and Canowindra in the north, about 30 kilometres apart. As a wine traveller it's practical to combine your Cowra travels with a trip to Orange.

A suggested route

Arriving in Cowra via Boorowa Road (Lachlan Valley Way) you land first at **Cowra Estate** (Boorowa Rd, Cowra; open Tue–Sun 10 am–4 pm; 02 6342 1136; www.winesofcowra.com), which is also the Quarry restaurant. The chardonnay is good and the Eagle Rock cabernet merlot isn't bad.

Windowrie Estate (Tastings at The Mill, Vaux St, Cowra; open Mon–Thu and weekends 11 am–5 pm, Fri 11 am–8 pm; 02 6344 3234; www.windowrie.com.au)

is arguably one of the better producers. The Pig in the House Shiraz and The Mill Verdelho are high quality and the Mill Range at $15 is very good value. The Mill is also a good spot to taste a few other locals.

Mulyan (North Logan Rd, Cowra; open weekends & public holidays 10 am–5 pm; 02 6342 1336; www.mulyanwines.com.au) is a grazing property that grew sweet corn and asparagus for canned-food company Edgell after World War II. The shiraz is the pick and not a bad wine for a couple of years in the cellar.

Taste Canowindra (2 Ferguson St, Canowindra; open Mon–Fri 10 am–4 pm and weekends from 8 am; 02 6344 2332; www.tastecanowindra.com.au) is a good spot to taste the products of ten local wineries that don't have cellar doors including Rosnay, Wallington and Swinging Bridge.

Just outside of Canowindra on the road to Orange is **Hamiltons Bluff** (Longs Corner Rd, Canowindra; open weekends 10 am–4 pm; 02 6344 2079; www.hamiltons bluff.com), which was nearly swallowed by financial sharks. Thankfully it survived and Jamie and Julie Andrews are still in business. The sangiovese is their passion and the best wine.

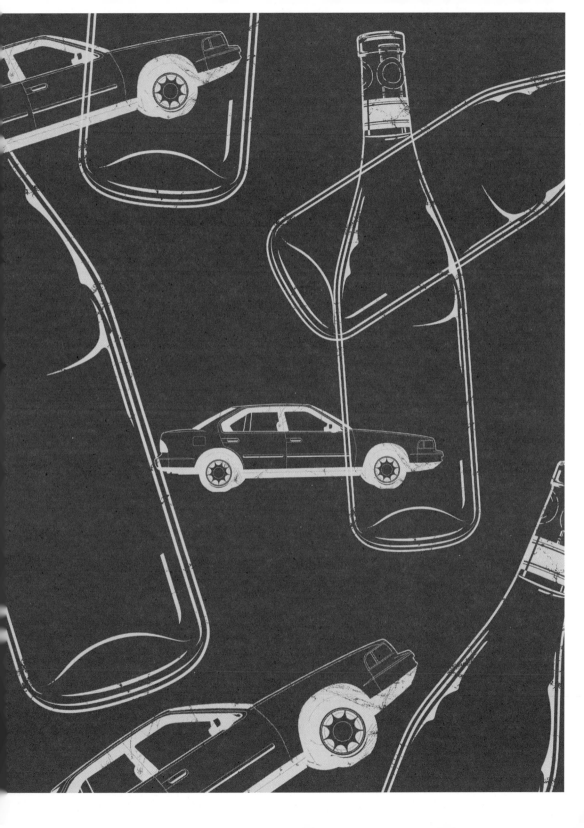

CANBERRA DISTRICT

WINERIES

1. Brindabella Hills
Woodgrove Close, Hall
02 6230 2583

2. Jeir Creek
122 Bluebell Ln, Murrumbateman
02 6227 5999

3. Shaw Vineyard Estate
34 Isabel Dr, Murrumbateman
02 6227 5827

4. Helm
Butts Rd, Murrumbateman
02 6227 5953

5. Clonakilla
Cripps Ln, Murrumbateman
02 6227 5877

6. Lambert Vineyards
810 Norton Rd, Wamboin
02 6238 3866

7. Lark Hill
521 Bungendore Rd, Bungendore
02 6238 1393

8. Mount Majura
Majura Rd, Majura, ACT
02 6262 3070

9. Pialligo Estate
18 Kallaroo Rd, Pialligo
02 6247 6060

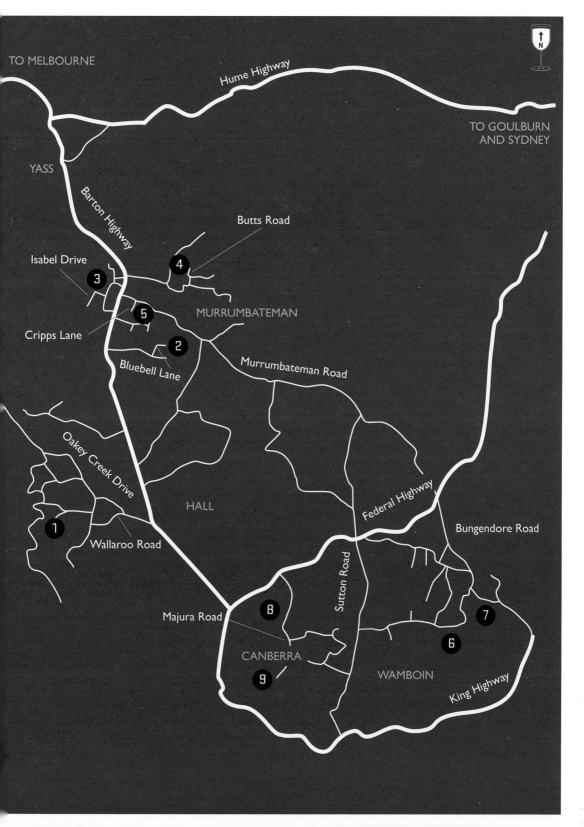

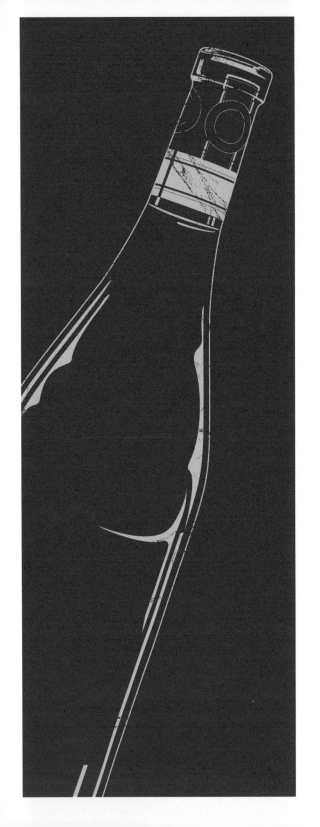

Snapshot

If you can say of the Hunter Valley that it wouldn't exist as a wine region if Sydney weren't just down the road, you could say the same for Canberra. If our forefathers had put Canberra at Orange (they nearly did but there wasn't enough water), one wonders how many wineries would be at Murrumbateman now. But the big difference between Canberra and the Hunter is that Sydney supports the Hunter jingoistically but Canberrans are yet to really embrace their wine region.

Canberra has the highest per capita consumption of wine in Australia but that isn't reflected in what's spent locally and being next door to Australia's most enthusiastic wine consumers hasn't done Canberra vignerons any favours. It is probably viewed with suspicion as just another choice for the tourists after the National Gallery of Australia and the Australian War Memorial. That's unfair because despite the political hot air in Canberra, it's a very cool wine region: conditions are tough and viticulture isn't easy but when all things fall into place the wines are fantastic.

The background

There were vineyards in the 1800s near Yass but the merino proved to be a better ride. That was until wine enthusiasts working in the national capital began to dabble with viticulture in the Whitlam era. Clonakilla was planted in 1971 and Helm in 1973. After this came Lark Hill (1978) and then crops in the 1980s including Brindabella Hills (1986) and Mount Majura (1988).

At the turn of the millennium, Hardys invested in the region with 40 hectares of vines and and also the Kamberra cellar door and winery near the showground. The adage normally goes that if one of the big wine companies invests in a region, it's made it. But Hardys has pulled out and the fancy architect-designed Kamberra wine centre has had a troubled history. What the future holds for Canberra is anyone's guess.

The wines

The Canberra region makes most of the bread-and-butter varieties very well and while it occasionally produces a very handy pinot noir and chardonnay, it is the riesling and shiraz and shiraz/viognier that are the main strengths year after year. The Clonakilla Shiraz Viognier is an absolute cult classic and most wineries produce a particularly good riesling. It is distinct, different and a worthy contribution to the wine world.

The prices

Prices aren't too bad. Expect to pay about $18 for entry levels and up to $50-plus for the famous wines. Most are around the $25 mark.

The layout

The district is split into two main districts. On one side of the Federal Highway you'll find the Murrumbateman/Yass wineries and this is the place where cellar doors are most closely concentrated. On the other side of the Federal Highway are the Bungendore wineries. There's also Mount Majura closer to Canberra and Piallago Estate is just near the airport. There are also a couple of wineries fronting what used to be Lake George on the Federal Highway near Collector.

A suggested route

Tourism brochures brag of 33 wineries within 35 minutes of Canberra; however, they are spread out. Starting from Canberra, head for Hall and **Brindabella Hills** (Woodgrove Close, Hall; open weekends & public holidays 10 am–5 pm; 02 6230 2583; www.brindabellahills.com.au). Winemaker Dr Roger Harris is one of the talents of the region and produces an excellent range of wines from a four-hectare vineyard. The shiraz is a particular favourite.

Back on the Barton Highway heading for Murrumbateman you'll come to **Jeir Creek** (122 Bluebell Ln, Murrumbateman; open Thu–Mon & public holidays 10 am–5 pm, weekends only in August 10 am–5 pm; 02 6227 5999; www.jeircreekwines.com.au). When the seasons are kind Jeir Creek produces some really good wines and one of the best stickies in the region.

Follow the signs once you get to Murrumbateman and you'll eventually come to the large yellow building that houses the cellar door for **Shaw Vineyard Estate** (34 Isabel Dr, Murrumbateman; open Wed–Sun & public holidays 10 am–5 pm; 02 6227 5827; www.shawvineyards.com.au). It is one of the newer players in the region—the vineyard was planted in the late 1990s—and is one of the most proactive marketers. The wines are really well made across the board but as is the case with most Canberra wineries, the riesling is the star. Flint in the Vines restaurant at Shaw Vineyard is also a good spot for lunch (open Sat & Sun for breakfast, Wed–Sun for lunch, Wed–Sat for dinner).

Back on the Barton Highway heading for Yass you'll find the turn-off to **Helm** (Butts Rd, Murrumbateman; open Thu–Mon 10 am–5 pm; 02 6227 5953; www.helmwines.com.au). Helm is one of the more established labels and the cellar door looks like it has been there forever. Ken Helm is a great character and if you're lucky enough, it might be the moustachioed one himself who will be pouring your wine. In a good year the reds are excellent, particularly cabernet sauvignon, but Ken has long been one of the loudest voices spruiking Canberra riesling (he is the organiser of the Canberra International Riesling Challenge) and his riesling is always one of the Canberra standouts.

Drive back into Murrumbateman, take the turn towards Bungendore and turn into Cripps Lane where you'll come to **Clonakilla** (Cripps Ln, Murrumbateman; open daily 10 am–5 pm; 02 6227 5877; www.clonakilla.com.au). Clonakilla has had some bad luck with the weather lately but still manages to produce fantastic wine. Hilltops fruit supplements the grapes. The shiraz viognier is an absolute classic but the quality is top-notch throughout the range.

Follow Murrumbateman Road towards the Federal Highway, turn right onto Sutton Road, cross over the two-lane highway and head for Bungendore. Take a left into Norton Road and you'll come to **Lambert Vineyards** (810 Norton Rd, Wamboin; open Thu–Sun 10 am–5 pm; 02 6238 3866; www.lambertvineyards. com.au). The cellar door is a bit of an ugly building but, after all, we're here for the wines not the architecture, and the wines are pretty good, especially the shiraz and riesling.

Back on the road to Bungendore, head up the hill and you'll get to **Lark Hill** (521 Bungendore Rd, Bungendore; open Wed–Mon 10 am–5 pm; 02 6238 1393; www.larkhillwine.com.au). Run by Sue and David Carpenter and their son Chris, they are pioneers of the region. The vineyard is high and cool and produces one of the best pinots in the Canberra region.

Get back on the Federal Highway heading for Canberra, turn off on the Majura Road and you'll get to **Mount Majura** (Majura Rd, Majura; open Thu–Mon 10 am–5 pm; 02 6262 3070; www.mountmajura.com.au), a singular spot with a pretty vineyard-covered hill and some smart wines. The Mount Majura Pinot Gris is one of the better versions of the variety.

Head down Majura Road towards Fyshwick, hang a left and you'll come to **Pialligo Estate** (18 Kallaroo Rd, Pialligo; open daily 10 am–5 pm; 02 6247 6060; www.pialligoestate.com.au), a little oasis between Fyshwick and the airport with some pretty good wines, especially the riesling and sangiovese.

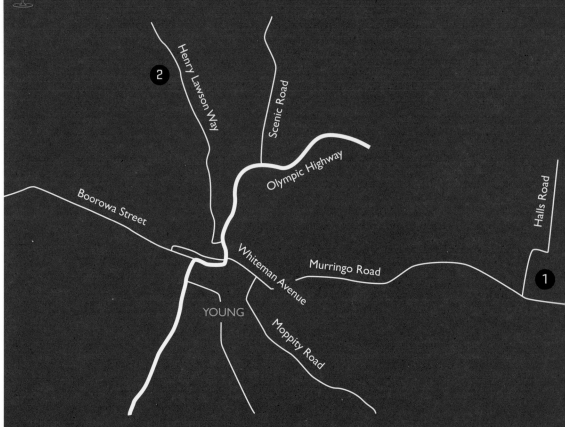

HILLTOPS

WINERIES

1. Grove Estate
Murringo Rd, Young
02 6382 6999

2. Chalkers Crossing
285 Henry Lawson Way, Young
02 6382 6900

Snapshot

Who came up with the name? It doesn't quite fit. There are hills, there are tops of hills but there are also valleys, gullys and ravines. One suspects that Young—the town around which the region centres— doesn't work very well on a wine label. 'Young shiraz' doesn't sound quite right, does it? Especially when the wine has a few years under its belt. Shiraz and cabernet sauvignon are what Hilltops is all about. The region is probably yet to fully realise its potential but deep, dark reds are a speciality. There's also some pretty good semillon and the odd chardonnay but it's the reds that will give it fame and possibly fortune.

The background

The place was first settled in the 1820s when Hamilton Hume took the first trip down the road that now bears his name. Gold fever hit in the mid-nineteenth century, causing Australia's first notable racial conflict at Lambing Flat (present- day Young) among the Chinese and Australian fossickers. Like many regions the wine history began on the back of the fossicker demand. A Dalmation by the name of Nichole Jasprizza started a vineyard to supply miners and by the turn of the century there were 240 hectares of vineyards around Young. While other wine regions succumbed to the sheep or the dairy cow, the cherry inundated Young's vineyards. The place is still the cherry capital of Australia. 1969 was a great year for music, protest and drug experimentation as well as the resurgent interest in table wine. It was the latter that prompted Peter Robertson to plant the Barwang vineyard that McWilliam's bought in 1989. Others have followed, moving from cherries to vines and taking their horticultural skills with them and sometimes growing both crops. The place has huge potential limited only by the available water.

The wines

If you enjoy big, bold Australian reds you'll like Young. It's shiraz, cabernet sauvignon, chardonnay and semillon. There are smatterings of Italian varieties and Chalkers Crossing sells wines made from the fruit of nearby Tumbarumba and Gundagai.

The prices

As far as prices go, Young is pretty good. Decent whites and reds can be purchased for less than $20.

The layout

The main highway running through Young is the Olympic Highway and the two cellar doors are on the eastern outskirts (Grove Estate) and just to the north of town (Chalkers Crossing). They're the only two cellar doors open to the public but with Young's star shining more brightly each year, it will become a tourist destination and others will no doubt follow.

A suggested route

From the northern or Sydney side, the first winery you get to is **Grove Estate** (Murringo Rd, Young; open weekends 10 am–5 pm; 02 6382 6999; www. groveestate.com.au), a cherry/vineyard business. Wine prices are good and many of the wines have been made by Tim Kirk (of Clonakilla fame) in exchange for grapes, and the quality is excellent.

Across town is **Chalkers Crossing** (285 Henry Lawson Way, Young; open weekdays 9 am–5 pm; 02 6382 6900; www. chalkerscrossing.com.au), which operates out of an efficient though not particularly attractive winery/shed. French winemaker Celine Rousseau has quickly got to grips with the local fruit and makes excellent whites and reds from Young fruit as well as fruit from Tumbarumba and Gundagai. The riesling and the Tumbarumba Chardonnay are particularly good.

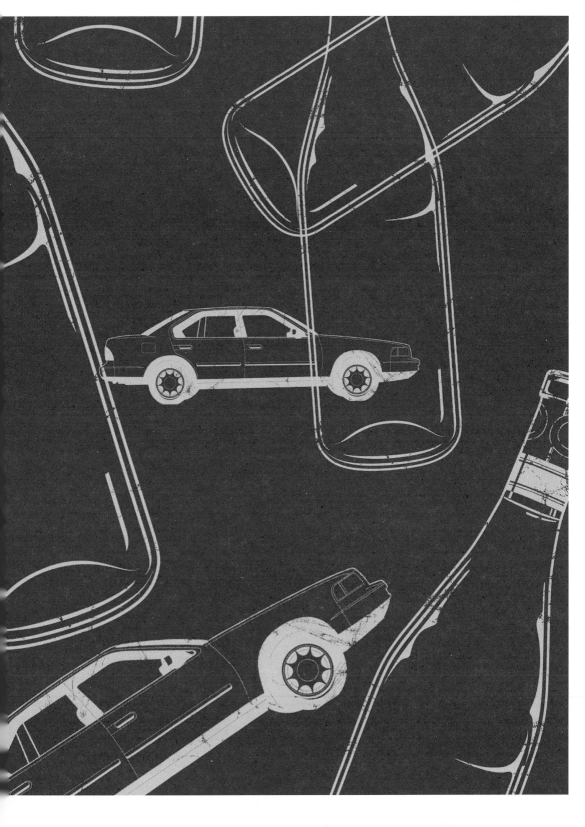

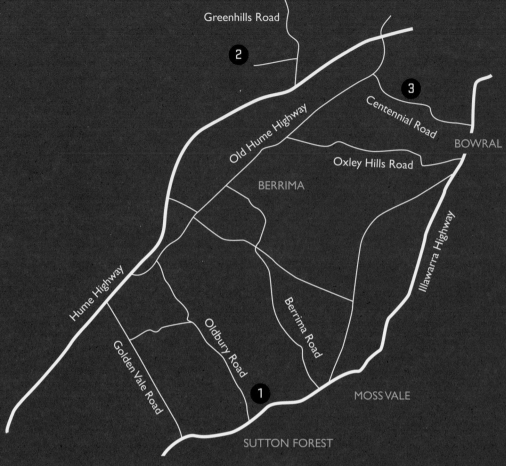

SOUTHERN HIGHLANDS

WINERIES

1. Southern Highland Wines
Oldbury Rd, Sutton Forest
02 4868 2300

2. Blue Metal Vineyard
Lot 18 Compton Park Rd, Berrima
02 4877 1877

3. Centennial Vineyards
Centennial Rd, Bowral
02 4681 8777

Snapshot

It used to be said that Tasmania was as close as Australia came to dear old Blighty but the people who said that had never been to the Southern Highlands. Almost eternally green, the rolling hills, soft mists and pastoral scenes have attracted Anglophiles and the pursuits have been more equestrian than viticultural—until now. Vineyards are proliferating and some of the wine being produced is surprisingly good.

The background

There were vines in the Highlands in the old days; after all, it's not that far from Camden and one of the original vineyards. Vines spread from Camden and there was viticulture up until the 1950s. Interest has been revived recently and most of the vineyards date from this millennium.

The wines

It's cool climate and at an altitude of around 700 metres above sea level, the fast-ripening varieties such as pinot noir and chardonnay have shown the most promise.

The prices

It's expensive land and cool-climate viticulture, and is catering to wealthy tourists not the retail trade. Don't expect much decent stuff under $20.

The layout

The region straddles the Hume Highway from the turn-off to Sutton Forest in the south to just north of Mittagong.

A suggested route

From the south, take the Sutton Forest Road towards Moss Vale and you'll come to **Southern Highland Wines** (Oldbury Rd, Sutton Forest; open daily 10 am–5 pm; 02 4868 2300; www.southernhighlandwines. com). It's an impressive-looking place. The whites have so far been better than the reds, particularly the chardonnay and riesling.

Just before Berrima on your left is **Blue Metal Vineyard** (Lot 18 Compton Park Rd, Berrima; open Thu–Mon 10 am–5 pm; 02 4877 1877; www.bluemetalvineyard.com). It's a quaint cellar door with a decent cafe and one of those large outdoor chess sets. There's a fruit salad of varieties and the Ignis Reserve Cabernet Sauvignon can be very good.

Back on the main road, heading left, drive past Berkelouw Books and take a right into Centennial Road. **Centennial Vineyards** (Centennial Rd, Bowral; open daily 10 am–5 pm; 02 4681 8777; www.centennial. net.au) has a building that befits its Bowral address. There is a wide range of wines, some decent sparkling and the Woodside Pinot Noir can be very good.

SOUTH COAST

WINERIES

1. Crooked River Wines
cnr Princes Hwy & Willowvale Road,
Gerringong
02 4234 0975

2. Coolangatta Estate
1135 Bolong Rd, Shoalhaven Heads
02 4448 7131

3. Cambewarra Estate
520 Illaroo Rd, Cambewarra
02 4446 0170

4. Kladis Estate
Princes Hwy, Wandandian
02 4443 5606

5. Cupitt's Winery
58 Washburton Rd, Ulladulla
02 4455 7888

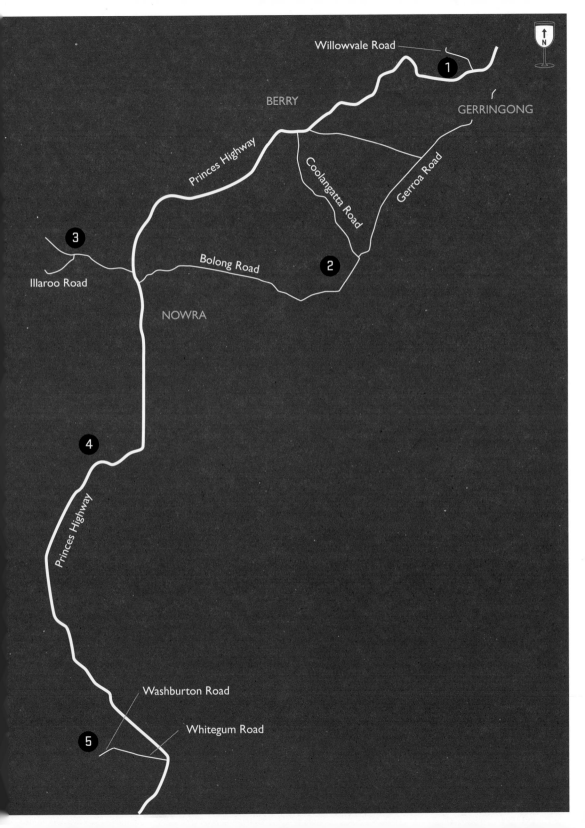

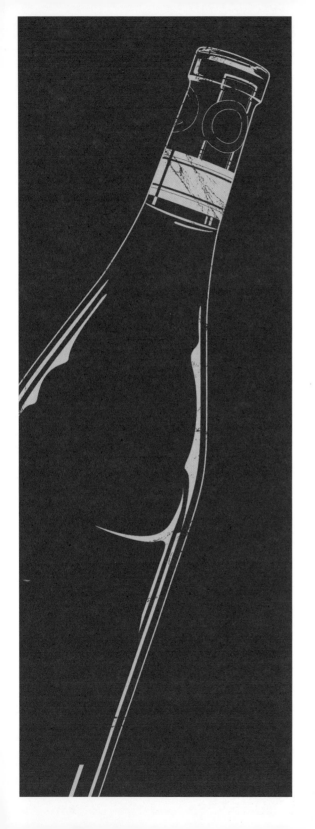

Snapshot

The stretch of coast from Kiama down to Bermagui is one of the best strips of coastline on this island and consequently is frequently visited. Where you've got tourists, sooner or later you will have wineries and as tourists discover the beauties of the South Coast, wineries have been springing up to capture their dollars. It is not the perfect climate for grapes—it rains in February when grapes are hanging on the vine and is often dry in winter when vines need rain. Mould-resistant varieties such as chambourcin have been favoured. It will never be a world-beating wine region but if you're in the area, the wineries are worth a visit.

The background

Apart from the odd experiment, there isn't much of a viticultural history on the South Coast. Apparently there used to be a huge table grapevine growing on the Marlin Hotel in Ulladulla in the 1950s but the number of birds and marsupials, combined with the weather made viticulture on a large scale a difficult business. In the late 1980s Coolangatta Estate was established and Cambewarra Estate followed in 1991. Both these wineries have had success with semillon in particular.

The wines

Where you've got mould you've got chambourcin—certainly not my favourite variety. There is also chardonnay, cabernet sauvignon, shiraz, semillon and verdelho.

The prices

The prices tend to reflect the difficulties of producing wine in the climate rather than the quality of the wine. So you can pay $20-plus for wine that is probably worth $15.

The layout

The region sits astride the Princes Highway, which runs from north to south.

A suggested route

Heading south from Sydney the first winery you get to is just after the turn-off to Gerringong. **Crooked River Wines** (cnr Princes Hwy & Willowvale Road, Gerringong; open 11 am–4.30 pm; 02 4234 0975; www.crookedriverwines.com.au) has a huge range available for tasting. Quality is variable but the occasional wine is OK.

Next on the highway is **Coolangatta Estate** (1135 Bolong Rd, Shoalhaven Heads; open daily 10 am–5 pm; 02 4448 7131; www.coolangattaestate.com.au), an impressive-looking affair with garden beds bursting with agapanthus and cannas. The wines are made at Tyrrell's in the Hunter Valley and are pretty good. The semillon is the standout and the tannat (a reasonably rare French variety) is worth a look, too.

Cambewarra Estate (520 Illaroo Rd, Cambewarra; open Thu–Sun 10 am–5 pm; 02 4446 0170; www.cambewarraestate.com.au) is the other highpoint on the South Coast with good semillon and a decent chambourcin.

Further down the road near the truck stop that is Wandandian is **Kladis Estate** (Princes Hwy, Wandandian; open daily 10 am–5 pm; 02 4443 5606; www.kladisestatewines.com.au). It's a big business and the wines are made from local fruit as well as grapes from elsewhere. The Dion Cabernet Sauvignon from an old Hunter Valley vineyard is a beauty (albeit expensive), and some of the local stuff is good, too.

Further south near Ulladulla is the recently opened vineyard **Cupitt's Winery** (58 Washburton Rd, Ulladulla; open Wed–Sun 10 am–5 pm; 02 4455 7888; www.cupittwines.com.au). The view is great and the buildings fit into the landscape wonderfully. The vines are still in their infancy and most of the wines are made from fruit grown outside the district. Quality is pretty good and it's a great spot for lunch.

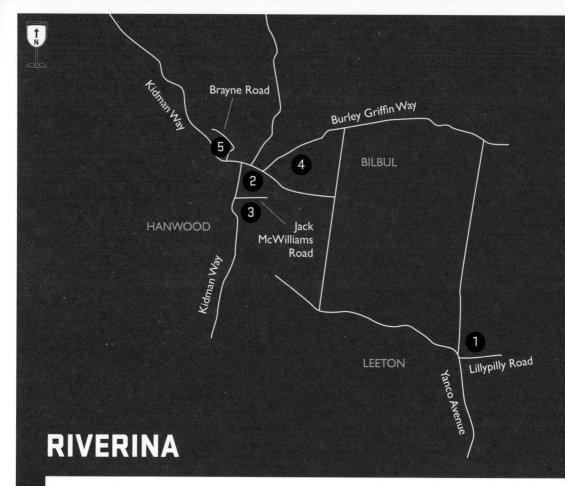

RIVERINA

WINERIES

1. Lillypilly Estate
Lillypilly Rd, Leeton
02 6953 4069

2. Nugan Estate
60 Banna Ave, Griffith
02 6962 1822

3. McWilliam's
Jack McWilliams Rd, Hanwood
02 6963 0001

4. De Bortoli
De Bortoli Rd, Bilbul
02 4993 8800

5. Westend Estate
1283 Brayne Rd, Griffith
02 6969 0800

Snapshot

To understand the concept of small you have to know what big looks like. And to properly appreciate the quaint little half-hectare vineyards and homemade operations so beloved of the cellar door pilgrim, everyone needs to go to a place like Griffith with vines stretching as far as the eye can see and wineries that look more like oil refineries. It isn't particularly pretty or quaint; it's viticulture and winemaking on a vast scale and used to taste like it, but not any more.

Those half-hectare vineyards where the winemaker has a name for each vine and has the time and luxury to observe the seasonal progress of each of his fledglings is impossible in the vast vineyards of Griffith. Technology takes the place of human care and lately the technology has improved. Vineyard monitoring has not only saved water, it has in fact made better fruit.

Griffith used to be about getting as many tonnes of grapes from a hectare of ground as possible; nowadays many grape growers are paid for quality not by the tonne and the divide between the Riverina and more poncy wine regions has narrowed. It will never be able to produce a stylish cool-climate chardonnay for instance, but for drinkable reds it's pretty good.

The background

If it hadn't been for the Murrumbidgee Irrigation scheme there would be no wine industry in the Riverina. The scheme was established between 1906 and 1912, but it would never happen now in our ecologically conscious times. Early explorers such as John Oxley, who discovered the place, described the land around Griffith as 'a country which for bareness and desolation has no equal'—he may have been having a bad-hair day as his pronouncements didn't stop graziers taking up the land along the Murrumbidgee River. In an attempt to drought-proof the place, channels were dug and this became the embryonic irrigation scheme inspired by the one on the Murray River.

By 1912 the water was running and J. J. McWilliam planted the first vines at Hanwood. The winery went up five years later. Italian immigrants came in after World War I and most of the big names in the region were well established by the 1950s. The Italian influence is what really sets it apart. It gives the architecture a certain style, the people a certain manner and is what gives Griffith its unique flavour.

The wines

It's an even divide of red and white: shiraz, semillon, cabernet sauvignon, chardonnay and sauvignon blanc. There's also a little bit of durif and petit verdot. The speciality of Griffith is the sticky. The dry autumns are perfect for leaving grapes hanging on the vine awaiting botrytis fungal infections and the metamorphosis into luscious dessert wine.

The prices

Dollar for dollar, Griffith is probably the most inexpensive wine region you can travel in.

The layout

Griffith is pretty much in the middle of nowhere. It's six hours from Sydney, five hours from Melbourne and four hours from Canberra, but if you're driving to South Australia (from Sydney or Canberra) it's a good stopover. Once in Griffith, the wine region is spread between Griffith, Yenda and Leeton; quite a large area but this is broad-acre viticulture.

A suggested route

Coming from Wagga Wagga the first town you hit is Leeton, and the must-visit winery there is **Lillypilly Estate** (Lillypilly Rd, Leeton; open Mon–Sat 10 am–5.30 pm; 02 6953 4069; www.lillypilly.com). It's a well-run family operation carefully tended by winemaker Robert Fiumara and home

to some brilliant stickies, a very good port and some good table wines.

Drive on into Griffith and you'll come to **Nugan Estate** (60 Banna Ave, Griffith; open Tue–Sun noon–3 pm; 02 6962 1822; www.nuganestate.com.au). This is a really successful business headed up by the energetic Michelle Nugan. There are wines here from Griffith but also other regions such as the King Valley and Coonawarra and they're all high quality.

Hang a left off Banna Avenue into Kidman Way and you'll eventually get to **McWilliam's** (Jack McWilliams Rd, Hanwood; open Mon–Sat 9 am–5 pm; 02 6963 0001; www.mcwilliams.com.au). You'll smell it before you get there—the Barter chicken factory is just across the road. The winery has had a big renovation and it needed it. It's a unique family-owned business that used to have its own railway going from Hanwood all the way to Chullora in Sydney. McWilliam's has brands in other areas in the Hilltops, the Barwang Range, the Yarra Valley and in Margaret River. Of the locally made Griffith wines, the Hanwood range always offers good value, especially the chardonnay, and McWilliam's produces some very good stickies.

Head back towards Griffith and turn right then left onto Burley Griffin Way and you'll get to **De Bortoli** (De Bortoli Rd,

Bilbul; open Mon–Sat 9 am–5 pm, Sun 9 am–4 pm; 02 4993 8800; www.debortoli.com.au). There's a huge range of local De Bortoli brands as well as those from their other regions. There are some real bargains and if you can't get value for money here you may as well give up.

Drive back into town, head west and you'll find the signs to **Westend Estate** (1283 Brayne Rd, Griffith; open weekdays 8.30 am–5 pm, weekends 10 am–4 pm; 02 6969 0800; www.westendestate.com.au). Westend is an example of how good Griffith wine can get: the 3 Bridges range is the best example—very good reds, whites and stickies. And the winemaker doesn't even drink!

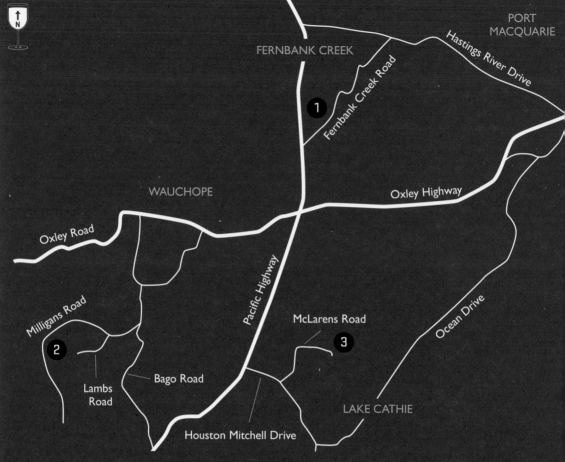

HASTINGS RIVER & PORT MACQUARIE

WINERIES

1. Cassegrain
764 Fernbank Creek Rd, Port Macquarie
02 6582 8377

2. Bago Vineyards
Milligans Rd, Wauchope
02 6585 7099

3. Long Point Vineyard
6 Cooinda Pl, Lake Cathie
02 6585 4598

Snapshot

Mention wine and the Hastings River or Port Macquarie and it's hard not to refer to Cassegrain. This one label dominates the region in a way that is not replicated in many other places. For such a small wine region, the label has a big presence Australia-wide and has managed, despite the climatic challenges, to produce very good wine and put the Hastings River region on the map.

The background

The wine history in this rather unsuitable grape-growing region dates back to 1837. In the 1860s there were 33 vineyards around Port Macquarie but as was the norm throughout the country, plantings fell into disrepair during World War I and eventually winemaking ceased. It was revived by Cassegrain in the 1980s and that success has encouraged a few others to stick a grapevine in the Hastings River dirt.

The wines

Chambourcin is the grape variety synonymous with this region. It is a French variety resistant to mould and mildew and a favourite of viticultural guru Richard Smart who helped with the set-up of Cassegrain. There are others such as semillon, shiraz, the ever-present chardonnay and cabernet sauvignon as well as a host of others.

The prices

Prices are fairly affordable—$15–$25.

The layout

Vineyards lie to the west of Port Macquarie. Bago Vineyards is closer to Wauchope and Long Point Vineyard is to the south near the town of Lake Cathie.

A suggested route

Cassegrain (764 Fernbank Creek Rd, Port Macquarie; open daily 9 am–5 pm; 02 6582 8377; www.cassegrainwines.com.au) should be on the top of your tasting list. Available for tasting are wines made from local fruit as well as others including New England and Tumbarumba. Quality is the best in the region and prices are very good. There's a good chardonnay, and the chambourcin is about as good as the variety gets.

Closer to Wauchope and at a little higher elevation is **Bago Vineyards** (Milligans Rd, Wauchope; open daily 11 am–5 pm; 02 6585 7099; www.bagovineyards.com.au), which has a large range of wines of fair quality.

Long Point Vineyard (6 Cooinda Pl, Lake Cathie; open Wed–Sun 10 am–5 pm; 02 6585 4598; www.longpointvineyard.com.au) has been around for 15 years and has an underground cellar door. The pick of the wines is the cabernet/chambourcin blend.

QUEENSLAND

The words Queensland and wine don't really go together. Not like Queensland and pineapples or Queensland and bananas. The common perception of Queensland is that it is a land kissed by sun with mangoes hanging from trees in the street, with palms swaying in balmy breezes—certainly not the climate for a grapevine. But if you've been to Stanthorpe in wintertime you'll know that the sun is only part of the picture. Stanthorpe is high (700–1000 metres above sea level) and that makes it a cool climate. Every time I've been there it's been freezing. Hail isn't uncommon and snow happens. There are less worthy wine regions in Queensland that aren't cool climate and rely on tourism more than wine quality to survive, but there are wineries that fall into that category in every state. The Queensland wine business is on the move. In the past 10 years it has grown faster than in any other state and Queensland was the first state sensible enough to have a minister for wine.

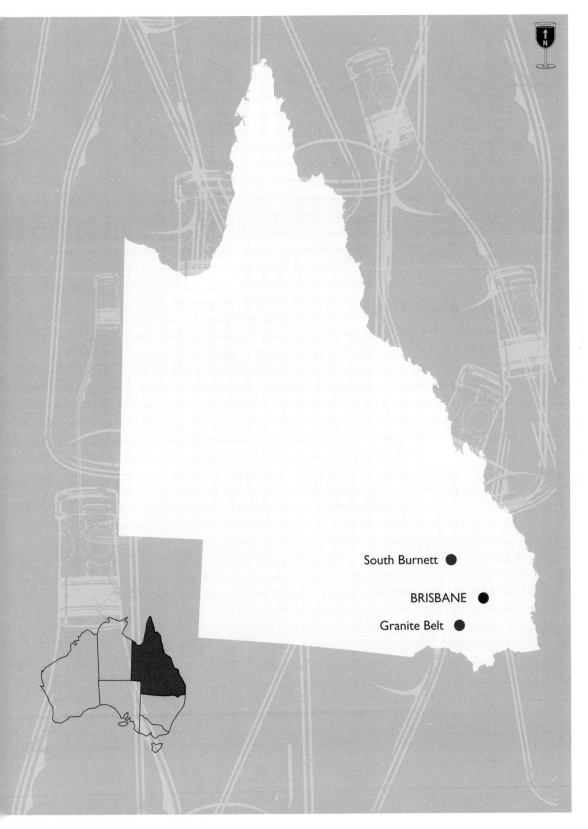

South Burnett ●

BRISBANE ●

Granite Belt ●

GRANITE BELT

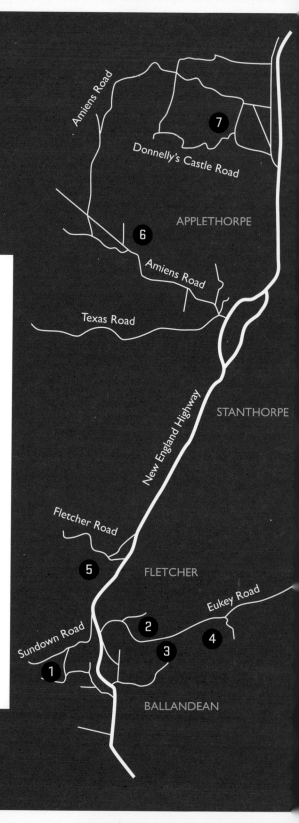

WINERIES

1. Golden Grove Estate
Sundown Rd, Ballandean
07 4684 1291

2. Just Red
2370 Eukey Rd, Ballandean
07 4684 3212

3. Hidden Creek
Eukey Rd, Ballandean
07 4684 1383

4. Symphony Hill
2017 Eukey Rd, Ballandean
07 4684 1388

5. Rumbalara Wines
137 Fletcher Rd, Fletcher
07 4684 1206

6. Robert Channon Wines
Amiens Rd, Stanthorpe
07 4683 3260

7. Boireann Winery
26 Donnelly's Castle Rd, The Summit
07 4683 2194

Snapshot

It's easy to dismiss Queensland wine. How can a state, that is notoriously sunny, produce half-decent wine or boast a cool-climate wine region? The Granite Belt rightly has claims to both. But there is more to a cool climate than longitude and latitude. Altitude is the critical third factor and the Granite Belt has lots of it. Perched at 800–1000 metres above sea level, it's in a different stratosphere to the sea level Gold Coast.

If you take the three-and-half-hour drive from Armidale Airport on the New South Wales side of the border, through Tenterfield to Ballandean, you're travelling on the Great Dividing Range in a very un-Queensland climate of four seasons, frosts and, on the odd occasion, snow. According to a local winemaker keen to show off the cool-climate credentials of his region, the mercury has plunged as low as −13 degrees Celsius. Not surprisingly, it has become a favourite spot for Queenslanders who want to experience the exquisite thrill of wearing an overcoat, sitting by a real log fire or tasting high-quality Queensland wines.

The background

The region was first planted in the 1860s, mainly by priests needing altar wine. Later it was Italian immigrants making wine from table grapes in bathtubs. In 1965 the real history began when a hectare of shiraz was planted. There was a splurge of interest in the 1990s and now a serious cellar door traveller can easily spend two or three days in the district, tasting very good wine products.

The wines

Like any new wine region it's a fruit salad. Shiraz, cabernet sauvignon, merlot and chardonnay make up 64 per cent of the plantings but there's also pinot grigio, sauvignon blanc, verdelho, viognier, tempranillo and a host of others. The strong suits are cabernet sauvignon, which hints at Margaret River elegance when it's good, and shiraz for which the region is best known. Of the newies, verdelho, tempranillo and pinot grigio look most promising.

The prices

There are some real bargains to be had in the Granite Belt. While some wines wear typical cool-climate prices, others are surprisingly affordable.

The layout

The Granite Belt is easy to get to from Brisbane or northern New South Wales. From Brisbane it's a cruisy two-and-a-half to three-hour drive. From Armidale it's three-and-a-half hours and from Sydney you should allow yourself 11 hours. The district lies from Ballandean to slightly north of Stanthorpe. From the New South Wales side you come in through Ballandean so it's practical to approach the Ballandean wineries first. From Brisbane you come in to Stanthorpe and it's wiser to travel north to south.

A suggested route

From the New South Wales side, head for Ballandean, turn onto Sundown Road and you'll come to the friendly family-run affair that is **Golden Grove Estate** (Sundown Rd, Ballandean; open daily 9 am–4 pm; 07 4684 1291; www.goldengroveestate. com.au). The property dates back to the 1940s and wine grapes were planted in 1972. The winemaker is the son of owner Sam Constanzo, Raymond, and he shows lots of skill. The shiraz is great, the sauvignon blanc is one of the best in the district, the durif is worth a look and there are also some good fortifieds, all at pretty attractive prices.

Head back to Ballandean, turn left into Eukey Road and you'll get to **Just Red** (2370 Eukey Rd, Ballandean; open weekends & public holidays 10 am–5 pm; 07 4684 3212; www.justred.com.au). The name says it all and if you're after some quaffers, this is

the place. The wines aren't world-beaters but they're not trying to be. There are decent reds to be had for $10!

A little further up the hill on the right is **Hidden Creek** (Eukey Rd, Ballandean; open Mon & Fri 11 am–3 pm, weekends & public holidays 10 am–4 pm; 07 4684 1383; www.hiddencreek.com.au). It's an attractive spot with three labels and a wide range of varietals available at the cellar door: Hidden Creek, Red Bird and Rooklyn. The Rooklyns are particularly good.

At the upper end of the sophistication scale is **Symphony Hill** (2017 Eukey Rd, Ballandean; open daily 10 am–4 pm; 07 4684 1388; www.symphonyhill.com.au). A very cleverly laid out cellar door with some interesting (and expensive) wines. The whole range is pretty smart, but try the Wild Child Viognier and the Family Reserve Cabernet Sauvignon if you're up for a thrill.

Get back on the New England Highway and head towards Stanthorpe. Turn left onto Fletcher Road and you'll come to **Rumbalara Wines** (137 Fletcher Rd, Fletcher; open daily 10 am–5 pm; 07 4684 1206; www.rumbalarawines.com.au). Run by an enthusiastic South African couple, the cellar door is a lively place with a restaurant and some very well priced wines. The place has an African safari theme and the Safari

Red Shiraz Merlot Cabernet Sauvignon blend is a bargain at $13.

Continue up the New England Highway. From the Stanthorpe bypass, turn left into Amiens Road. Here you'll find **Robert Channon Wines** (Amiens Rd, Stanthorpe; open weekdays 11 am–5 pm, weekends & public holidays 10 am–5 pm; 07 4683 3260; www.robertchannonwines.com). There's a vast range of high-quality wines. The winery is famous for verdelho but don't ignore the chardonnay or the cabernet—it's a beauty.

Back on the highway you'll go past the quaint town of Applethorpe and see the signs to **Boireann Winery** (26 Donnelly's Castle Rd, The Summit; open daily 10 am–4.30 pm; 07 4683 2194; www.boireannwinery.com.au), the best red producer in the region. The cabernet sauvignon is regularly brilliant but don't forget to taste the mourvèdre shiraz.

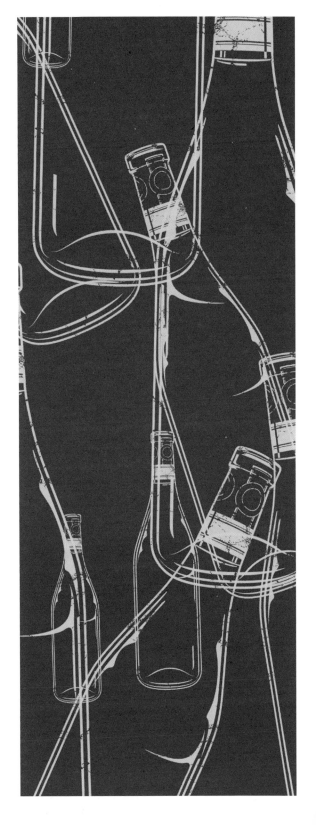

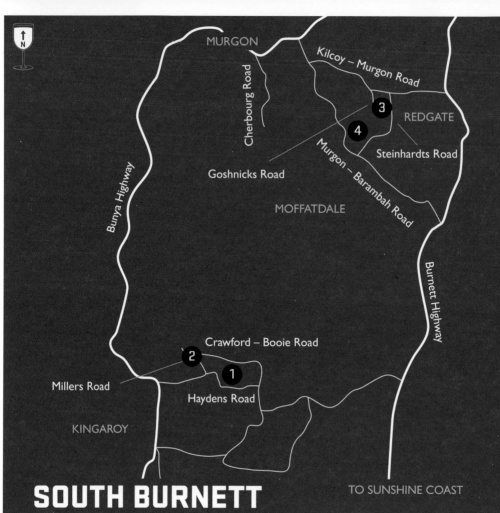

SOUTH BURNETT

WINERIES

1. Crane Wines
Haydens Rd, Kingaroy
07 4162 7647

2. Captain's Paddock
18 Millers Rd, Kingaroy
07 4162 4534

3. Barambah
79 Goshnicks Rd, Redgate, via Murgon
1300 781 815

4. Clovely Estate
Steinhardts Rd, Moffatdale, via Murgon
07 3876 3100

Snapshot

Never heard of it? The place doesn't get much publicity outside Queensland. To place it geographically, it's centred around Joh Bjelke-Petersen's home town of Kingaroy and about 100 kilometres west of Noosa as the galah flies, which suggests that peanuts might be a better crop than grapes. But viticulture can be surprisingly adaptable and some of the wines are good. The Granite Belt will always outshine South Burnett but if you're in the district it's worth a look.

The background

This is an area not new to the vine; there have been table grapes planted since the late 1800s but the region's retail wine history really hit its straps in the 1990s.

The wines

It's half/half white and red with shiraz and chardonnay being dominant There's some verdelho and cabernet sauvignon, too.

The prices

Prices aren't too bad: there's a few wines for under $15 but most sit at the $20 mark.

The layout

The region is around the towns of Kingaroy in the south and Murgon to the north; this is about a two-hour drive from Brisbane and about the same if you're coming from the Sunshine Coast.

A suggested route

Starting from the south about seven kilometres from Kingaroy is **Crane Wines** (Haydens Rd, Kingaroy; open daily 10 am–4 pm; 07 4162 7647; www.cranewines. com.au). The wines are acceptable; the dry verdelho and cabernet sauvignon are the picks and the grappa is worth a taste if you're into fiery spirits.

Next stop is **Captain's Paddock** (18 Millers Rd, Kingaroy; open daily 10 am–5 pm; 07 4162 4534; www.captainspaddock. com.au). The top-of-the-range double-pruned shiraz has a good reputation but is not available for tasting. Also check out the standard shiraz and the verdelho.

North of the region is Murgon and a lot of cellar doors. One is **Barambah** (79 Goshnicks Rd, Redgate, via Murgon; open Thu–Sun 10 am–5 pm; 1300 781 815; www.barambah.com.au), a professionally run operation with good whites by ex-wine writer and MW Peter Scudamore-Smith.

The biggest and probably the best is **Clovely Estate** (Steinhardts Rd, Moffatdale, via Murgon; open daily 10 am–5 pm; 07 3876 3100; www.clovely.com.au). The wines are good; there's a large range, particularly the chardonnay and verdelho.

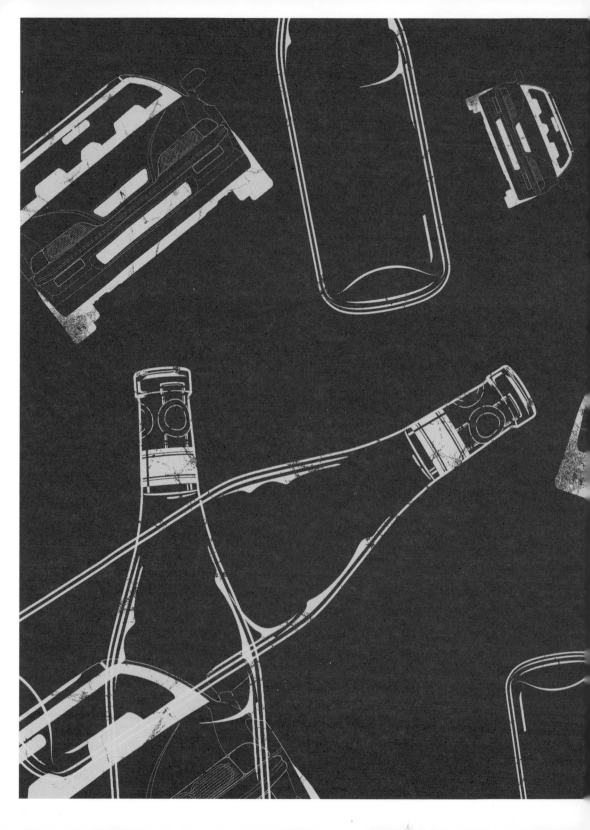

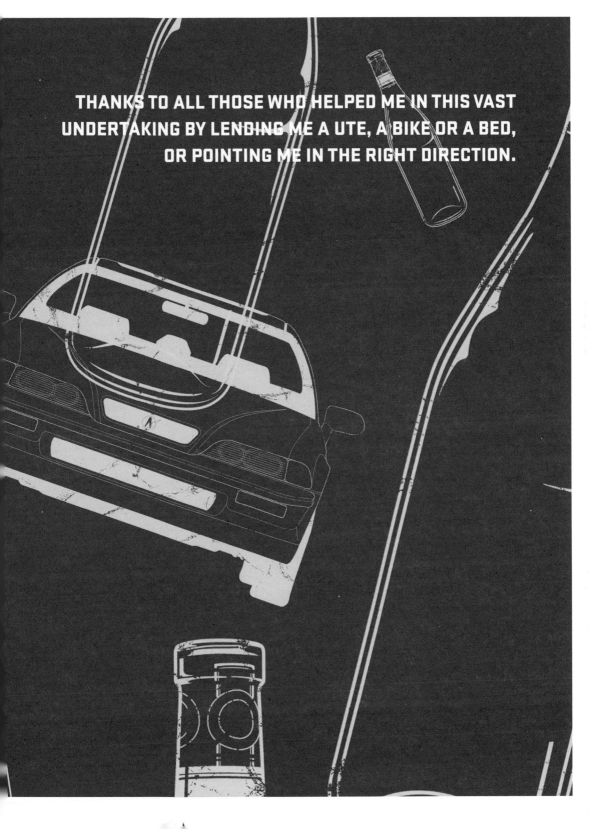

THANKS TO ALL THOSE WHO HELPED ME IN THIS VAST
UNDERTAKING BY LENDING ME A UTE, A BIKE OR A BED,
OR POINTING ME IN THE RIGHT DIRECTION.

Published in 2011 by Murdoch Books Pty Limited

Murdoch Books Australia
Pier 8/9
23 Hickson Road
Millers Point NSW 2000
Phone: +61 (0) 2 8220 2000
Fax: +61 (0) 2 8220 2558
www.murdochbooks.com.au

Murdoch Books UK Limited
Erico House, 6th Floor
93–99 Upper Richmond Road
Putney, London SW15 2TG
Phone: +44 (0) 20 8785 5995
Fax: +44 (0) 20 8785 5985
www.murdochbooks.co.uk

Publisher: Diana Hill
Designer: Hugh Ford
Editor: Melissa Penn
Project Editor: Laura Wilson
Production: Joan Beal

National Library of Australia Cataloguing-in-Publication entry
Author: Powell, Greg Duncan.
Title: Glovebox guide to wine touring / Greg Duncan Powell
ISBN: 978-1-74196-815-6 (pbk.)
Subjects: Wineries—Australia—Guidebooks
                 Wine tasting—Australia—Guidebooks
                 Wine and wine making—Australia—Guidebooks.
Dewey Number: 641.220994
A catalogue record for this book is available from the British Library.

Printed by 1010 Printing International Limited, China

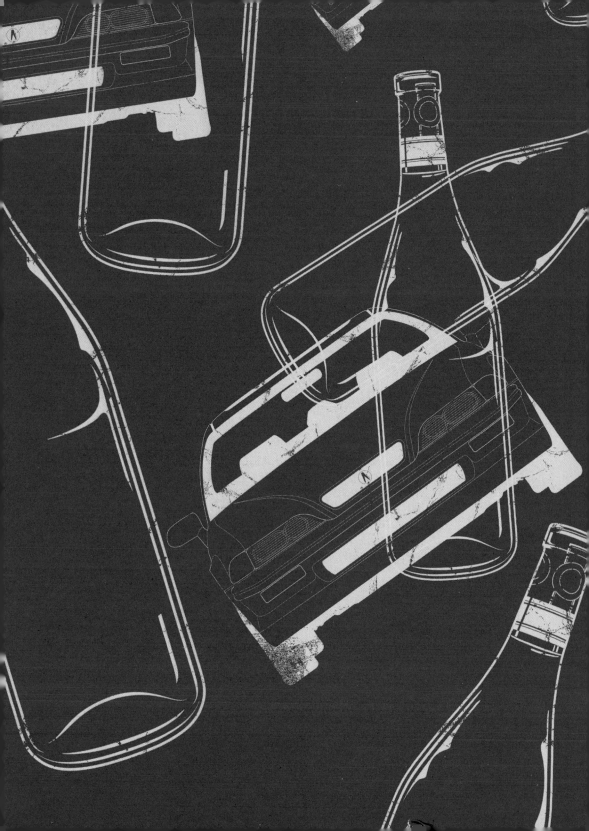